BURMA CHRONICLES

GUY DELISLE WAS BORN IN QUEBEC CITY IN 1966 AND HAS SPENT THE LAST DECADE LIVING AND WORKING IN FRANCE. HE HAS WRITTEN AND DRAWN FOUR GRAPHIC NOVELS INCLUDING *SHENZHEN*, AN ACCOUNT OF HIS TRAVELS IN CHINA, AND *PYONGYANG*, AN ACCOUNT OF HIS EXPERIENCES IN NORTH KOREA.

ALSO BY GUY DELISLE

PYONGYANG: A JOURNEY IN NORTH KOREA
SHENZHEN: A TRAVELOGUE FROM CHINA
ALBERT & THE OTHERS
ALINE & THE OTHERS

Guy Delisle
BURMA CHRONICLES

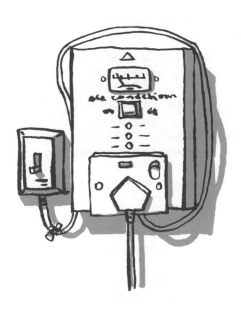

JONATHAN CAPE
LONDON

THIS EDITION PUBLISHED BY JONATHAN CAPE 2011

8 10 9

COPYRIGHT © GUY DELISLE 2009
TRANSLATION © HELGE DASCHER 2009

GUY DELISLE HAS ASSERTED HIS RIGHT UNDER THE COPYRIGHT, DESIGNS
AND PATENTS ACT, 1988 TO BE IDENTIFIED AS THE AUTHOR OF THIS WORK

THIS BOOK IS SOLD SUBJECT TO THE CONDITION THAT IT SHALL NOT,
BY WAY OF TRADE OR OTHERWISE, BE LENT, RESOLD, HIRED OUT,
OR OTHERWISE CIRCULATED WITHOUT THE PUBLISHER'S PRIOR
CONSENT IN ANY FORM OF BINDING OR COVER OTHER THAN THAT
IN WHICH IT IS PUBLISHED AND WITHOUT A SIMILAR CONDITION,
INCLUDING THIS CONDITION, BEING IMPOSED
ON THE SUBSEQUENT PURCHASER

FIRST PUBLISHED IN GREAT BRITAIN IN 2009 BY
JONATHAN CAPE
RANDOM HOUSE, 20 VAUXHALL BRIDGE ROAD,
LONDON SW1V 2SA

WWW.VINTAGE-BOOKS.CO.UK

ADDRESSES FOR COMPANIES WITHIN THE RANDOM HOUSE GROUP LIMITED CAN BE FOUND AT:
WWW.RANDOMHOUSE.CO.UK/OFFICES.HTM

THE RANDOM HOUSE GROUP LIMITED REG. NO. 954009

A CIP CATALOGUE RECORD FOR THIS BOOK IS AVAILABLE FROM THE BRITISH LIBRARY

ISBN 9780224096188

PRINTED AND BOUND IN INDIA BY
REPLIKA PRESS PVT. LTD.

MYANMAR

OFFICIAL NAME SINCE 1989, ADOPTED BY THE UN.

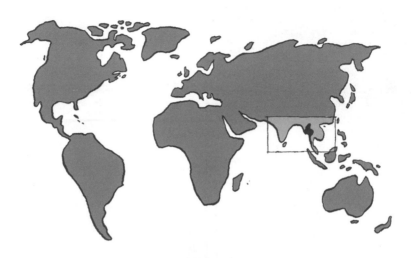

BURMA

FORMER NAME, STILL USED BY COUNTRIES THAT DO NOT
ACCEPT THE LEGITIMACY OF THE GOVERNMENT THAT TOOK
POWER IN 1989. SUCH AS FRANCE, AUSTRALIA AND THE US.

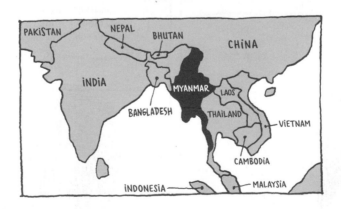

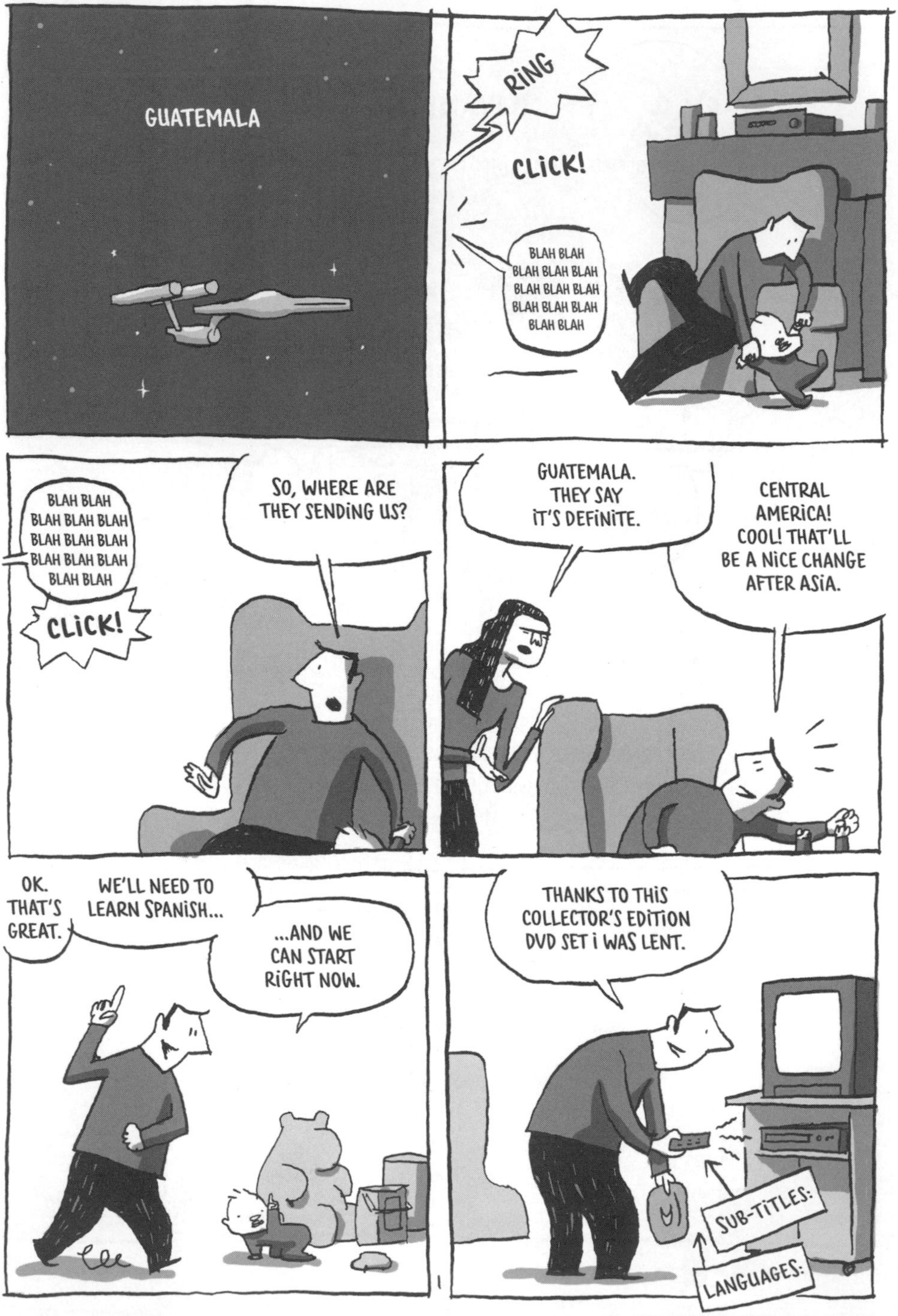
GUATEMALA
RING
CLICK!
BLAH BLAH BLAH BLAH BLAH BLAH BLAH BLAH BLAH BLAH BLAH BLAH BLAH
BLAH BLAH BLAH BLAH BLAH BLAH BLAH BLAH BLAH BLAH BLAH BLAH BLAH
CLICK!
SO, WHERE ARE THEY SENDING US?
GUATEMALA. THEY SAY IT'S DEFINITE.
CENTRAL AMERICA! COOL! THAT'LL BE A NICE CHANGE AFTER ASIA.
OK. THAT'S GREAT.
WE'LL NEED TO LEARN SPANISH...
...AND WE CAN START RIGHT NOW.
THANKS TO THIS COLLECTOR'S EDITION DVD SET I WAS LENT.
SUB-TITLES:
LANGUAGES:

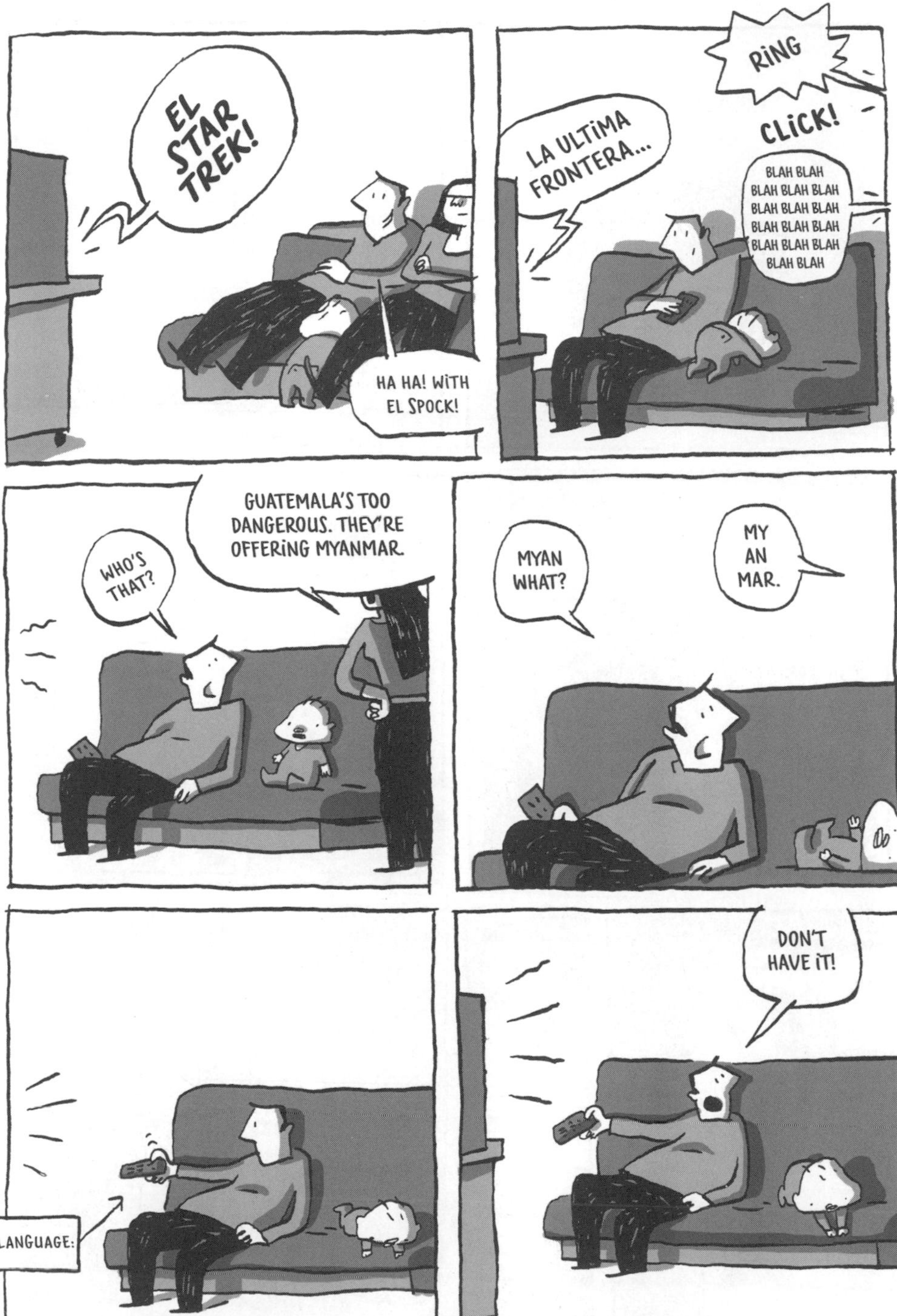
EL STAR TREK!
HA HA! WITH EL SPOCK!
LA ULTIMA FRONTERA...
RING
CLICK!
BLAH BLAH BLAH BLAH BLAH BLAH BLAH BLAH BLAH BLAH BLAH BLAH BLAH BLAH BLAH BLAH
GUATEMALA'S TOO DANGEROUS. THEY'RE OFFERING MYANMAR.
WHO'S THAT?
MYAN WHAT?
MY AN MAR.
LANGUAGE:
DON'T HAVE IT!

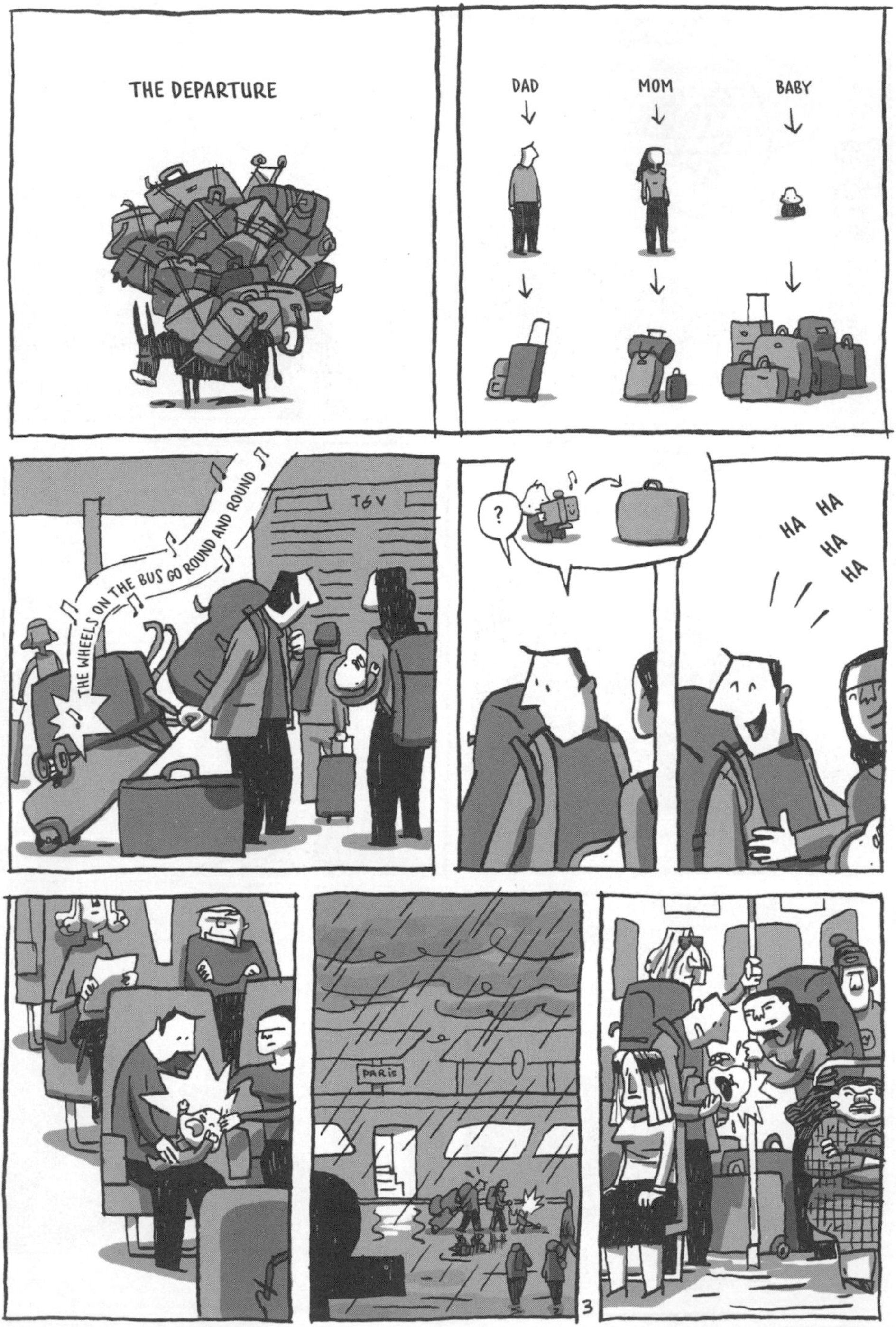
THE DEPARTURE
DAD
MOM
BABY
THE WHEELS ON THE BUS GO ROUND AND ROUND
TGV
?
HA HA HA HA
PARIS

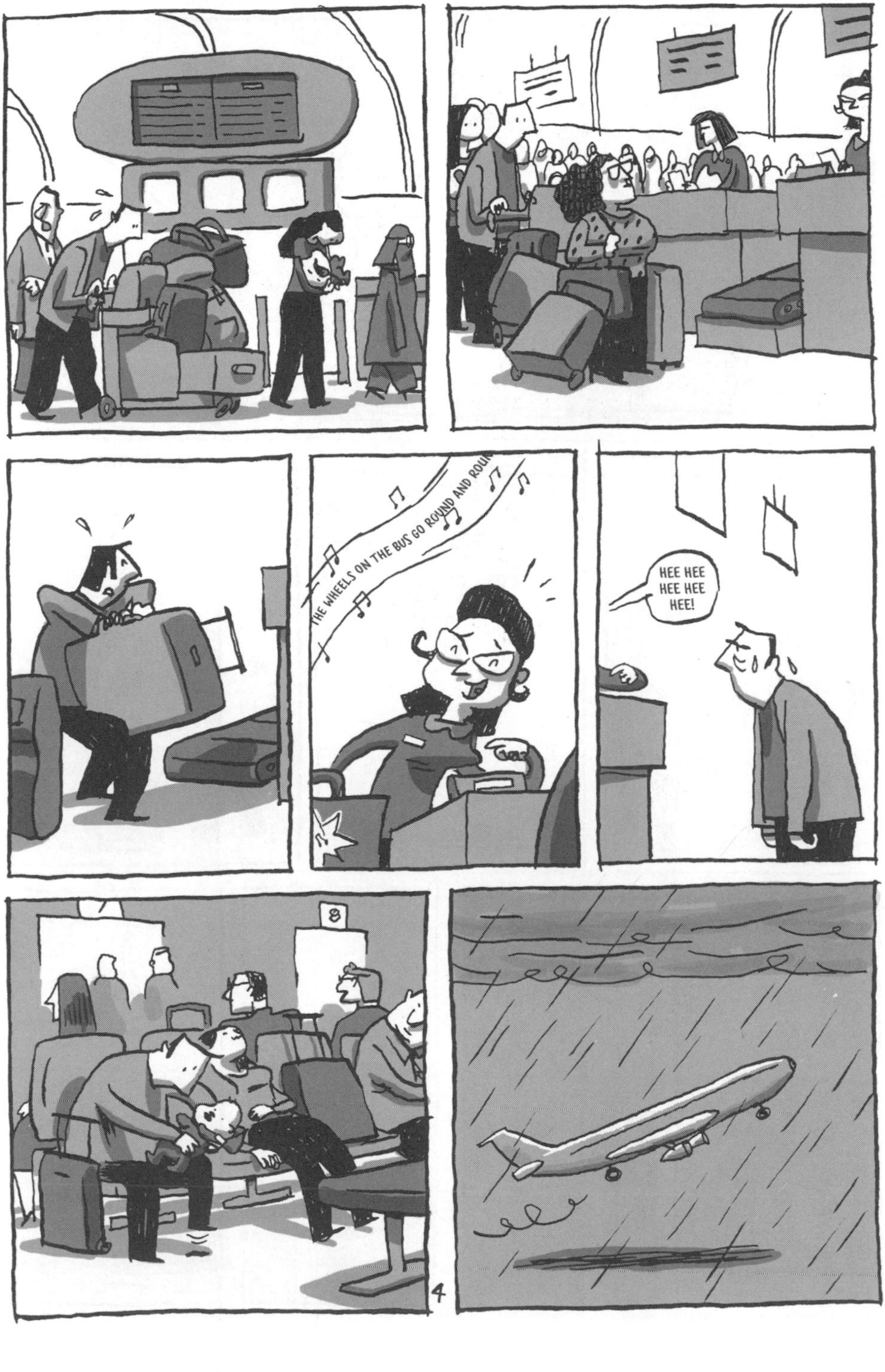
THE WHEELS ON THE BUS GO ROUND AND ROUND
HEE HEE HEE HEE HEE!
8

WAAA!
BANGKOK
THE WHEELS ON THE BUS GO ROUND AND ROUND...
SLAM

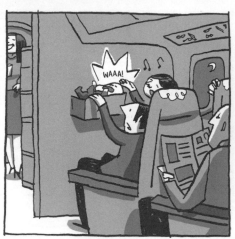

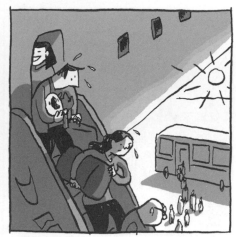

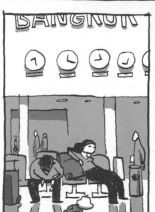

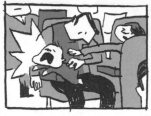

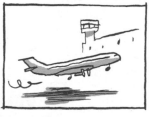

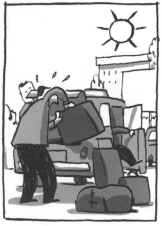

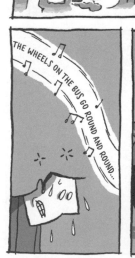

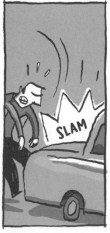

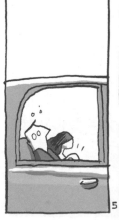

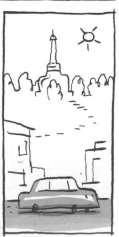

GUEST HOUSE

IT TURNS OUT THAT MSF* HAS NO HOUSE FOR US. WE'RE GOING TO HAVE TO FIND ONE.

OH.

*MSF = MÉDECINS SANS FRONTIÈRES, AKA DOCTORS WITHOUT BORDERS

IN THE MEANTIME, WE'RE LIVING IN THE "GUEST HOUSE". IT'S WHERE EXPAT FIELD WORKERS LIVE WHEN THEY PASS THROUGH THE CAPITAL.

6

THE GROUND FLOOR IS TAKEN UP BY MSF OFFICES.

FOR THE FIRST FEW DAYS, I HOLE UP ON THE TOP FLOOR, WHILE NADÈGE TAKES ON HER NEW DUTIES.

UPSTAIRS, I KEEP MY EYES GLUED ON LOUIS.

BECAUSE THERE ARE POWER OUTLETS ALL OVER THE PLACE, AND THEY'RE REAL BABY TRAPS.

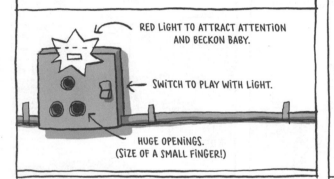

RED LIGHT TO ATTRACT ATTENTION AND BECKON BABY.

SWITCH TO PLAY WITH LIGHT.

HUGE OPENINGS. (SIZE OF A SMALL FINGER!)

ADD TO THAT A TRANSFORMER BOLTED TO THE FLOOR WITH TWO THICK RED CABLES ON EITHER SIDE.

ADA?

SHORTLY BEFORE WE LEFT, AN ER PHYSICIAN TOLD ME ABOUT ALL THE ELECTRIC SHOCK INJURIES KIDS CAN SUFFER.

THAT, COMBINED WITH THE JETLAG, HAS ME PLUNGED INTO A STATE OF NEAR-PANIC.

7

AS THE WEEK GOES BY, I COVER UP THE OPENINGS WITH LUGGAGE STICKERS.

I GET A WASHBOWL ORGANIZED, SINCE SHOWERS ARE HARDLY IDEAL FOR BABIES.

I SET OUT A PLAY PERIMETER USING A MATTRESS SURROUNDED BY SUITCASES.

LITTLE BY LITTLE, THINGS SHAPE UP AND I MANAGE TO RELAX.

TO THE POINT THAT, OVER THE NEXT FEW DAYS, I SPEND MOST OF MY TIME SLEEPING, DOZING OR VAGUELY POKING THROUGH MAGAZINES.

TIME

EXPATS OFTEN LEAVE BEHIND THE BOOKS THEY BRING. SOME HOUSES END UP WITH A NICE LITTLE LIBRARY AS A RESULT.

BUT THERE'S NOT MUCH HERE: TWO GUIDES TO BURMA, ONE TO THAILAND AND THE REST ON HUMANITARIAN ACTION.

MEKONG MALARIA FORUM

THERE'S A TIME MAGAZINE SUBSCRIPTION, AND I READ IT CHRONOLOGICALLY.

HEY! THIS ONE'S MISSING PAGES.

IN MYANMAR, ALL MAGAZINES GO THROUGH THE CENSORSHIP BUREAU. ARTICLES THAT ARE UNFLATTERING TO THE COUNTRY ARE SYSTEMATICALLY REMOVED.

OH, RIGHT! I ALMOST FORGOT! WE'RE UNDER DICTATORSHIP HERE.

9

CITY MART

ONE OF THE FIRST FIXTURES OF OUR NEW EVERYDAY LIFE IS THE "CITY MART," WHICH STOCKS ALL BASIC CONSUMABLES.

SEE THIS? THEY EVEN HAVE DIAPERS.

WHEN I THINK THAT WE WENT TO THE TROUBLE OF BRINGING THREE HUGE PACKS FROM FRANCE.

I WAS TOLD WE WOULDN'T FIND ANY.

A HOUSE BUT NO DIAPERS, HUH?

AH! FOOD AISLES IN FOREIGN COUNTRIES! I'VE GOT TO ADMIT THAT I FIND THEM TOTALLY EXOTIC.

THEY'RE A PART OF LOCAL CULTURE THAT TOURISTS MISS OUT ON COMPLETELY.

IF I HAD TO WRITE A GUIDEBOOK, I'D MENTION THEM.

***MIDDLE OF THE 3RD ROW, TO THE LEFT: DON'T MISS THE DISPLAY OF CANNED FOOD: TUNA, SARDINES AND MACKEREL IMPORTED FROM SINGAPORE.

THERE ARE SOME REAL GRAPHIC TREASURES. I OFTEN BUY CANS AND EMPTY THEM WITH-OUT REALLY KNOWING WHAT'S INSIDE TO MAKE PENCIL HOLDERS.

I'VE GOT A WHOLE COLLECTION BACK HOME THAT EVERYONE COVETS.

HEY! NOT BAD AT ALL!

KENYA 2002.

OH MAN, NO WAY!

SOME PRODUCTS HAVE MANAGED TO TAKE OVER THE ENTIRE WORLD. YOU CAN'T GO ANYWHERE WITHOUT FINDING NESCAFE AND THE LAUGHING COW.

HERE, THIS IS THE REAL FACE OF GLOBALIZATION: A GRINNING RED COW.

STAFF MUST COME CHEAP AROUND HERE.

THERE ARE MORE CLERKS THAN CUSTOMERS IN SOME AISLES.

EXCUSE ME.

AND LIKE THEY SAY: NOTHING KILLS SERVICE LIKE TOO MUCH SERVICE.

OH! THANK YOU.

HEY! ISN'T THAT THE GUY FROM THE UN? OR WAS IT THE RED CROSS? I CAN'T REMEMBER.

HCR, ICRC, WFP, AAH, AZG, AMI, MDM.* I ALWAYS GET THEM MIXED UP.

DAMN, HE SAW ME.

HELLO!

*HIGH COMMISSION FOR REFUGEES, INTERNATIONAL COMMITTEE OF THE RED CROSS, WORLD FOOD PROGRAM, ACTION AGAINST HUNGER, ARTSEN ZONDER GRENZEN (MSF HOLLAND), ACTION MÉDICALE INTERNATIONALE, MÉDECINS DU MONDE.

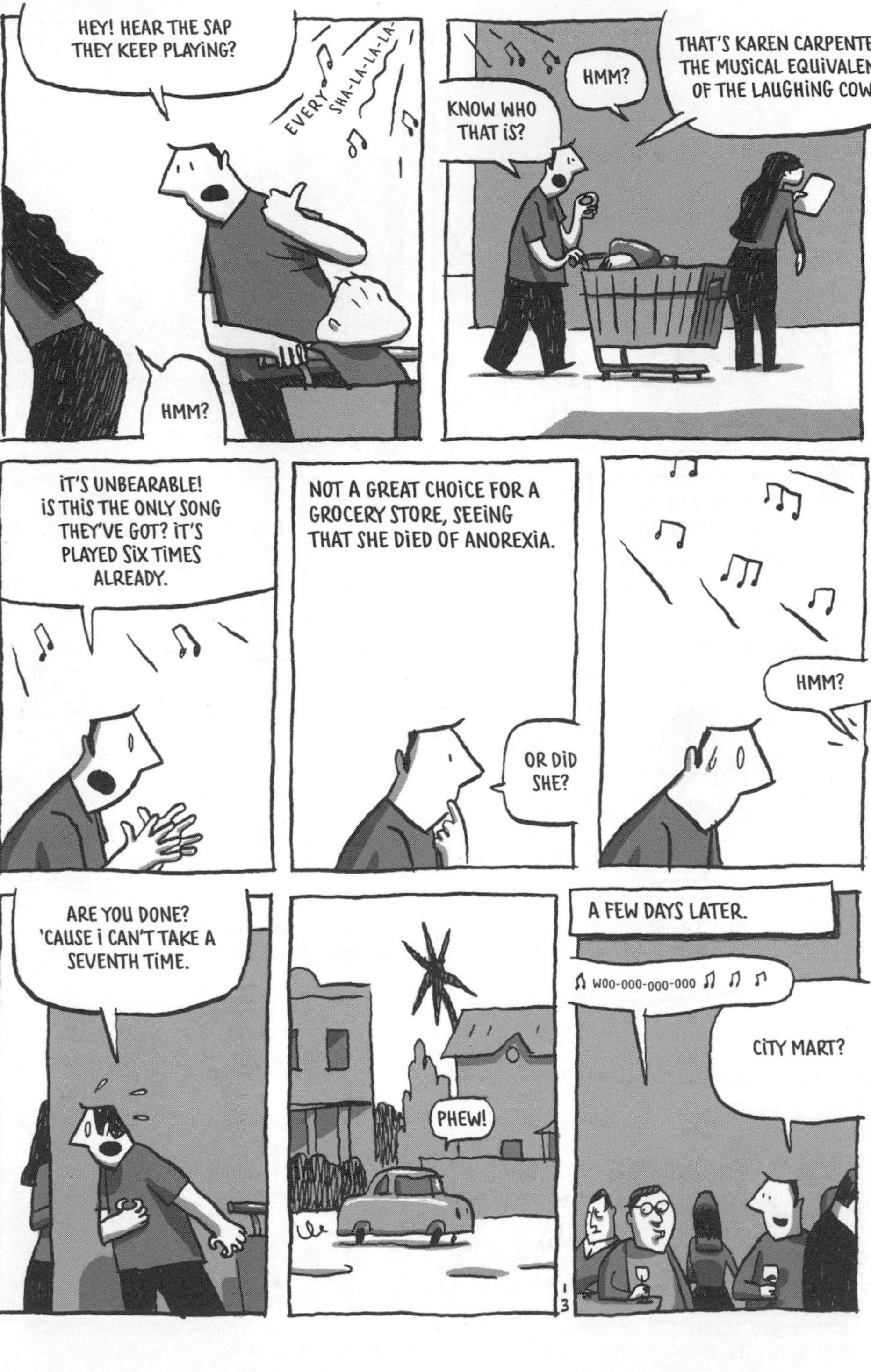
HEY! HEAR THE SAP THEY KEEP PLAYING?
EVERY SHA-LA-LA-LA-
HMM?
KNOW WHO THAT IS?
HMM?
THAT'S KAREN CARPENTER. THE MUSICAL EQUIVALENT OF THE LAUGHING COW.
IT'S UNBEARABLE! IS THIS THE ONLY SONG THEY'VE GOT? IT'S PLAYED SIX TIMES ALREADY.
NOT A GREAT CHOICE FOR A GROCERY STORE, SEEING THAT SHE DIED OF ANOREXIA.
OR DID SHE?
HMM?
ARE YOU DONE? 'CAUSE I CAN'T TAKE A SEVENTH TIME.
PHEW!
A FEW DAYS LATER.
WOO-000-000-000
CITY MART?

THE AC

BURMA HAS A HOT SEASON, A VERY HOT SEASON AND A RAINY SEASON.

IN FEBRUARY, YOU SWEAT FROM MORNING TO EVENING.

AND APPARENTLY IT'S JUST THE START.

YOU'LL SEE, THE TEMPERATURE'LL GO UP TILL THE RAINS START IN SUMMER.

WHAT? IT'S GOING TO GET HOTTER?

CRIPES, HOW'S THAT POSSIBLE?

AS IT IS, I PRETTY MUCH WAIT TILL SUNDOWN TO TAKE THE BABY OUT.

WHOA!

ANOTHER HALF HOUR AND THEN WE'LL GO.

14

LUCKILY, MOST OF THE HOUSES HERE HAVE AIR CONDITIONING.

ONE OF THE BLESSINGS OF OUR TIMES.

BUT POWER OUTAGES ARE FREQUENT AS WELL.

ABOUT A MINUTE LATER.

15

ON ARCHITECTURE IN THE TROPICS

We've got a real estate agent to help us find a house, and she calls at all hours.

RRING

We keep telling her we're looking for something small and inexpensive, but she takes us all over the place anyway.

There's no shortage of rentals. Foreigners have been streaming out since the American embargo.

No air conditioning? Forget it.

For a poor country, there's plenty of building going on. New places are popping up on every corner.

The reason is simple: the banks are unreliable. Those who have money prefer to invest in something solid.

In early 2005, the government shut down the Asia Wealth Bank and the Mayflower Bank without notice.

16

SHE KEEPS SHOWING US A MODEL I'D CLASSIFY AS GRECO-BURMO-CHINESE.

THIS WAY PLEASE.

– NARROW THREE-STORY

– CLADDING: SMALL CERAMIC TILES

– ROOF: BLUE PLASTIC TILES

– BLUE-TINTED REFLECTIVE WINDOWS

– BALCONIES ALL OVER

– AND GREEK COLUMNS

THE COLUMNS ARE A BIT NOUVEAU RICHE, AREN'T THEY?

IT'S NO BETTER INSIDE. THE SPACES LOOK LIKE THEY WERE CARVED UP BY A MAD ARCHITECT.

A LIVING ROOM BETWEEN TWO FLOORS?

HEY! COME SEE! A ONE-PERSON BALCONY!

REALLY? GET IN, I WANNA TRY.

IN SHORT: MODERN HOMES THAT ARE ENTIRELY INAPPROPRIATE FOR THE REGION. THE AIR CIRCULATION IS LOUSY. TWO MINUTES WITHOUT AC AND YOU'RE ROASTING.

PLEASE, GOD, MAKE IT COME BACK ON!

WHILE THE TRADITIONAL MODEL LETS THE AIR PASS THROUGH UNDER THE ROOF AND HAS A SHADY SPOT BELOW THAT STAYS COOL YEAR-ROUND.

AESTHETIC AND PRACTICAL CONSIDERATIONS ASIDE, IT'S NOT THE MSF WAY TO SPEND DONOR MONEY ON PALACES FOR ITS EXPATS.

... WITH JUST ONE FLOOR.

SEE THAT? THERE'S A POOL.

I DON'T THINK SHE GETS IT.

BY THE END OF THE DAY, WE DON'T EVEN BOTHER GETTING OUT OF THE CAR.

NO.

NO.

NO.

WE COME HOME EMPTY-HANDED AND IRRITABLE. TO TOP IT OFF, I'M SURE I GOT A SUNBURN.

YOU'RE PINK.

WE WIND UP CHANGING REAL ESTATE AGENTS, AND A WEEK LATER, HE TAKES US AROUND TO ALL THE SAME PLACES.

ADVENTURES
iN BURMA
I

FED UP WITH THE HEAT, i SHAVE MY HAIR SHORT.

BUT iT iSN'T EASY TO DO ON YOUR OWN.

ONE FALSE MOVE AND THE CLiPPER GUiDE FLiES OFF, SO i END UP WITH A BALD TRiANGLE ON MY HEAD.

FASCiNATED BY THE SENSA-TiON, i CAN'T STOP TOUCHiNG MY SKULL.

SCRATCH!
SCRATCH!

i GET A MiNi SUNBURN...

THAT GiVES ME MiNi MiGRAiNES...

AND MiNi CHiLLS.

BRRR...

STROLLER

C'MON, A BIT OF FRESH AIR AT THE END OF THE DAY WILL DO US GOOD.

ADA!

OUR NEIGHBORHOOD IS NICE AND PEACEFUL, WITHOUT MUCH TRAFFIC.

LUCKILY, SINCE SIDEWALKS ARE NONEXISTENT IN THIS PART OF TOWN.

ADA!

HUH? WHERE?

LOUIS HAS DEVELOPED A FASCINATION FOR FLOWERS.

20

FFFFLLLOWERR.

ADA!

THE THING I LIKE ABOUT THE STROLLER IS THAT I GO VIRTUALLY UNNOTICED.

THANKS TO LOUIS, WHO GETS ALL THE ATTENTION.

OF COURSE, HE IS ESPECIALLY CUTE.

I KNOW, I KNOW, ALL PARENTS SAY THAT.

EXCEPT IN THIS CASE, IT HAPPENS TO BE TRUE.

JUST LOOK AT THAT FACE!

HE'S GOT IT GOOD, WITH BURMESE GIRLS COMING OUT TO COVER HIM WITH SMILES AND KISSES.

BUT ALL THE ATTENTION LEAVES HIM COLD.

YOU'LL SEE, ANOTHER TWENTY YEARS AND IT WON'T BE SO EASY.

21

ALONG THE STREETS, PITCHERS AND GLASSES ARE SET OUT FOR THIRSTY PASSERS-BY.

I COULD BE DYING OF THIRST, YOU STILL COULDN'T PAY ME TO TAKE A SIP.

ADA.

FURTHER ALONG, ANOTHER ADORING FAN CROSSES THE STREET TO ADMIRE THE BABY.

HER SISTERS WAVE US OVER FROM THE OTHER SIDE. THEY DON'T NEED TO TWIST MY ARM.

BOY OR GIRL?

BOY, IT'S A BOY!

GOOD LORD, IT'S HIGH TIME I CUT THAT KID'S HAIR.

LOUIS IS BEING PASSED FROM ONE GIRL TO THE NEXT WHEN THE PATRIARCH APPEARS.

ONE OF HIS DAUGHTERS HAS BROUGHT HIM OUT.

HE'S STIFF AS A STATUE. HE MUST BE SICK. IN ANY CASE, HE'S VERY THIN.

HE LOOKS HAPPY TO SEE AN OCCIDENTAL BABY. I THINK.

EVEN THOUGH I'VE HARDLY STRAYED FROM THE HOUSE, I MANAGE TO GET LOST.

I WANDER AROUND THE NEIGH- BORHOOD TILL NIGHTFALL.

OK, OK...NO NEED TO PANIC. WHAT NOW?

FIELDWORK

TO COMPLETE THE HANDOVER FROM THE LAST MANAGER, NADÈGE NEEDS TO GO OUT IN THE FIELD TO VISIT ONE OF THE MISSION'S TWO PROJECTS.

THE BUS TRIP TAKES A WHOLE NIGHT. SHE'LL BE GONE FOR THREE DAYS.

THIS WILL BE HER FIRST TIME AWAY FROM LOUIS SINCE HIS BIRTH.

2
4

AND MY FIRST TIME ALONE WITH HIM FOR SO LONG.

BABIES NEED CONSTANT ATTENTION THROUGHOUT THE DAY. AND IT'S CRAZY TO SEE HOW TIME SEEMS TO SLOW DOWN WHEN IT PASSES MINUTE BY MINUTE.

SOMETIMES I TELL MYSELF:

OK, THAT SHOULD KEEP HIM BUSY FOR AT LEAST FIVE MINUTES. THAT'LL BE FIVE MINUTES DOWN.

LUCKILY THERE'S NAPTIME.

AH HA! YOU RUBBED YOUR EYES! I SAW YOU!

WAH

NO... ALREADY?

LOUIS' LATEST GAME INVOLVES LETTING SMALL OBJECTS FALL INTO HARD-TO-REACH PLACES.

25

AND THEN CRYING FOR THEM.

ADA

ADA

A

ADA

ADA

HANG ON, I'M COMING.

AND THE HARDER IT IS FOR ME TO GET AT THE OBJECT, THE MORE HE LAUGHS.

ALRIGHT, I THINK WE'LL PLAY SOMETHING ELSE NOW.

WAAH

FINE, OK, BUT THIS IS THE LAST TIME.

WAAH

OK. BUT THIS REALLY IS THE LAST TIME. OR ELSE I'LL BLOW ALL MY CREDIBILITY.

NADÈGE COMES IN LATE AT NIGHT. SHE HASN'T BREASTFED IN THREE DAYS AND HER BREASTS ARE SORE.

HE'S SLEEPING?

YEAH.

OUCH.

LUCKILY, HE WAKES UP JUST IN TIME.

WAAH

AH HA!

AAAAAH PHEW!

HOME
(ALMOST)
SWEET
HOME

WE'RE MOVING TODAY.

WE STILL HAVEN'T FOUND A HOUSE, SO FOR NOW WE'RE TAKING OVER THE ROOM OF THE LAST MANAGER, WHO HAS GONE BACK TO FRANCE.

WE'LL BE LIVING WITH THE HEAD OF THE MISSION, ASIS, WHO IS ALREADY PUTTING UP PIERRE, A LOGISTICS EXPERT JUST BACK FROM AN EMERGENCY MISSION IN SRI LANKA FOLLOWING DECEMBER'S TERRIBLE TSUNAMI.

PFF... WHAT A MESS...

ASIS, LIKE JUST ABOUT ALL THE MSF DOCTORS I'VE MET, SMOKES A PACK OF CIGARETTES A DAY.

AND PIERRE PROBABLY MORE.

BUT AT LEAST THIS WILL BE MORE COMFORTABLE THAN THE "GUEST HOUSE".

GOOD LORD, THE BED IS HARD AS BRICK.

HEY, THERE'S A DESK IN THE ROOM. MAYBE I CAN GET BACK TO WORK.

I DON'T MIND PLAYING HOUSEDAD FOR A WHILE, BUT I'D LIKE TO GET DRAWING AGAIN.

DURING THE DAY, I'M ON MY OWN WITH SEGN NAN, THE HOUSEKEEPER, WHO EVENTUALLY BECOMES LOUIS' BABYSITTER.

AND MAUNG AYE, OUR GUARD, WHO DOESN'T HAVE MUCH TO GUARD IN A COUNTRY AS QUIET AS BURMA. QUIET IN TERMS OF BURGLARY, THAT IS.

28

LIKE MANY BURMESE, MAUNG EYE HAS A THING FOR BETELNUT, AND HE CHEWS IT MORNING AND NIGHT.

WHEN HE FLASHES A SMILE, IT'S SOMETHING TO SEE. HIS TEETH ARE STAINED DEEP RED, VERGING ON BLACK, FROM THE BETEL JUICE.

ACTUALLY, TO BE PRECISE, THEY'RE BLACK ON THE SIDE HE CHEWS ON, AND FADE TO CHERRY RED ON THE OTHER SIDE.

IT REALLY MAKES THE PALE PINK OF THE GUMS STAND OUT.

HMM...I WONDER HOW BLACK TEETH GO OVER WITH THE GIRLS.

BUT HE'S YOUNG AND HE'S GREAT WITH KIDS, AND THAT'S ALL THAT MATTERS TO LOUIS.

BABIES ARE EASY.

ADA.

ADA.

29

THE BURMESE LOVE CHILDREN. AND WITH MAUNG AYE AS A BUDDY, LOUIS GOT TO KNOW THE WHOLE NEIGHBORHOOD IN NO TIME. A WHITE-SKINNED BABY IS A BIG DRAW HERE.

AND SO ONE DAY, ON OUR STROLL...

LOUIS!

LOUIS!

WHO'S THAT? I DON'T KNOW HER.

LOUIS!

LOUIS!

LOUIS!

LOUIS!

WHOA! TALK ABOUT POPULAR!

AMONG OUR NEIGHBORS IS AN OLD SMILING GUY WHO KNOCKS HIMSELF OUT TRYING TO TEACH LOUIS TO SAY HELLO IN BURMESE.

MIN

GA

LA

BA.

BUT WHEN I MEET HIM ON MY OWN, HE COMPLETELY IGNORES ME.

MING'LABA!

I FEEL A BIT SLIGHTED.

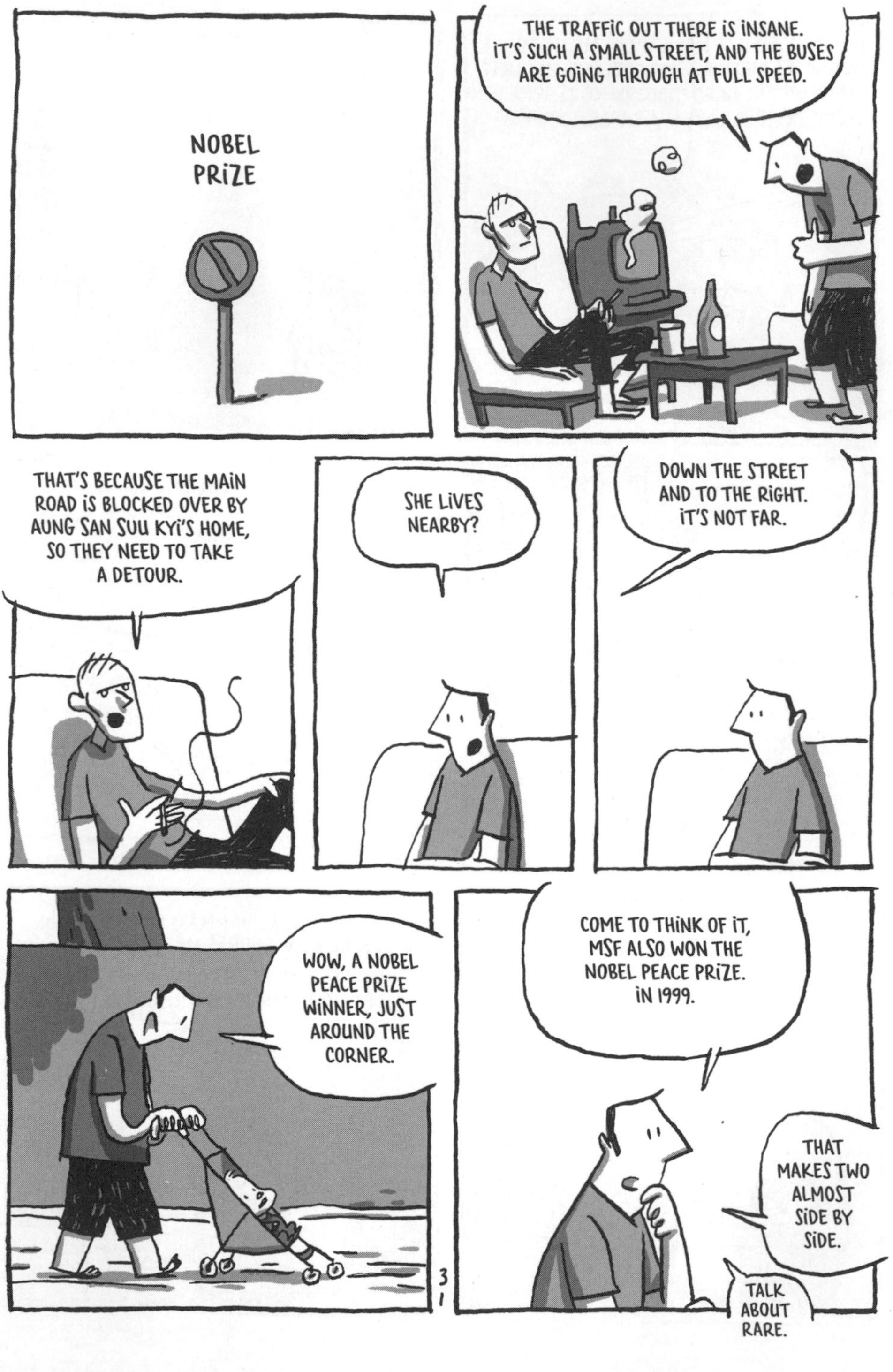
NOBEL PRIZE
THE TRAFFIC OUT THERE IS INSANE. IT'S SUCH A SMALL STREET, AND THE BUSES ARE GOING THROUGH AT FULL SPEED.
THAT'S BECAUSE THE MAIN ROAD IS BLOCKED OVER BY AUNG SAN SUU KYI'S HOME, SO THEY NEED TO TAKE A DETOUR.
SHE LIVES NEARBY?
DOWN THE STREET AND TO THE RIGHT. IT'S NOT FAR.
WOW, A NOBEL PEACE PRIZE WINNER, JUST AROUND THE CORNER.
COME TO THINK OF IT, MSF ALSO WON THE NOBEL PEACE PRIZE. IN 1999.
THAT MAKES TWO ALMOST SIDE BY SIDE.
TALK ABOUT RARE.

WELL, LET'S HAVE A LOOK. DOWN THE STREET AND THEN RIGHT.

OH, OF COURSE. OVER BY THE CHECKPOINT, WHERE ALL THE CARS COME INTO OUR STREET INSTEAD OF GOING STRAIGHT.

TURNING OUR QUIET LITTLE STREET INTO A DANGEROUS BOULEVARD.

AND IT'S ALL BECAUSE OF AUNG SAN SUU KYI.

HMPF. THANKS A LOT.

OK, HERE GOES, BABY.

ADA!

I CAN'T IMAGINE THEY'D KEEP AN INNOCENT DAD AND HIS KID FROM GOING THROUGH.

I PLAY STUPID AND PRETEND NOT TO UNDER-STAND, BUT IT'S NO USE. WE WON'T BE GET-TING A LOOK AT THE HOME OF THE WORLD'S MOST FAMOUS POLITICAL PRISONER.

IN FACT, SHE'S NOT REALLY A PRISONER. SHE CAN'T LEAVE HER HOME, BUT SHE'S FREE TO LEAVE THE COUNTRY. EXCEPT SHE HAS CHOSEN TO STAY AND, BY HER SIMPLE PRESENCE, RESIST ONE OF THE MOST OPPRESSIVE REGIMES IN THE WORLD.

SINCE HER RETURN TO BURMA IN 1988, SHE HAS BEEN AT THE FOREFRONT OF THE OPPOSITION MOVEMENT WITH HER PARTY, THE NLD (NATIONAL LEAGUE FOR DEMOCRACY). THOUGH UNDER HOUSE ARREST, SHE WON THE ELECTION WITH MORE THAN 80% OF THE VOTE. BUT THE GENERALS DIDN'T STEP DOWN. INSTEAD, REPRESSION INTENSIFIED, ESPECIALLY FOR THE MEMBERS OF HER PARTY.

SHE HAS SPENT MOST OF THE PAST FIFTEEN YEARS REDUCED TO SILENCE. SHE HAS NO ACCESS TO NEWSPAPERS, TELEVISION OR THE INTERNET. A RADIO IS HER ONLY SOURCE OF OUTSIDE INFORMATION. TODAY, AT AGE 60, SHE HAS TWO EMPLOYEES WHO HELP WITH DAILY CHORES. ONCE A MONTH, A PHYSICIAN IS AUTHORIZED TO VISIT.

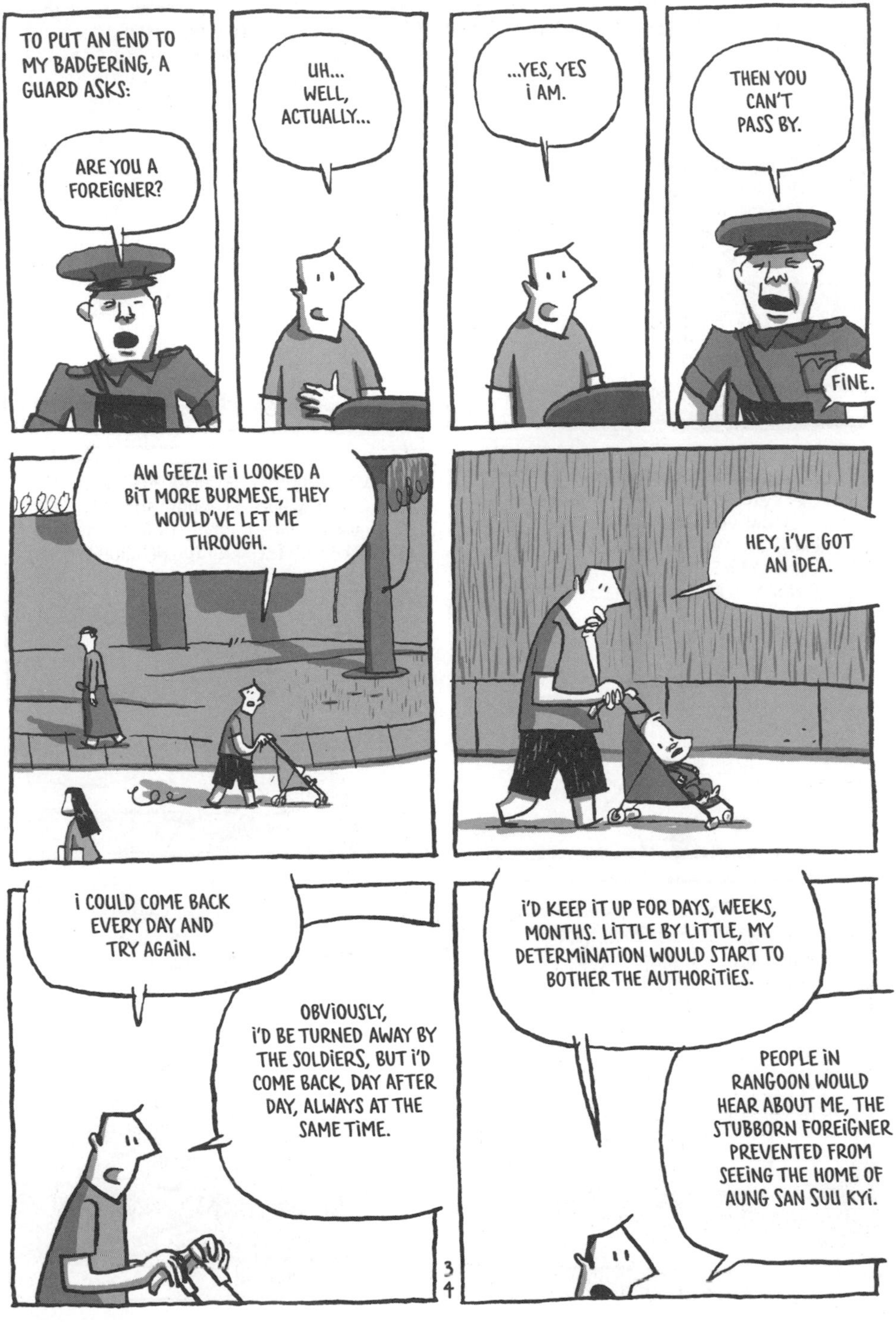
TO PUT AN END TO MY BADGERING, A GUARD ASKS:
ARE YOU A FOREIGNER?
UH... WELL, ACTUALLY...
...YES, YES I AM.
THEN YOU CAN'T PASS BY.
FINE.
AW GEEZ! IF I LOOKED A BIT MORE BURMESE, THEY WOULD'VE LET ME THROUGH.
HEY, I'VE GOT AN IDEA.
I COULD COME BACK EVERY DAY AND TRY AGAIN.
OBVIOUSLY, I'D BE TURNED AWAY BY THE SOLDIERS, BUT I'D COME BACK, DAY AFTER DAY, ALWAYS AT THE SAME TIME.
I'D KEEP IT UP FOR DAYS, WEEKS, MONTHS. LITTLE BY LITTLE, MY DETERMINATION WOULD START TO BOTHER THE AUTHORITIES.
PEOPLE IN RANGOON WOULD HEAR ABOUT ME, THE STUBBORN FOREIGNER PREVENTED FROM SEEING THE HOME OF AUNG SAN SUU KYI.

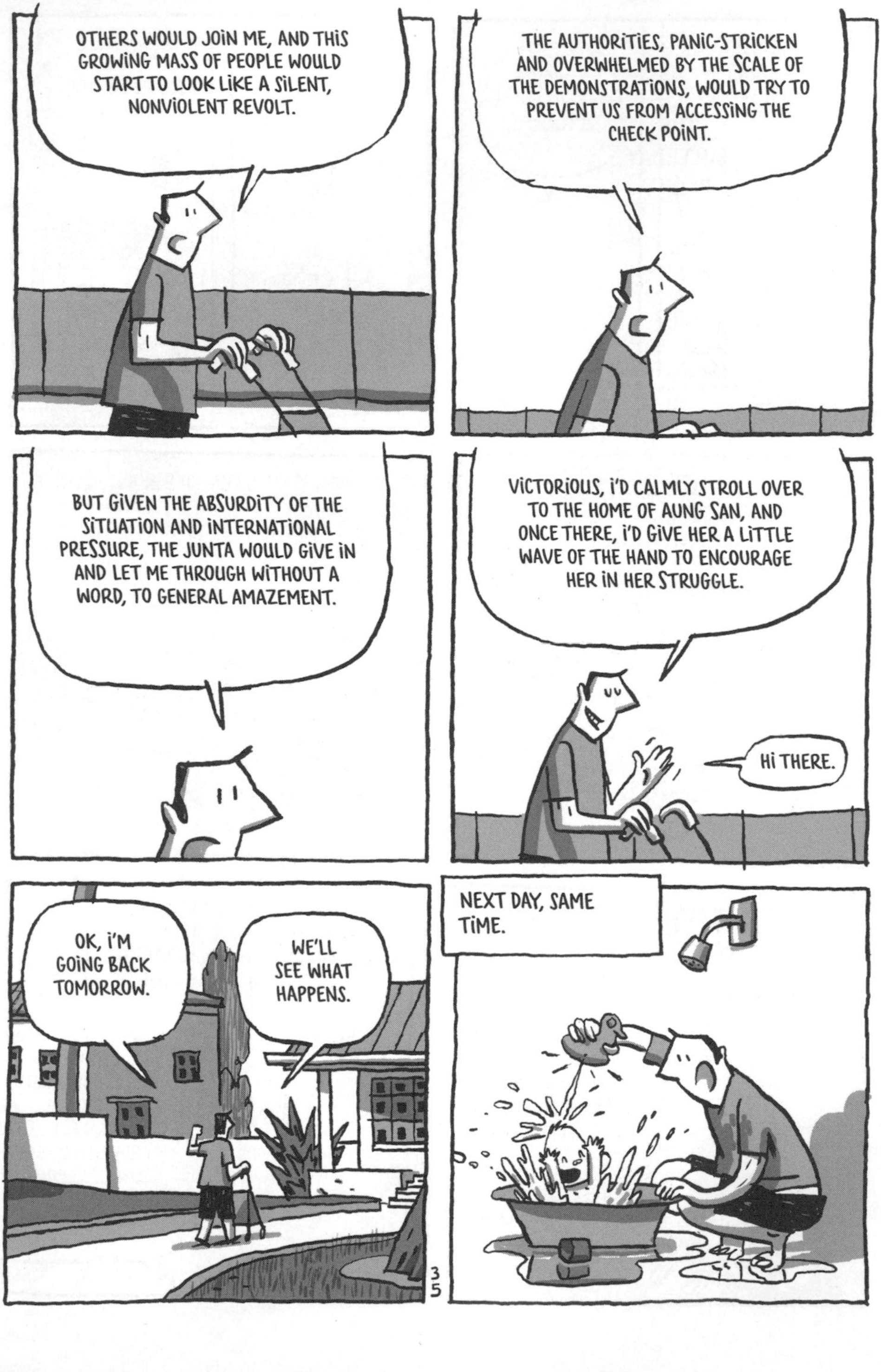
OTHERS WOULD JOIN ME, AND THIS GROWING MASS OF PEOPLE WOULD START TO LOOK LIKE A SILENT, NONVIOLENT REVOLT.
THE AUTHORITIES, PANIC-STRICKEN AND OVERWHELMED BY THE SCALE OF THE DEMONSTRATIONS, WOULD TRY TO PREVENT US FROM ACCESSING THE CHECK POINT.
BUT GIVEN THE ABSURDITY OF THE SITUATION AND INTERNATIONAL PRESSURE, THE JUNTA WOULD GIVE IN AND LET ME THROUGH WITHOUT A WORD, TO GENERAL AMAZEMENT.
VICTORIOUS, I'D CALMLY STROLL OVER TO THE HOME OF AUNG SAN, AND ONCE THERE, I'D GIVE HER A LITTLE WAVE OF THE HAND TO ENCOURAGE HER IN HER STRUGGLE.
HI THERE.
OK, I'M GOING BACK TOMORROW.
WE'LL SEE WHAT HAPPENS.
NEXT DAY, SAME TIME.

THE BIRTHDAY PARTY

TODAY, THE MSF ASSISTANT PROGRAM MANAGER IS THROWING A PARTY FOR HIS SON'S FIRST BIRTHDAY AND WE'RE INVITED.

GREAT, WE'LL GET TO SEE A BURMESE INTERIOR.

THIS IS WHEN HE'LL ANNOUNCE HIS SON'S NAME, BECAUSE SO FAR, EVERYONE HAS BEEN USING THE NICKNAME HIS PARENTS CHOSE BASED ON A SOUND HE MADE SOON AFTER HIS BIRTH.

AGOU!

AGOU!

THAT'S HOW IT USUALLY GOES IN BURMA: FIRST THE NICKNAME, THEN THE NAME. AND MOST OF THE TIME, IT'S THE NICKNAME THAT STICKS.

THEY LIVE IN AN APARTMENT IN A WORKING CLASS NEIGHBORHOOD.

SUPER.

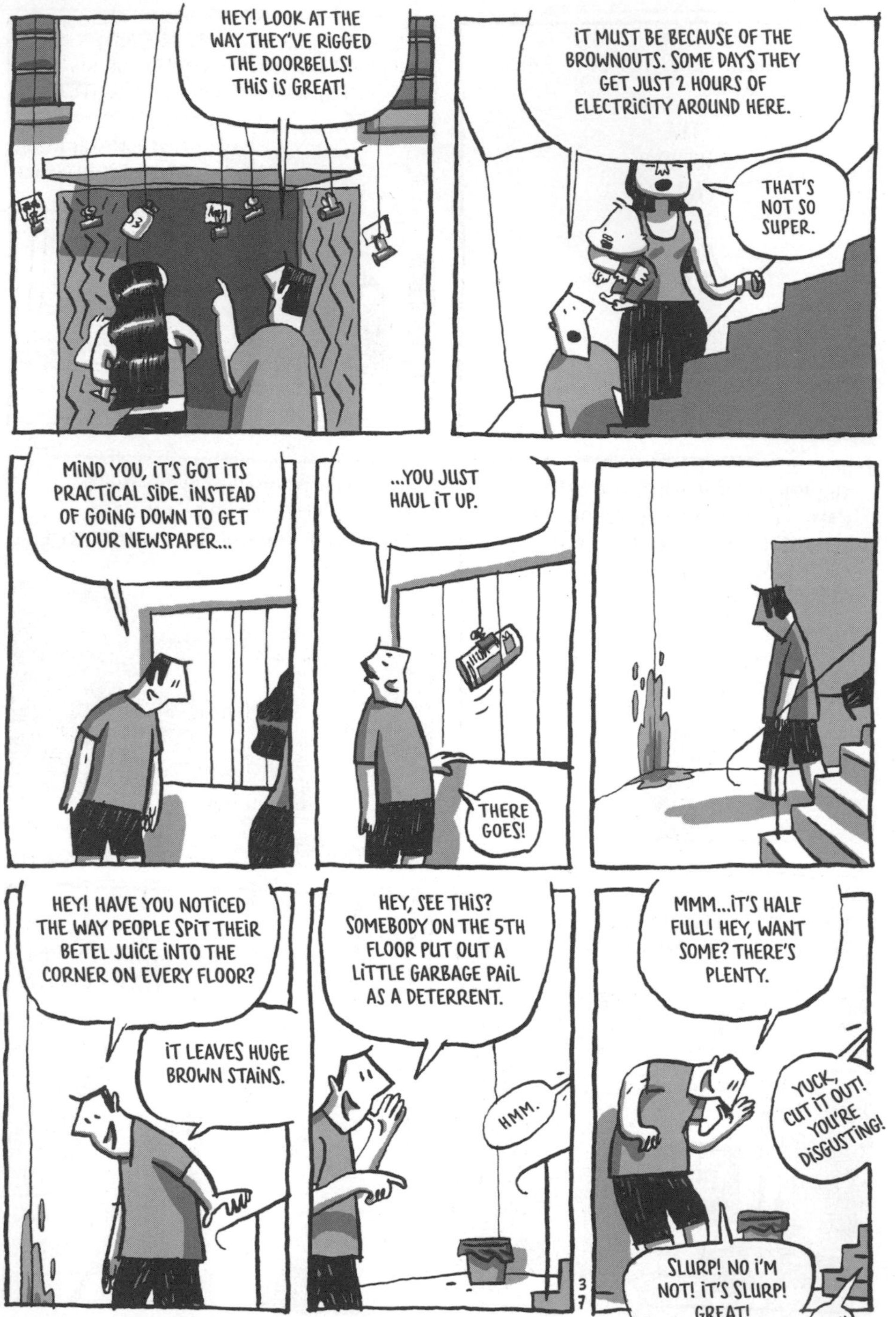
HEY! LOOK AT THE WAY THEY'VE RIGGED THE DOORBELLS! THIS IS GREAT!
IT MUST BE BECAUSE OF THE BROWNOUTS. SOME DAYS THEY GET JUST 2 HOURS OF ELECTRICITY AROUND HERE.
THAT'S NOT SO SUPER.
MIND YOU, IT'S GOT ITS PRACTICAL SIDE. INSTEAD OF GOING DOWN TO GET YOUR NEWSPAPER...
...YOU JUST HAUL IT UP.
THERE GOES!
HEY! HAVE YOU NOTICED THE WAY PEOPLE SPIT THEIR BETEL JUICE INTO THE CORNER ON EVERY FLOOR?
IT LEAVES HUGE BROWN STAINS.
HEY, SEE THIS? SOMEBODY ON THE 5TH FLOOR PUT OUT A LITTLE GARBAGE PAIL AS A DETERRENT.
HMM.
MMM...IT'S HALF FULL! HEY, WANT SOME? THERE'S PLENTY.
YUCK, CUT IT OUT! YOU'RE DISGUSTING!
SLURP! NO I'M NOT! IT'S SLURP! GREAT!
ARGH

WE GET THERE RIGHT ON TIME. PEOPLE ARE ALREADY SEATED ON THE GROUND, EATING.

SO, WHAT'S THE BABY'S NEW NAME?

I DON'T KNOW. I COULDN'T MAKE IT OUT.

AS ONE GROUP OF PEOPLE LEAVES, ANOTHER ARRIVES. THE TABLES EMPTY AND REFILL STEADILY.

OK, WELL, I GUESS WE SHOULD GET GOING. MORE PEOPLE JUST SHOWED UP.

IT'S ALL VERY EFFICIENT. HARDLY AN HOUR AFTER ARRIVING, WE'RE BACK AT THE CAR.

WE DIDN'T EXPECT TO BE DONE SO QUICKLY.

SO WHAT DO WE DO NOW?

I DON'T KNOW. VISIT A PAGODA?

NOT ANOTHER PAGODA?

REBOOT

WE FINALLY VISIT A HOUSE THAT'S NOT BAD, BUT TOO SMALL FOR A COUPLE WITH A CHILD.

ASIS OFFERS TO TAKE THE LITTLE HOUSE AND LEAVE US HIS OWN.

I'VE GOT TO ADMIT THAT I'M STUNNED. THERE ARE ALL KINDS OF PROGRAM MANAGERS. WE'VE MET ONES IN OTHER COUNTRIES AND THEY WEREN'T THE TYPE TO HAND OVER THEIR HOMES. NOT AT ALL.

ASIS IS THE KIND OF GUY WHO DOESN'T LEAVE HIS HUMANITARIAN VALUES BEHIND WHEN HE WALKS OUT THE OFFICE DOOR.

WE INHERIT HIS TV AS WELL, ALONG WITH ITS SATELLITE DISH.

RATS, NO STAR TREK.

I BUY A TABLE, SET UP A WORK SPACE IN A CORNER AND GET BACK TO MY COMICS ACTIVITIES.

LUCKILY, THIS LITTLE ROOM HAS A SECOND DOOR THAT LEADS OUTSIDE.

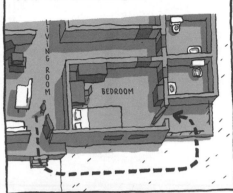

WHICH MEANS THAT MORNINGS, I GET TO LOOK LIKE I'M GOING TO WORK.

SEE YOU LATER! DADDY'S GOING TO WORK!

MAN OH MAN. JUST THINKING ABOUT PEOPLE WHO SPEND HOURS IN SUBWAYS...

MIND YOU, THEY DON'T NEED TO WORRY ABOUT SNAKES IN THE GRASS.

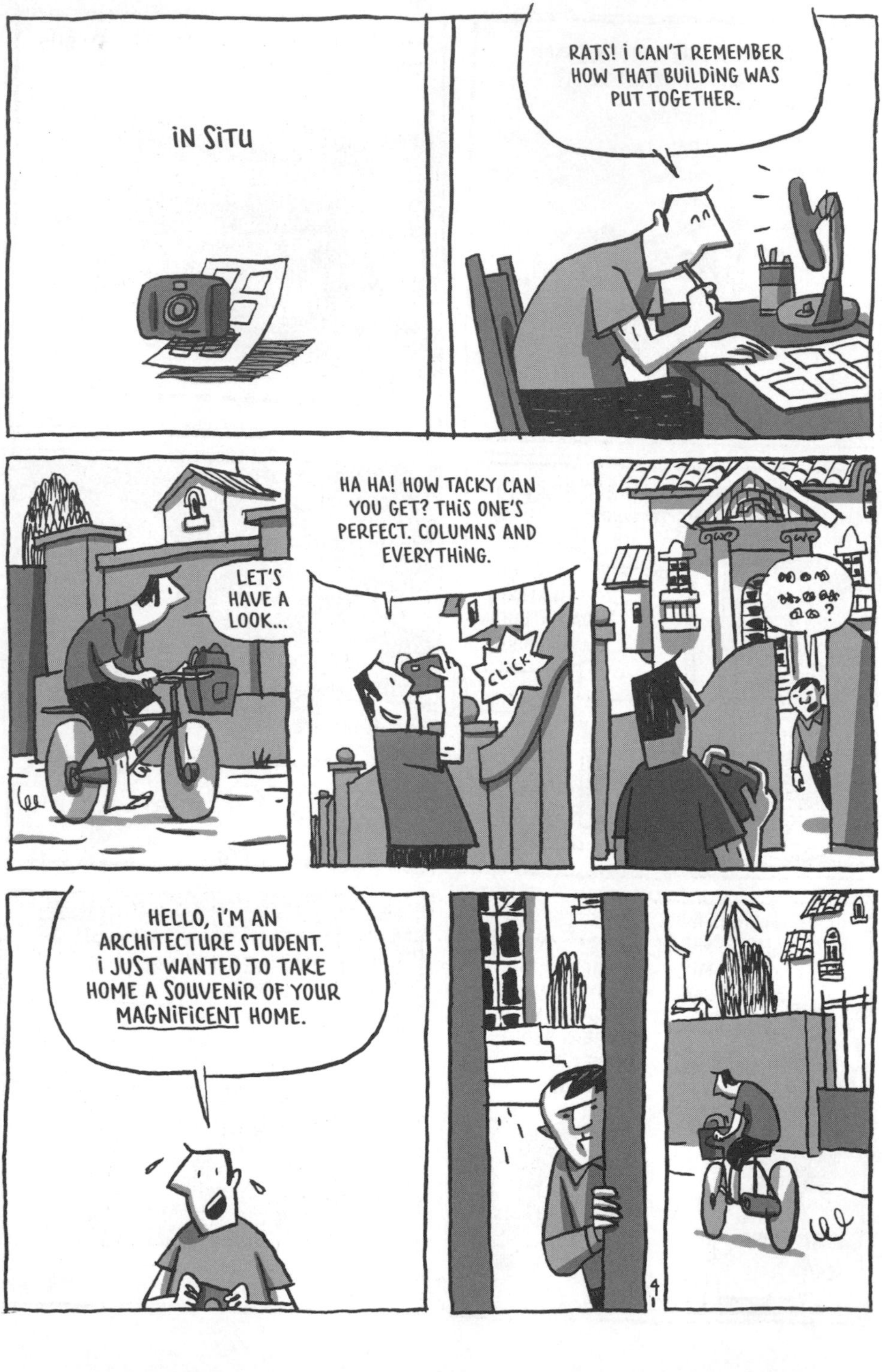
IN SITU
RATS! I CAN'T REMEMBER HOW THAT BUILDING WAS PUT TOGETHER.
LET'S HAVE A LOOK...
HA HA! HOW TACKY CAN YOU GET? THIS ONE'S PERFECT. COLUMNS AND EVERYTHING.
CLICK
HELLO, I'M AN ARCHITECTURE STUDENT. I JUST WANTED TO TAKE HOME A SOUVENIR OF YOUR MAGNIFICENT HOME.

GOOD OLD
PABLO

WHILE I WORK, SENG NAN TAKES CARE OF LOUIS AND THE HOUSE.

SENG NAN IS KACHIN, ONE OF THE COUNTRY'S THREE MAJOR ETHNIC GROUPS. THEIR TERRITORY IS IN THE FAR NORTH, BETWEEN INDIA AND CHINA.

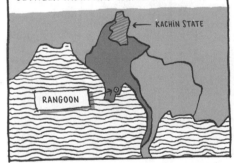

← KACHIN STATE

RANGOON

SHE SPEAKS SEVERAL LANGUAGES: KACHIN, BURMESE AND A LITTLE ENGLISH.

SHE SLEEPING.

HE SLEEPING.

HER ENGLISH IS A BIT ROUGH, THOUGH. FOR EXAMPLE, SHE GETS THE MASCULINE AND FEMININE MIXED UP WHEN SHE TALKS ABOUT LOUIS.

SHE VERY TIRED.

HE VERY TIRED.

AND IT GETS TO ME, SEEING THAT I JUST CUT HIS HAIR AND THERE'S NO REAL REASON FOR CONFUSION ANYMORE.

JEEZUS, I GUESS I'LL USE THE 9 MM CLIPPER GUIDE INSTEAD OF THE 13 MM ONE NEXT TIME.

OH MAN, I DON'T BELIEVE IT! SHE CLEANED MY DESK AGAIN!
I KEEP TELLING HER NOT TO, BUT SHE CAN'T STOP HERSELF. EVERY DAY, SHE TIDIES MY THINGS.
ONE DAY, I FOUND MY INK BOTTLE TOPPLED OVER ON A PAGE I HAD JUST FINISHED.
AAAHHH...
I'LL WIND UP LIKE PICASSO.
ACCESS PROHIBITED AT ALL TIMES
THE DUST WILL ACCUMULATE OVER THE YEARS.
AH-CHOO!
AH-CHOO!
AND TO GET MY ATTENTION, MY WIFE WILL SLIDE NOTES UNDER THE DOOR.
Darling. Jean Cocteau just stopped in to say hello.
AH, THAT PAIN IN THE BUTT!

SMALL VEHICLE

EVERY MORNING AT AROUND 8 AM, A GUY PASSES BY THE HOUSE, TAPPING ON A BELL.

HE'S FOLLOWED BY A DOZEN BAREFOOT NOVICE MONKS WHO COLLECT ALMS FROM OUR NEIGHBORS.

THEY EACH CARRY A RICE BOWL.

OTHER FOODS ARE MANAGED BY A CIVILIAN WHO CLOSES THE LINE, PUSHING A LITTLE CANTEEN AS HE GOES.

ONE SLEEPLESS NIGHT, I DISCOVER THAT THEY FILE BY AT 4 AND 6 A.M. AS WELL.

IT'S EASY TO UNDERSTAND WHY THEY GET UP EARLY WHEN YOU KNOW THEY CAN'T EAT AFTER NOON.

BUDDHISTS (87% OF THE POPULATION) GO ON THEIR FIRST MONASTIC RETREAT AT ABOUT AGE 10. THEY GENERALLY RETURN AS ADULTS AND STAY FOR A LONGER PERIOD OF TIME.

DING! DING!

DING.

HEY! IT'S THE LITTLE MONKS! LET'S GO GIVE THEM SOME RICE.

MINGALABA!

MINGALABA!

MINGALABA

ALMOST ALL MY NEIGHBORS ARE OUTSIDE AND WAITING.

THE SIZE OF THE BOWLS AND THE AMOUNT OF RICE IN THEM SAYS A LOT ABOUT THE GENEROSITY OF PEOPLE HERE.

IT'S NOT A MATTER OF BEGGING. GIVING TO THE MONKS IS CONSIDERED A GREAT HONOR.

EVERY DONATION INCREASES A PERSON'S MERITS, AND MERITS LIGHTEN ONE'S KARMA IN THE NEXT LIFE.

45

MERITS CAN BE OBTAINED IN ANY NUMBER OF WAYS: BY MAKING TEMPLE OFFERINGS, HELPING TO MAINTAIN A PAGODA OR, BETTER YET, BUILDING ONE.

AS DID NE WIN, THE FIRST IN A LONG LINE OF GENERALS WHO HAVE RULED THE COUNTRY WITH AN IRON FIST SINCE 1962.

AFTER SPENDING ONE WHOLE LIFETIME OPPRESSING A NATION, HE WANTED TO AVOID COMING BACK AS A RAT OR A FROG IN THE NEXT.

THERE! THAT WAS NICE, HUH?

AREN'T THOSE LITTLE MONKS CUTE?

FROM NOW ON, WE'LL GO GIVE THEM RICE EVERY MORNING.

NEXT DAY, SAME TIME.

ZZZ!

THE BURMESE PRACTICE THERAVADA BUDDHISM, WHICH DRAWS ON THE MOST ANCIENT WRITINGS COLLECTED BY THE DISCIPLES OF BUDDHA. AS SUCH, THEY CONSIDER THEIR DOCTRINE AS THAT CLOSEST TO THE TRUTH AND MOST PURE.

IN THE THERAVADA, BUDDHA IS NOT A GOD, BUT A MAN WHO HAS ATTAINED ENLIGHTENMENT. THERE'S NO USE PRAYING TO HIM, HE PROTECTS NO ONE.

IT'S UP TO YOU TO WORK ON YOUR OWN SALVATION BY BECOMING A MONK OR ADOPTING THE MONASTIC LIFE AND ITS MANY PRECEPTS.

BECAUSE THE PATH TO NIRVANA IT OFFERS IS SO RESTRICTIVE AND ACCESSIBLE TO SO FEW, THERAVADA IS REFERRED TO AS THE "SMALL VEHICLE."

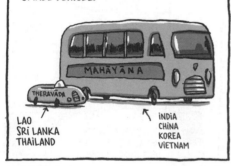

MAHAYANA

THERAVADA

LAO
SRI LANKA
THAILAND

INDIA
CHINA
KOREA
VIETNAM

GOOD GRIEF! REACHING NIRVANA MUST BE SOMETHING ELSE.

I BETTER GET STARTED ONE OF THESE DAYS.

NEARBY, THERE'S ONE OF THOSE CENTERS THAT CATERS MOSTLY TO FOREIGNERS.

INTERNATIONAL MEDITATION CENTER

LET'S HAVE A LOOK.

I INQUIRE, BUT SINCE YOU NEED TO COMMIT TO A 10-DAY RETREAT, I BACK OFF.

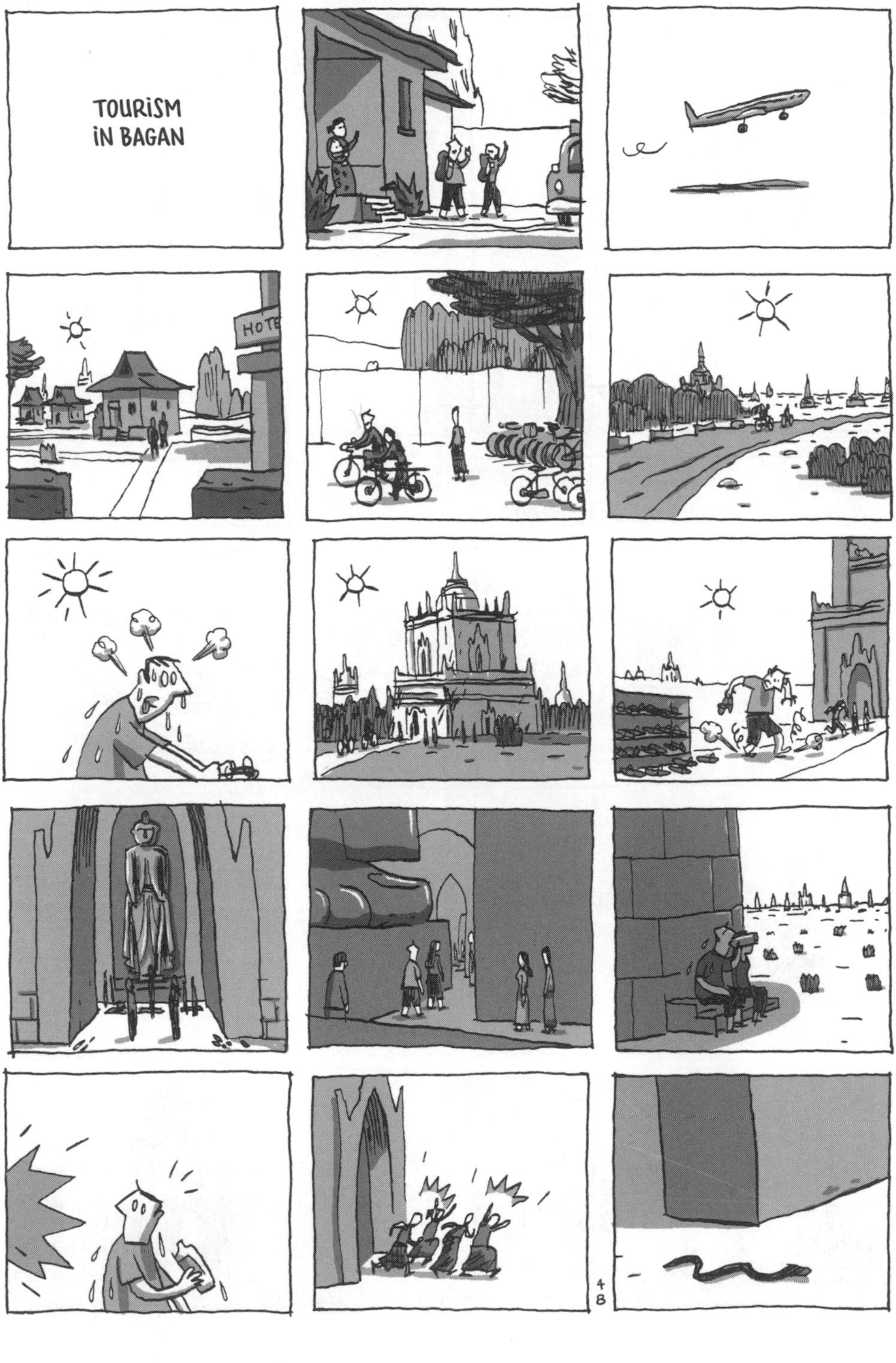
TOURISM
IN BAGAN
HOTE

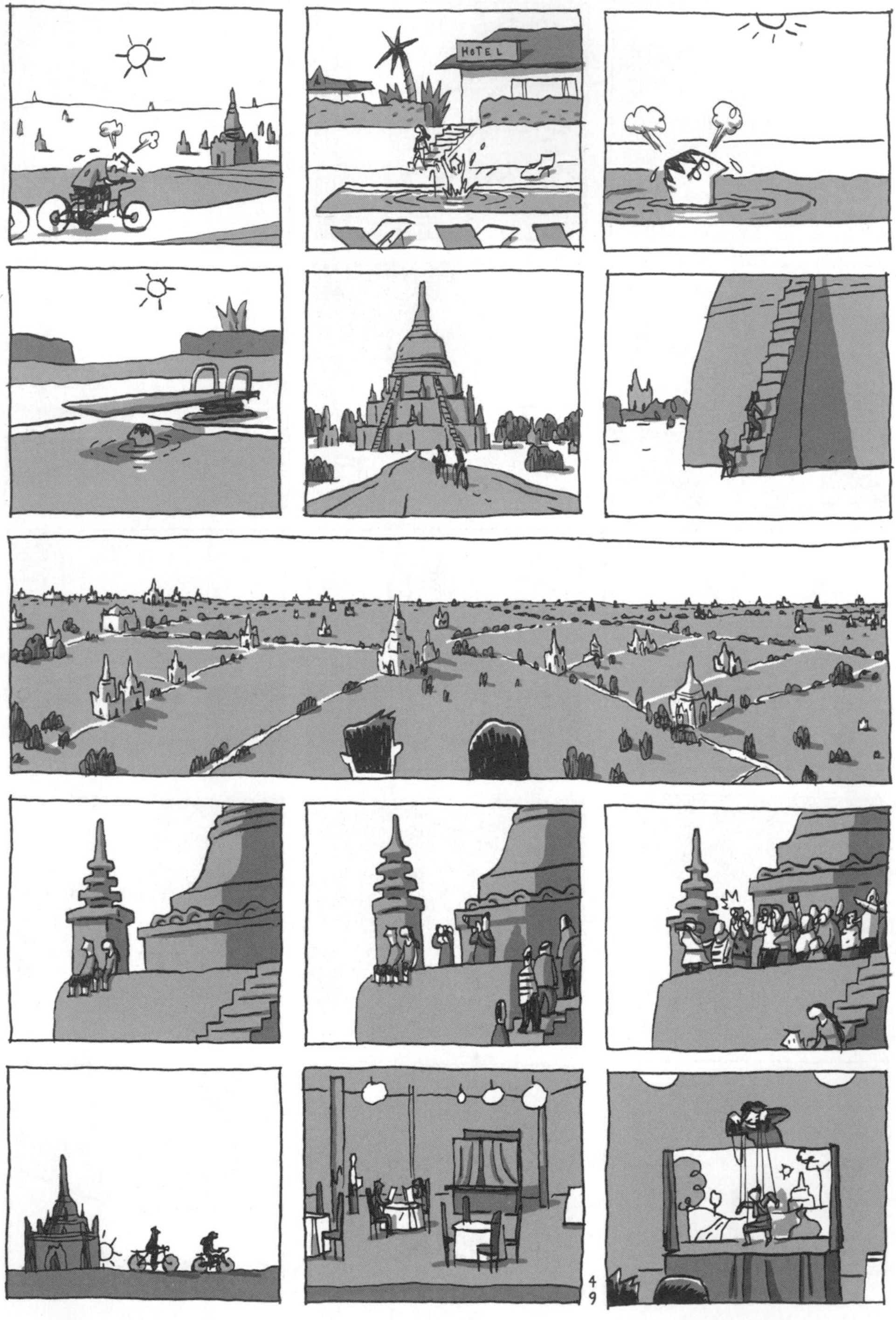
HOTEL

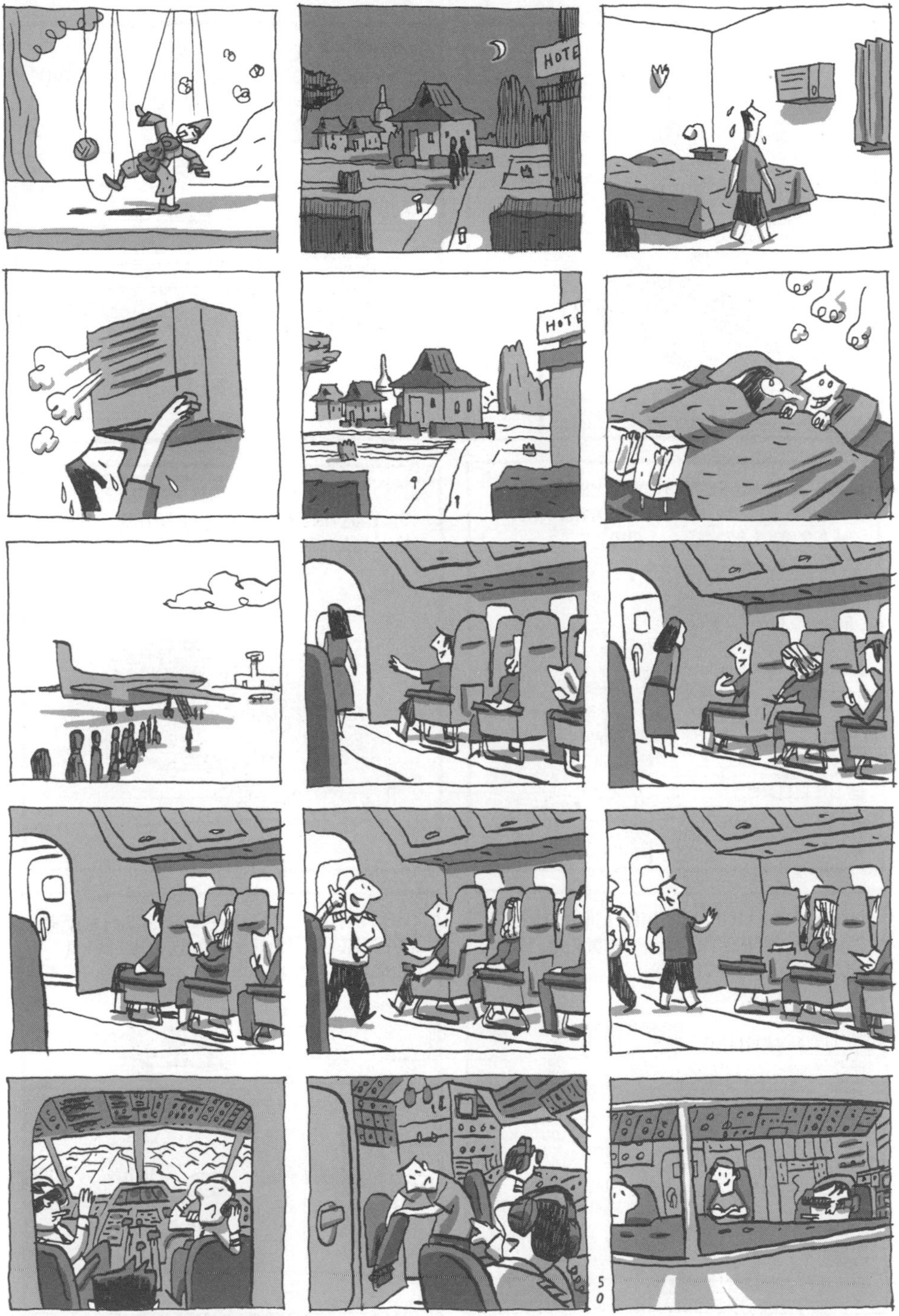
HOTE
HOTE

MSF
(DOCTORS
WITHOUT
BORDERS)

THREE MSF SECTIONS WORK IN BURMA: MSF HOLLAND, MSF SWITZERLAND AND THE ONE I CAME WITH, MSF FRANCE.

EACH OF THESE SECTIONS WORKS IN SEVERAL REGIONS OF THE COUNTRY AND ON A RANGE OF MEDICAL PROJECTS.

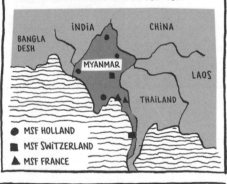

● MSF HOLLAND
■ MSF SWITZERLAND
▲ MSF FRANCE

AIDS, TUBERCULOSIS, FIRST AID, SUPPORT FOR EXISTING MEDICAL INFRASTRUCTURE, MALARIA, ETC.

MSF FRANCE WORKS IN THE EAST OF THE COUNTRY ALONG THE THAI BORDER, IN THE MON AND KAREN STATES.

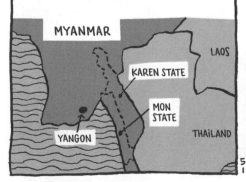

TWO POLITICALLY SENSITIVE REGIONS WHERE INDEPENDENT ARMED GROUPS CONTROL A NUMBER OF ZONES.

INSIDE THESE ZONES, WHICH HAVE NO HEALTH SYSTEMS, THE POPULATION IS LEFT TO FEND FOR ITSELF, WITHOUT ACCESS TO MEDICAL CARE. VICTIMS OF POLITICAL DISCRIMINATION, THESE ARE THE PEOPLE MSF WANTS TO REACH BY OFFERING THE GOVERNMENT A PROGRAM TO TREAT MALARIA, THE LEADING CAUSE OF DEATH IN THE REGION AND THROUGHOUT THE COUNTRY.

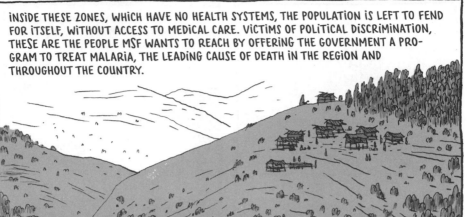

A PROPOSAL TO OPEN A VILLAGE CLINIC HAS TO PASS THROUGH A LONG CHAIN OF BUREAUCRATS.

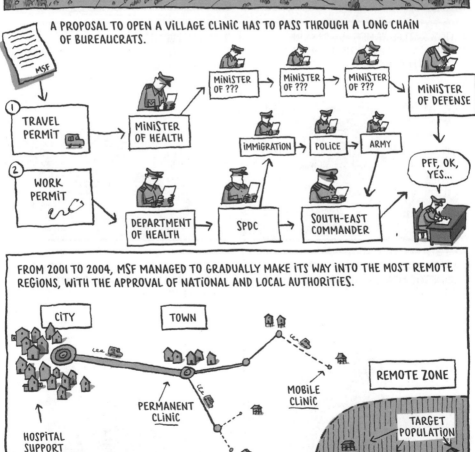

FROM 2001 TO 2004, MSF MANAGED TO GRADUALLY MAKE ITS WAY INTO THE MOST REMOTE REGIONS, WITH THE APPROVAL OF NATIONAL AND LOCAL AUTHORITIES.

EVENINGS, AFTER A DAY AT HOME WITH LOUIS, I JUMP ON ANY OPPORTUNITY TO HAVE SOME ADULT CONVERSATION.

WITH NADÈGE AT MSF, MOST OF THE PEOPLE WE KNOW WORK FOR NON-PROFIT ORGANIZATIONS.

AND SO I'VE OFTEN SAT IN ON ALL THE BIG QUESTIONS THAT ARE THE FODDER OF DEBATE IN HUMANITARIAN CIRCLES.

I DON'T HAVE MUCH TO SAY. WITH MY DOMESTIC ACTIVITIES, I FEEL A BIT OUTSIDE THE FRAY.

THE ONLY NEWS I HAVE TO SHARE IS THAT CITY MART JUST RECEIVED A NEW SHIPMENT OF JAPANESE DIAPERS.

ဟွန်မတီးရ

*NO HONKING WITHIN CITY LIMITS.

WHEN WE ARRIVED, THERE WAS A FLOURISH-
ING MARKET FOR PIRATED DVDS. YOU COULD
FIND ANY MOVIE FOR THE PRICE OF A COFFEE.

MATRIX

NEW

SPIDERMAN

KUROSAWA

BERGMAN

W.ALLEN

WE MANAGED, FOR EXAMPLE, TO WATCH THE
LATEST STAR WARS THE SAME WEEK IT CAME
OUT IN THEATRES.

THEY LOOK WEIRD,
DON'T THEY?

I THINK IT
WAS FILMED WITH
A CELL PHONE.

ALL THIS BOUNTY FLOWED IN FROM CHINA
AND THAILAND, WHERE LINER NOTES ARE
NOT ALWAYS COPIED WITH CARE.

"THE COW AND THE PRISONER"
WITH FERNONDEL... HA HA!

WINNER OF 2
OSCARS? NO,
REALLY?...WHADDA
YA KNOW...

"THIS DVD IS PROTECT-
ED AGAINST COPYING."
NO KIDDING.

"ALL RITS OF
REPROPUCTION AND
DISRIBUTION RESERVES.
PROJECTION OF THIS
VIDEOGRAM IN PUBLIC.
WITH OR WITHOUT AN
ADSMISION CHARGE.

TALK ABOUT
POETRY!

BUT THOSE DAYS ARE OVER. LAST NIGHT, THE GOVERNMENT DECIDED TO BAN THE SALE OF FOREIGN FILMS, AND THIS MORNING, THE SHELVES ARE EMPTY.

NEW RELEASES

WHOA! THAT'S EXTREME.

THEY'VE ONLY GOT BURMESE MOVIES SHOT IN 5 DAYS WITH A VIDEO CAMERA. WANNA TRY ONE?

DO THEY HAVE SUBTITLES?

I DOUBT IT.

FOR NEW RELEASES, WE FALL BACK ON PEOPLE COMING FROM BANGKOK. PIRATED FILMS ARE ILLEGAL THERE TOO, BUT COPY-RIGHT LEGISLATION IS HARDER TO ENFORCE IN THE COUNTRIES NEXT DOOR.

WHAT IS THIS SHIT?

HERE, UNDER THE MILITARY JUNTA, PEOPLE OBEY AND DON'T ASK QUESTIONS.

SO, WHY THE SUDDEN CRACKDOWN ON FOREIGN MOVIES?

NO IDEA.

"FOREIGN FILMS ENCOURAGE ACTS OF SEXUAL AGGRESSION."

← NEW LIGHT OF MYANMAR

OH, RIGHT, THAT IS A DRAG.

55

THE OFFICIAL EXPLANATION DOESN'T FOOL ANYONE, AND SPECULATION ABOUT THE REAL REASONS IS RUNNING HIGH.

IT'S TO ISOLATE US EVEN MORE.

I BET THE GOVERNMENT WANTS IN ON THE MARKET.

IT'S LIKE THE QUESTION OF WHY MOTORBIKES ARE NOT ALLOWED IN THE CITY. EVERYBODY HAS A THEORY.

...THAT'S WHAT MOST PEOPLE THINK, BUT I KNOW THE REAL REASON...

HMM...

HUH...

YOU DO?

THE MORE OR LESS OFFICIAL VERSION IS THAT THEY'RE TOO DANGEROUS.

WHATEVER...

DANGEROUS FOR WHO?

THEN THERE'S THE STORY ABOUT THE MOTORCYCLIST WHO PASSED THE TOP GENERAL'S CAR, POINTING HIS FINGER LIKE A GUN.

BANG!

AND THE ONE ABOUT THE MOTORCYCLIST WHO THREW A BOMB AT A HOTEL. BECAUSE HE WAS RIDING AN ENFIELD, THE POLICE COULDN'T KEEP UP.

IT'S HARD TO BELIEVE THAT THERE USED TO BE MOTORBIKES LIKE THIS ONE IN THE CITY STREETS...

ROYAL ENFIELD BULLET 1950

THAT WAS BACK WHEN BURMA HAD A MOVIE INDUSTRY THAT WAS THE ENVY OF ITS NEIGHBORS.

RANGOON

BOMBAY

HONG KONG

BAD DAD
MANUAL
MILK
MILK
57

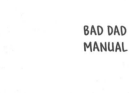

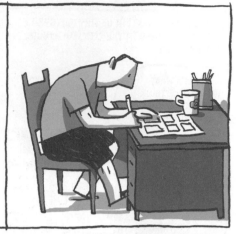

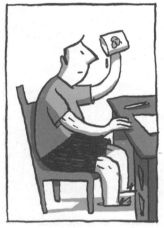

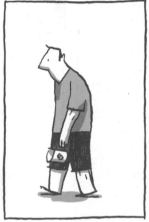

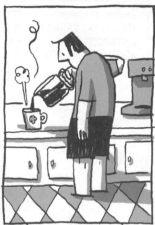

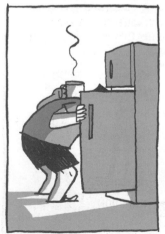

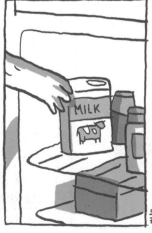

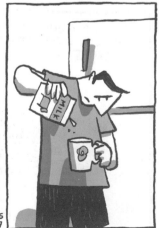

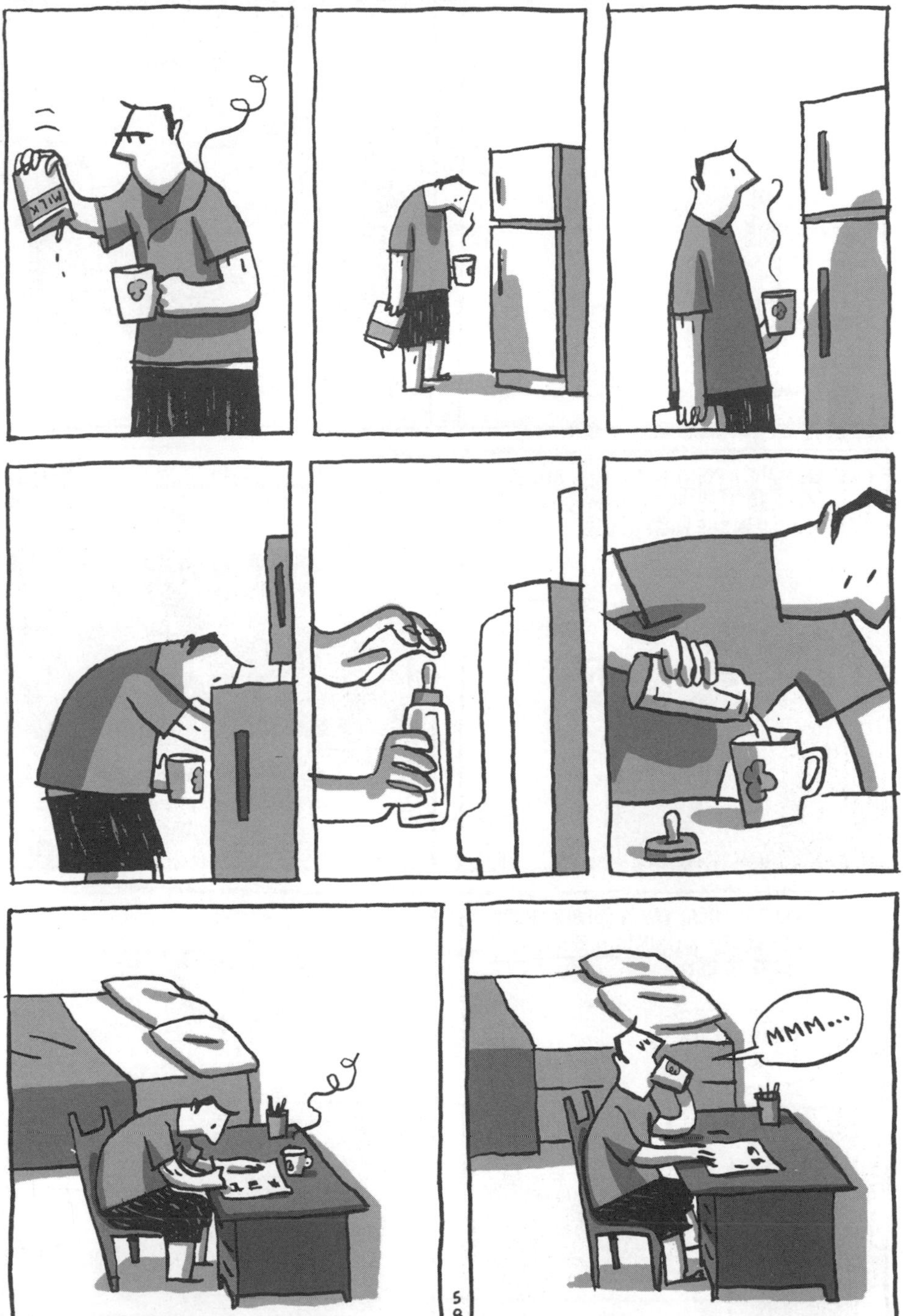
MILK
MMM...

CHINESE INK

DAMN...NO MORE INK!

PAGE 32

I'D EVEN MADE A POINT OF PACKING ALONG TWO EXTRA BOTTLES, BUT THEY MYSTERIOUSLY DISAPPEARED IN THE FIRST HOUSE.

VANISHED!

GOD KNOWS WHERE THOSE TWO BOTTLES OF CHINESE INK ENDED UP.

RIGHT HERE...!

I CHECK ALL THE LOCAL PAPER SUPPLY SHOPS, BUT THEY ONLY STOCK FOUNTAIN PEN INK, WHICH IS SURE TO RUN.

THAT'LL NEVER WORK.

4,000 KYATS.

59

IT DOESN'T WORK.

I KNEW IT.

A BURMESE FRIEND TELLS ME ABOUT A SHOP IN TOWN THAT SHOULD HAVE WHAT I NEED.

32 STREET PLEE-ZE*

*FRENCH ACCENT

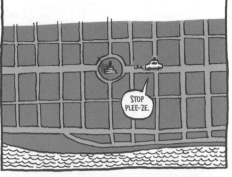

A LEGACY OF BRITISH COLONIAL RULE, THE DOWNTOWN STREETS ARE ALL AT RIGHT ANGLES. NOT TOO PRETTY, BUT PRACTICAL.

STOP PLEE-ZE.

THERE'S NOT A SHADOW OF A CHINESE INK BOTTLE ANYWHERE ON 32ND STREET. IN FACT, THE SHOPKEEPERS HERE SELL ONLY PAPER, WITH BIG STACKS IN FRONT OF EVERY STORE.

SHOOT! TOO BAD I'M NOT LOOKING FOR PAPER.

AFTER A STREET OF DVD PLAYERS AND ANOTHER OF PHOTOCOPIERS, I FIND THE INK STREET.

GOOD LORD. I HOPE THEY'VE GOT MORE PORTABLE FORMATS.

ARE THESE FOR PRINT SHOPS?

60

INSIDE, I'M SHOWN TWO KINDS OF INK, ONE OF WHICH IS A BIT THICK.

WHAT'S THE DIFFERENCE BETWEEN THE TWO?

3,000 KYATS!

RIGHT, BUT I MEANT IN TERMS OF QUALITY.

IN A DUSTY CORNER, I FIND SOME VINTAGE ENGLISH NIBS.

2040 HINKS WELLES & Cº RED INK PEN ENGLAND

WOW, THIS SHOP IS A REAL TRIP BACK IN TIME.

OH JOY!

I FIND ROTRING INK THAT MUST HAVE BEEN LYING HERE FOR YEARS, BECAUSE ACCORDING TO THE EXPIRY DATE, IT'S ONLY GOOD FOR ANOTHER MONTH.

HM... THIS SHOULD BE ENOUGH TO FINISH THE BOOK.

THERE. AFTER A WEEK OF SEARCHING, MISSION ACCOMPLISHED.

FOR THE NEXT FEW DAYS, IT'S LIKE THE WORD IS OUT, AND I SEE IT EVERYWHERE: AT THE CORNER SHOP, THE SUPERMARKET, ETC.

"ROTRING" INK

ARGH!!... TALK ABOUT IRRITATING!

MIGHT AS WELL START FRESH.

RINSING OUT THE LITTLE BOTTLE I USE FOR MY INK...

HEY! AN OLD NIB!

INCREDIBLE! IT MUST HAVE BEEN IN THERE FOR YEARS!

HMM... WHEN COULD I HAVE LOST IT?

I REMEMBER SOMETHING, BUT...

TOO BAD I'VE GOT SUCH A LOUSY MEMORY.

HMM! OH! THAT'S IT! IT JUST CAME BACK!

DAMN! MY NIB!

WHAT THE HECK. IT WON'T RUST. I'LL FISH IT OUT SOME OTHER DAY.

HA HA! THAT WAS AGES AGO! I WAS STILL SINGLE AND CHILDLESS!

I HADN'T GOT ANYTHING PUBLISHED YET. I WAS WORKING IN ANIMATION AND BETWEEN JOBS I WAS DOING A COMIC FOR L'ASSOCIATION©.*

6 2

*COMICS PUBLISHER IN FRANCE.

OH MAN! THAT'S CRAP! HEY, YOU COULDN'T GET THAT PUBLISHED TODAY, BUDDY.

SCREW YOU. I CAN DO WHATEVER I LIKE.

LITTLE BRAT.

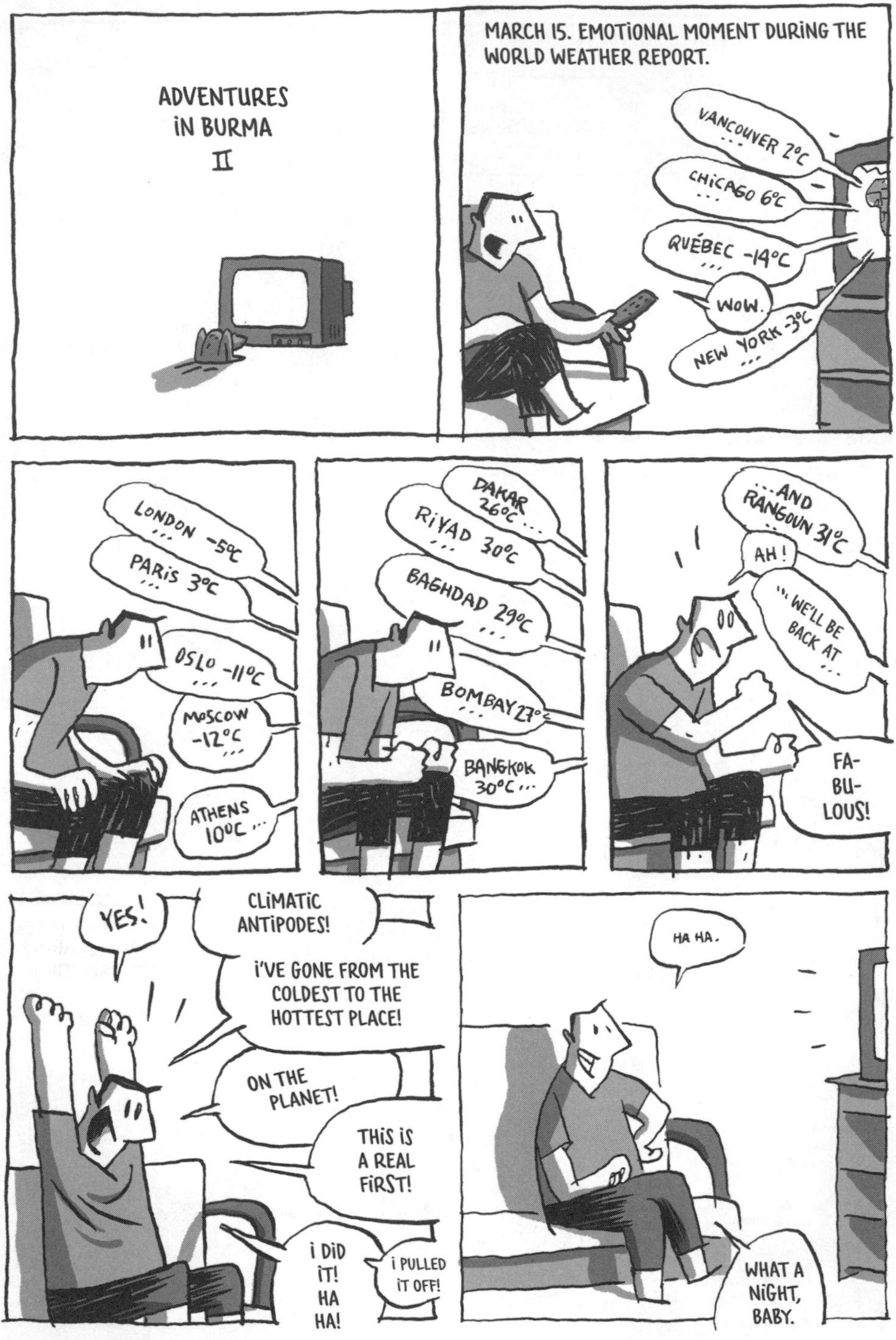
ADVENTURES IN BURMA II
MARCH 15. EMOTIONAL MOMENT DURING THE WORLD WEATHER REPORT.
VANCOUVER 2°C ...
CHICAGO 6°C ...
QUÉBEC -14°C ...
WOW.
NEW YORK -3°C ...
LONDON -5°C ...
PARIS 3°C ...
OSLO -11°C ...
MOSCOW -12°C ...
ATHENS 10°C ...
DAKAR 26°C ...
RIYAD 30°C ...
BAGHDAD 29°C ...
BOMBAY 27°C ...
BANGKOK 30°C ...
...AND RANGOUN 31°C ...
AH!
... WE'LL BE BACK AT ...
FA-BU-LOUS!
YES!
CLIMATIC ANTIPODES!
I'VE GONE FROM THE COLDEST TO THE HOTTEST PLACE!
ON THE PLANET!
THIS IS A REAL FIRST!
I DID IT! HA HA!
I PULLED IT OFF!
HA HA.
WHAT A NIGHT, BABY.

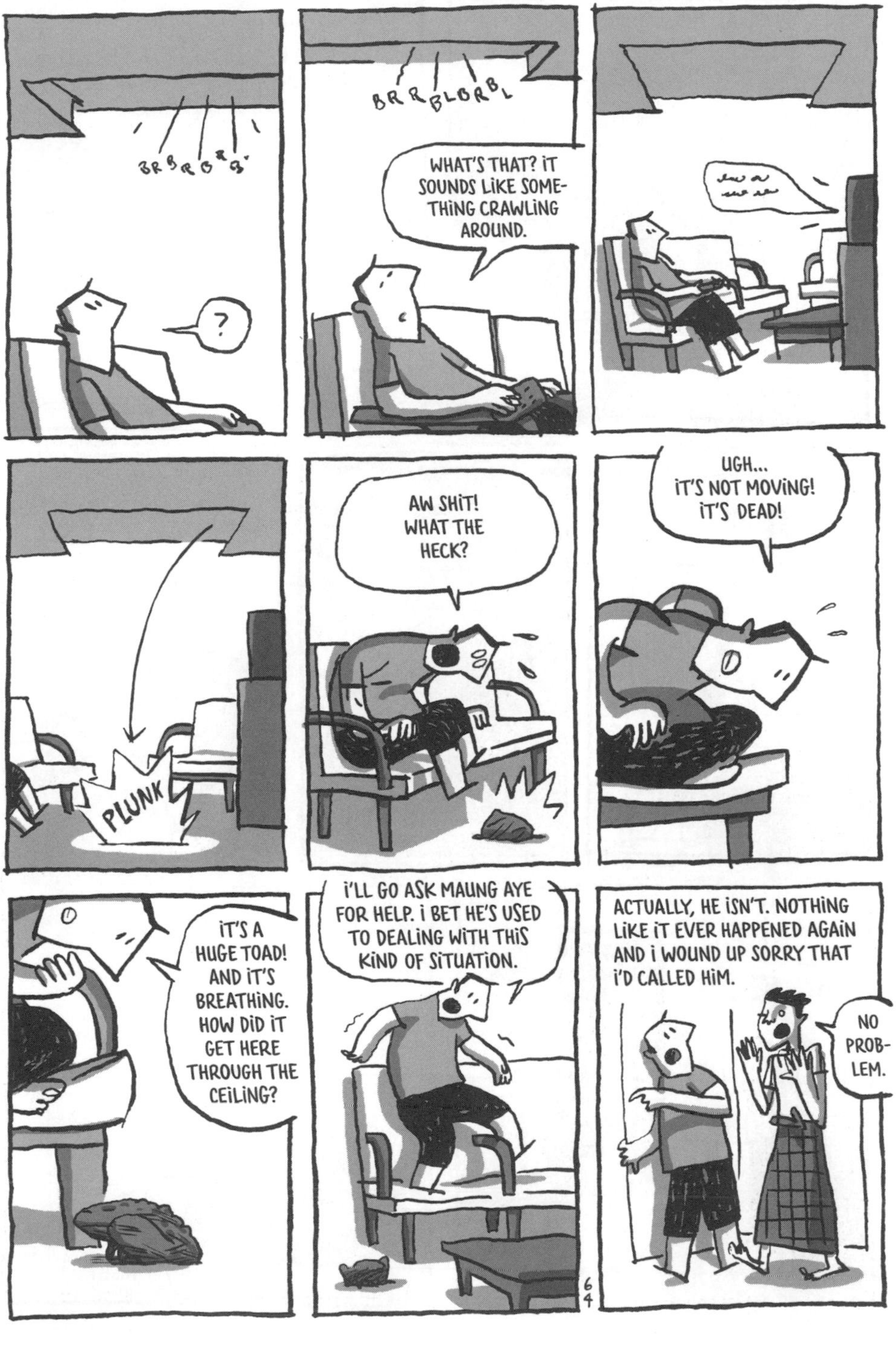
BRBRBRBB
?
BRRBLORBL
WHAT'S THAT? IT SOUNDS LIKE SOMETHING CRAWLING AROUND.
PLUNK
AW SHIT! WHAT THE HECK?
UGH... IT'S NOT MOVING! IT'S DEAD!
IT'S A HUGE TOAD! AND IT'S BREATHING. HOW DID IT GET HERE THROUGH THE CEILING?
I'LL GO ASK MAUNG AYE FOR HELP. I BET HE'S USED TO DEALING WITH THIS KIND OF SITUATION.
ACTUALLY, HE ISN'T. NOTHING LIKE IT EVER HAPPENED AGAIN AND I WOUND UP SORRY THAT I'D CALLED HIM.
NO PROBLEM.

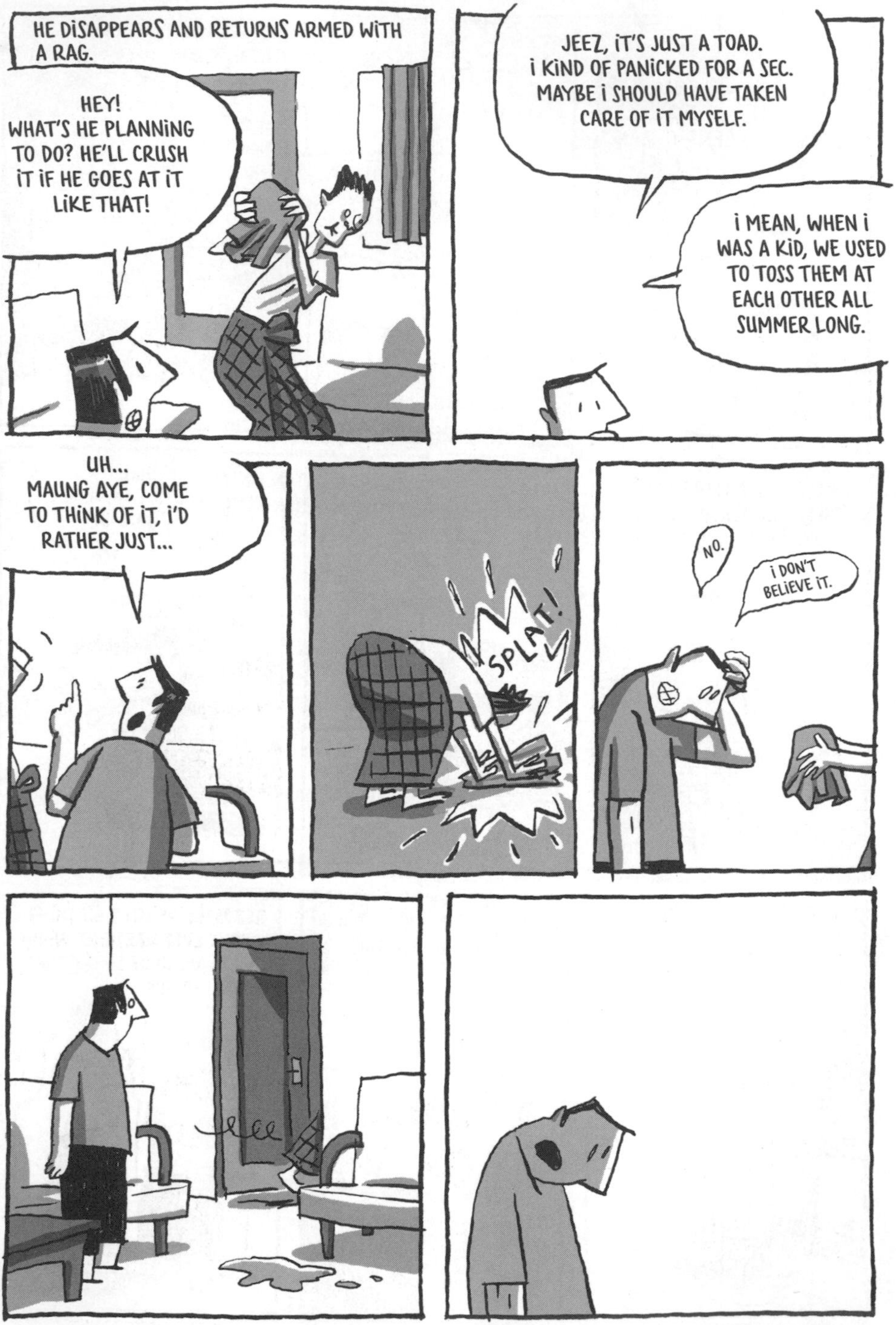

HE DISAPPEARS AND RETURNS ARMED WITH A RAG.
HEY! WHAT'S HE PLANNING TO DO? HE'LL CRUSH IT IF HE GOES AT IT LIKE THAT!
JEEZ, IT'S JUST A TOAD. I KIND OF PANICKED FOR A SEC. MAYBE I SHOULD HAVE TAKEN CARE OF IT MYSELF.
I MEAN, WHEN I WAS A KID, WE USED TO TOSS THEM AT EACH OTHER ALL SUMMER LONG.
UH... MAUNG AYE, COME TO THINK OF IT, I'D RATHER JUST...
SPLAT!
NO.
I DON'T BELIEVE IT.

CENS-O-RAMA

MANY MAGAZINES ARE PUBLISHED IN MYANMAR. MORE THAN 80 A WEEK, I'M TOLD.

SOME IN COLOR, BUT MOST IN BLACK AND WHITE ON LOUSY PAPER.

THERE ARE A FEW DAILIES, TOO. AND ALL THESE PUBLICATIONS NEED TO GO THROUGH A CENSOR BEFORE HITTING THE STREET.

YOU CAN OFTEN FIND TRACES OF THE CENSOR'S WORKMANSHIP.

TIME MAGAZINE: WHOLE PAGE REMOVED.

EMPTY WORD BALLOONS.

I'VE HEARD THAT IN THE PAST, PUBLISHERS HAD TO COVER UP ARTICLES DEEMED INAPPROPRIATE WITH A LAYER OF THICK SILVER PAINT.

3,000

OR THEY COULD USE SCISSORS AND BRING THE CENSOR AS MANY CUTTINGS AS THERE WERE COPIES PRINTED.

3,000

BUT SOMETIMES, A THIRD OF THE PRINT RUN WOULD ALREADY HAVE BEEN SENT OUT. INSTEAD OF RUNNING AFTER IT, PUBLISHERS WOULD REPRINT THE MISSING PAGES AND CUT THEM UP TO FILL THE TALLY.

ADVERTISERS WOULD WORRY ABOUT THE CONTENT ON THE FLIP SIDE OF THEIR ADS.

NO WAY! NOT A CARTOONIST! OUR STUFF GETS CUT EVERY TIME WITH THAT GUY.

AND SO, FOR YEARS, YOU COULD SEE BLANK SPOTS FORMERLY OCCUPIED BY ARTICLES YOU'D NEVER GET TO READ.

AH, THE BASTARDS!

← BEFORE

THESE DAYS, WITH COMPUTER ASSISTED PUBLISHING, PAGES ARE EASILY RESET, AND NO ONE'S THE WISER.

WOW, ANOTHER GREAT DAY IN BURMA.

← NOW

YOU CAN IMAGINE WHAT A FEW WESTERN PAPERS WOULD LOOK LIKE UNDER THE BURMESE EDITORIAL SYSTEM.

ALL DONE?

ONE SEC, I'M LOOKING FOR AN ARTICLE.

The NEW LIGHT OF MYANMAR

IS THE NATION'S OFFICIAL NEWSPAPER. IT'S AVAILABLE EVERYWHERE, IN ENGLISH AND IN BURMESE. THE PROPAGANDA IS LAID ON SO THICK THAT YOU WONDER WHETHER A SINGLE PERSON IN THE ENTIRE COUNTRY BELIEVES IT.

WHAT? IT'S NOT TRUE?

THE FRONT PAGE INVARIABLY LISTS THE PROFESSED OBJECTIVES OF THE PEOPLE, DIVIDED INTO 3 CATEGORIES.

THE 4 ECONOMIC OBJECTIVES

THE 4 POLITICAL OBJECTIVES

THE 4 SOCIAL OBJECTIVES

AND IT GOES ON WITH THE "DESIRES" OF THE PEOPLE ON PAGE 2. THESE FOUR SENTENCES ARE EVERYWHERE, PRINTED ON THE COVER OF EVERY BOOK, MAGAZINE AND DVD, SHOWN BEFORE EVERY FILM AND EVEN POSTED AT THE ENTRANCE TO THE PARK NEXT DOOR.

PEOPLE'S DESIRES

* OPPOSE THOSE RELYING ON EXTERNAL ELEMENTS, ACTING AS STOOGES, HOLDING NEGATIVE VIEWS
* OPPOSE THOSE TRYING TO JEOPARDIZE STABILITY OF THE STATE AND PROGRESS OF THE NATION
* OPPOSE FOREIGN NATIONS INTERFERING IN INTERNAL AFFAIRS OF THE STATE
* CRUSH ALL INTERNAL AND EXTERNAL DESTRUCTIVE ELEMENTS AS THE COMMON ENEMY

OPPOSE... CRUSH... PFF!...

NOTE THE XENOPHOBIC, PARANOID AND HAWKISH RHETORIC THAT ALL DICTATORSHIPS USE.

ALL THE ONES I'VE VISITED, ANYWAY.

LET'S SEE THE HEADLINES: AGREEMENT REACHED WITH THE AMBASSADOR OF SLOVAKIA — JADE SALE ATTRACTS 483 MERCHANTS — FOREST SECTOR CONTINUES TO GROW — OPENING OF A FLORAL ARRANGEMENT CLASS

THERE'S ALSO A QUOTE FROM NR. I GENERAL THAN SHWE: "THE DEVELOPMENT OF OUR HUMAN RESOURCES IS VITAL FOR THE NATION. DEMOCRACY ALONE CANNOT GUARANTEE BURMA'S DEVELOPMENT AND SUSTAINABILITY IN THE LONG TERM."

WHEW!

QUOTATIONS GENERALLY TAKE UP A QUARTER OF A PAGE.

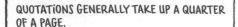

"CONTINUOUS EFFORT IS REQUIRED TO CREATE A STRONGER AND MORE MODERN ARMY."
SENIOR GENERAL THAN SHWE

Nº 1

THE "NEW LIGHT OF MYANMAR" BASICALLY HAS THREE SECTIONS:

—INTERNATIONAL NEWS, ALL OF IT BLEAK.

SUICIDE BOMB IN IRAQ.

PLANE CRASH IN INDIA.

EARTHQUAKE IN AFGHANISTAN.

FLOODING IN VIETNAM.

OVER 2 PAGES

—NATIONAL NEWS, WITH SLOW BUT STEADY PROGRESS ON ALL FRONTS, THANKS TO THE EFFORTS OF OUR HARD-WORKING ARMY

MINISTER OF FOREIGN AFFAIRS UNYAN WIN LEAVING FOR BANGLADESH.

SENIOR GENERAL THAN SHWE INSPECTING KANDANGI NATIONAL PARK.

PRIME MINISTER GENERAL SOE WIN AT THE MALAYSIAN DINNER GALA.

LIEUTENANT GENERAL THEIN SEIN PRESIDING OVER THE NATIONAL ASSEMBLY.

SENIOR VICE GENERAL MUNG AYE WELCOMING PRIME MINISTER GENERAL SOE WIN AT THE AIRPORT.

DAW KYI KYI, WIFE OF THE MINISTER OF INFORMATION, AT AN EDUCATION CONFERENCE.

ETC.

Senior General Than Shwe delivers ...

(from page 1)

Commander-in-Chief (Navy) Vice-Admiral Soe Thein, Commander-in-Chief (Air) Lt-Gen Myat Hein, Commander of Central Command Maj-Gen Khin Zaw, Ministers Maj-Gen Htay Oo, U Aung Thaung, Maj-Gen Saw Tun, Brig-Gen Ohn Myint, Brig-Gen Thein Zaw, Col Thein Nyunt, Maj-Gen Thein Swe, Brig-Gen Lun Thi, U Thaung, Dr Chan Nyein, Dr Kyaw Myint and Brig-Gen Thein Aung, Military Appointment-General Maj-Gen Hsan Hsint of the Ministry of Defence, Defence Services Inspector-General Maj-Gen Thein Htaik, Maj-Gen Kyi Win of the Ministry of Defence, Vice-Chief of Armed Forces Training Maj-Gen Aung

↑
SOME ARTICLES CONTAIN NOTHING BUT A LIST OF OFFICIALS PRESENT AT A GIVEN EVENT.

AND LASTLY, <u>SPORTS AND CULTURE</u>, THE SECTION MOST READ BY THE BURMESE, WHO HAVE FIGURED OUT WHAT TO MAKE OF THE REST OF THE PAPER...

...SEEING THAT THEY ALSO HAVE ACCESS TO BURMESE-LANGUAGE RADIO BROADCASTS FROM THAILAND.

HEY!

AS I WAS DRAWING THE VARIOUS OFFICIALS, I NOTICED A SMALL SARTORIAL DETAIL.

SHIRT OF A CIVILIAN OR UNRANKED SOLDIER.
↓

SHIRT WITH POCKETS ADJUSTED FOR HIGH-RANKING OFFICERS.
↓

NOT EXACTLY PRACTICAL, BUT ESSENTIAL FOR THE DISPLAY OF MILITARY DECORATIONS.

GOLDEN VALLEY

WE LIVE IN GOLDEN VALLEY, A V.I.P. NEIGHBORHOOD.

IN OTHER WORDS, WE'RE SURROUNDED BY BUSINESSMEN WITH CLOSE TIES TO THE REGIME AND THE GENERALS. AS A RESULT OF WHICH WE HAVE A STEADY SUPPLY OF ELECTRICITY AND WATER THROUGHOUT THE DRY SEASON.

SOME OF THE HOUSES ARE MASSIVE. EQUALLY MASSIVE WALLS SURROUND THEM, WITH ONLY ROOFTOPS VISIBLE BEYOND.

DAMN! IT'S HIDDEN...

DESPITE THE HEIGHT OF THE WALLS, THEY'VE ADDED BARBED WIRE ON TOP.

7
1

YOU GET THE PROTECTION YOU CAN AFFORD.

GLASS SHARDS FOR SMALL HOUSES.

FENCES WITH POINTED STAKES FOR MEDIUM ONES.

BARBED WIRE AND SURVEILLANCE CAMERAS FOR THE LARGEST AND MOST SOPHISTICATED.

BARBED WIRE LOOKS A BIT NOUVEAU RICHE, HUH?

ADA!

THOSE GUARDED DAY AND NIGHT BY SOLDIERS BELONG TO ARMY OFFICERS.

SINCE CRIME IS VIRTUALLY NON-EXISTENT HERE AND BREAK-INS ARE RARE, YOU'VE GOT TO WONDER WHAT ALL THE SECURITY IS ABOUT.

THE THING MILITARY OFFICERS FEAR MOST IN THIS COUNTRY IS OTHER MILITARY OFFICERS.

THEIR POWER STRUGGLES ARE THE CAUSE OF CONSTANT POLITICAL INFIGHTING.

HEY, THE MINISTER OF TRANSPORT WAS REPLACED.

AGAIN?

THE CASE OF PRIME MINISTER KHIN NYUT IN OCTOBER 2004 IS STILL FRESH IN LOCAL MEMORY.

CONSIDERED A MODERATE REFORMER, KHIN NYUT TRIED TO MEDIATE BETWEEN THE NO. I GENERAL AND HIS SWORN ENEMY, AUNG SAN SUU KYI. UNSUCCESSFULLY, AS WE ALL KNOW.

HE MAINTAINED MANY CONTACTS WITH THE OUTSIDE WORLD, TRYING TO BREAK BURMA'S ISOLATION. HE WAS ALSO ONE OF THE FEW MILITARY OFFICERS WITH A UNIVERSITY DEGREE.

AND THEN, DESPITE HIS FUNCTION AS HEAD OF THE SECRET SERVICE, CHARGES WERE BROUGHT AGAINST HIS OFFICE, AND THE ENTIRE MINISTRY WAS THROWN INTO JAIL.

SINCE THAT PURGE, WHICH OCCURRED A FEW MONTHS BEFORE OUR ARRIVAL, THE GOVERNMENT HAS TOUGHENED ITS STANCE AND THE COUNTRY HAS REVERSED COURSE.

HA HA
HA HA

N.G.O.S AND INTERNATIONAL ORGANIZATIONS ARE UNDER INCREASING SCRUTINY BY THE GENERALS.

ALL THESE OUTSIDE ELEMENTS SPREAD NEGATIVE IDEAS.

AND THE POPULATION CAN ONLY LOOK ON IN SILENCE AS THE LEADERS FIGHT IT OUT.

YOU CAN'T LOSE HOPE. AT 76, THAN SHWE IS BOUND TO CROAK SOON.

AND ONCE HE'S GONE, THINGS WILL CHANGE.

YOU KNOW, THAT'S WHAT WE THOUGHT ABOUT THE DEPARTURE OF NE WIN, THE LAST DICTATOR.

HE HELD ALL STRINGS FROM 1962 ON...

...IN '88, THERE WERE DEMONSTRATIONS THAT ENDED IN BLOODSHED, AND THEN THAN SHWE WAS MADE HEAD OF STATE.

SO I DON'T SEE MUCH REASON FOR HOPE.

74

OFF DAYS

ALRIGHT, I'LL GO OUT AND DO A FEW SKETCHES. THAT'LL CLEAR MY HEAD.

I SHOULD DO THIS MORE OFTEN, INSTEAD OF STAYING HOLED UP IN MY ROOM.

WHAT TO DRAW?

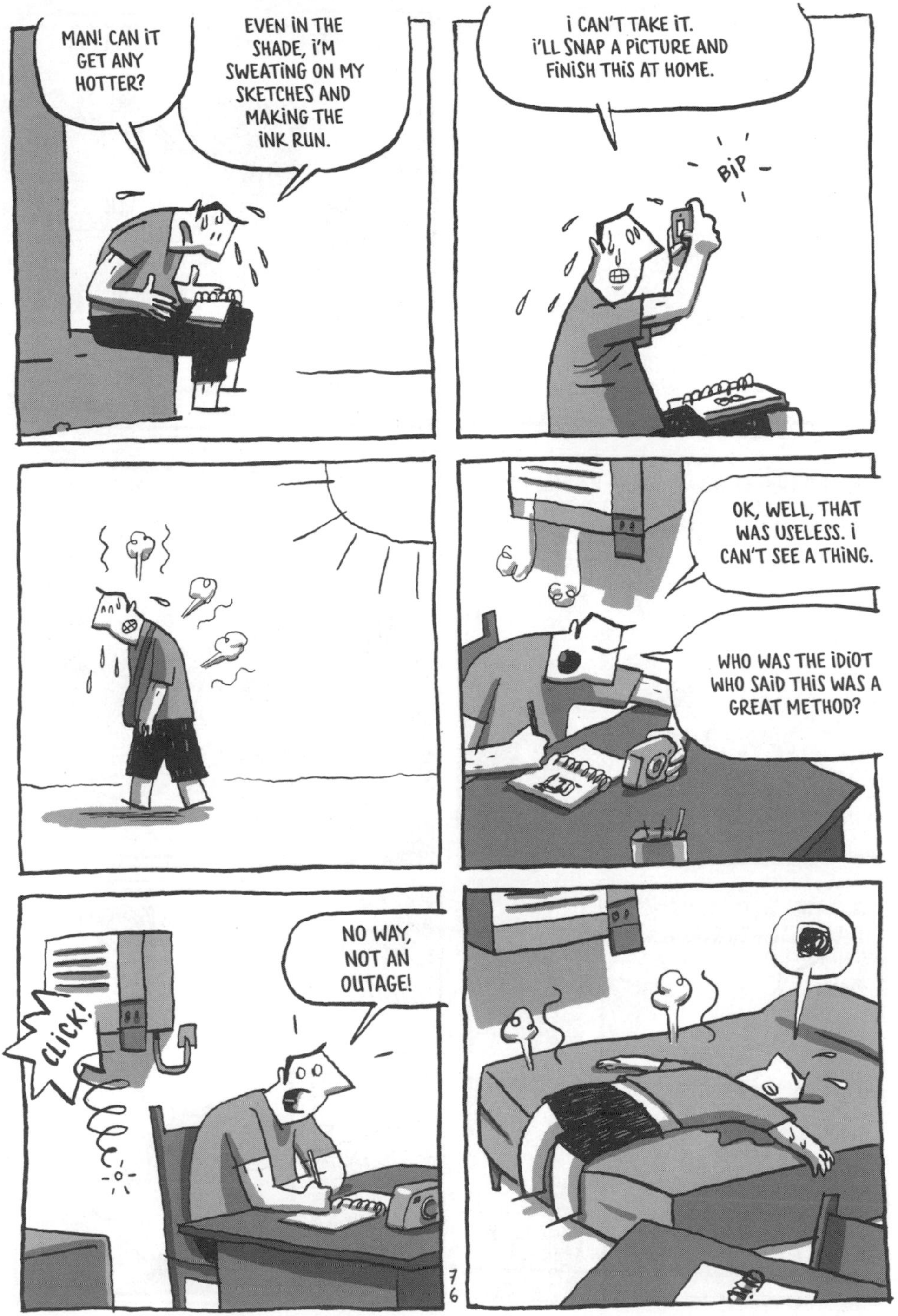
MAN! CAN IT GET ANY HOTTER?
EVEN IN THE SHADE, I'M SWEATING ON MY SKETCHES AND MAKING THE INK RUN.
I CAN'T TAKE IT. I'LL SNAP A PICTURE AND FINISH THIS AT HOME.
BIP
OK, WELL, THAT WAS USELESS. I CAN'T SEE A THING.
WHO WAS THE IDIOT WHO SAID THIS WAS A GREAT METHOD?
CLICK!
NO WAY, NOT AN OUTAGE!

ARMED
FORCES
DAY

LATELY, THE STREETS HAVE BEEN FULL OF MILITARY.

ARMED FORCES DAY IS COMING UP, AND THE REGIME ALWAYS WORRIES THAT A FEW AGITATORS MAY STIR THINGS UP.

WHICH SEEMS UNLIKELY TO ME. FOR WEEKS, SECURITY OFFICERS HAVE BEEN POSTED EVERY 200 YARDS ALONG THE PARADE ROUTE, DAY AND NIGHT.

AND THEY NEED TO CHECK THEIR ASSIGNED STRETCH OF GROUND REGULARLY FOR MINES.

FROM THE LOOK ON THEIR FACES, YOU CAN TELL THEY'RE NOT THRILLED BY THE TASK.

WALKING
STREET
VENDORS

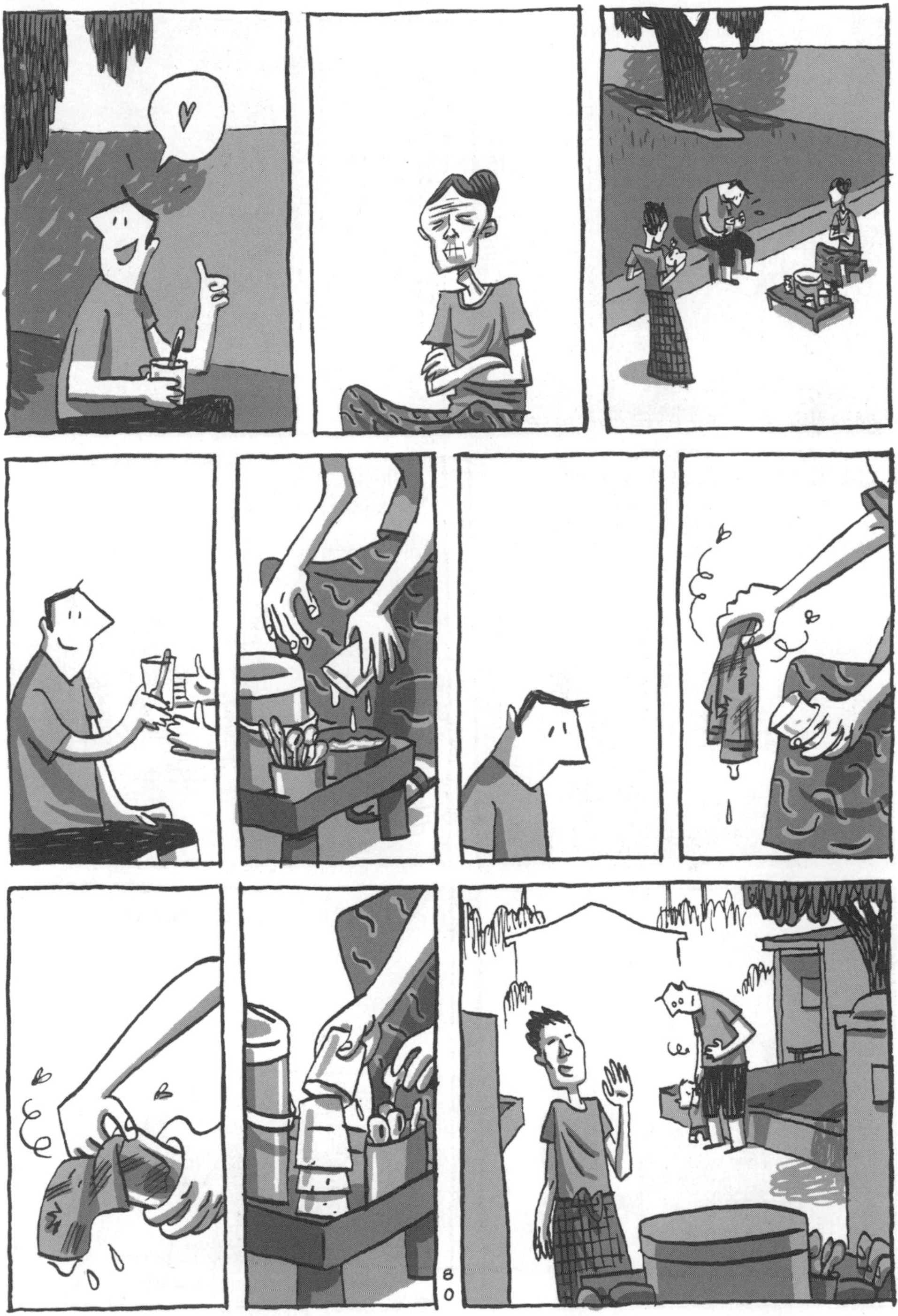

DURING MY FEW DAYS IN PARIS BEFORE COMING TO BURMA, I CAME ACROSS A KNIFE GRINDER.

I FOUND THAT PRETTY EXOTIC. I THOUGHT THEY ONLY LIVED ON IN DOISNEAU'S PHOTOS. IT SEEMS IMMIGRANTS FROM THE EAST ARE REVIVING THE TRADITION. WHICH IS GREAT.

A COUPLE OF DAYS LATER, I GOT TO SEE THE BURMESE VERSION.

81

RUSTIC, BUT MUCH MORE EFFICIENT.

AT THE
AUSTRALIAN
CLUB

FRIENDS WHO ARE MEMBERS HAVE INVITED US TO SPEND SUNDAY AT THE AUSTRALIAN CLUB.

SQUASH COURT

POOL

WADING POOL

SWINGS AND SLIDE

LAWN

BUFFET

BARBECUE

TENNIS COURT

NOT BAD.

IT'S A WHOLE OTHER WORLD.

TODAY'S PROGRAM: SQUASH, POOL AND BBQ.

"CASCADE" —WHAT'S THIS, AN AUSTRALIAN BREW?

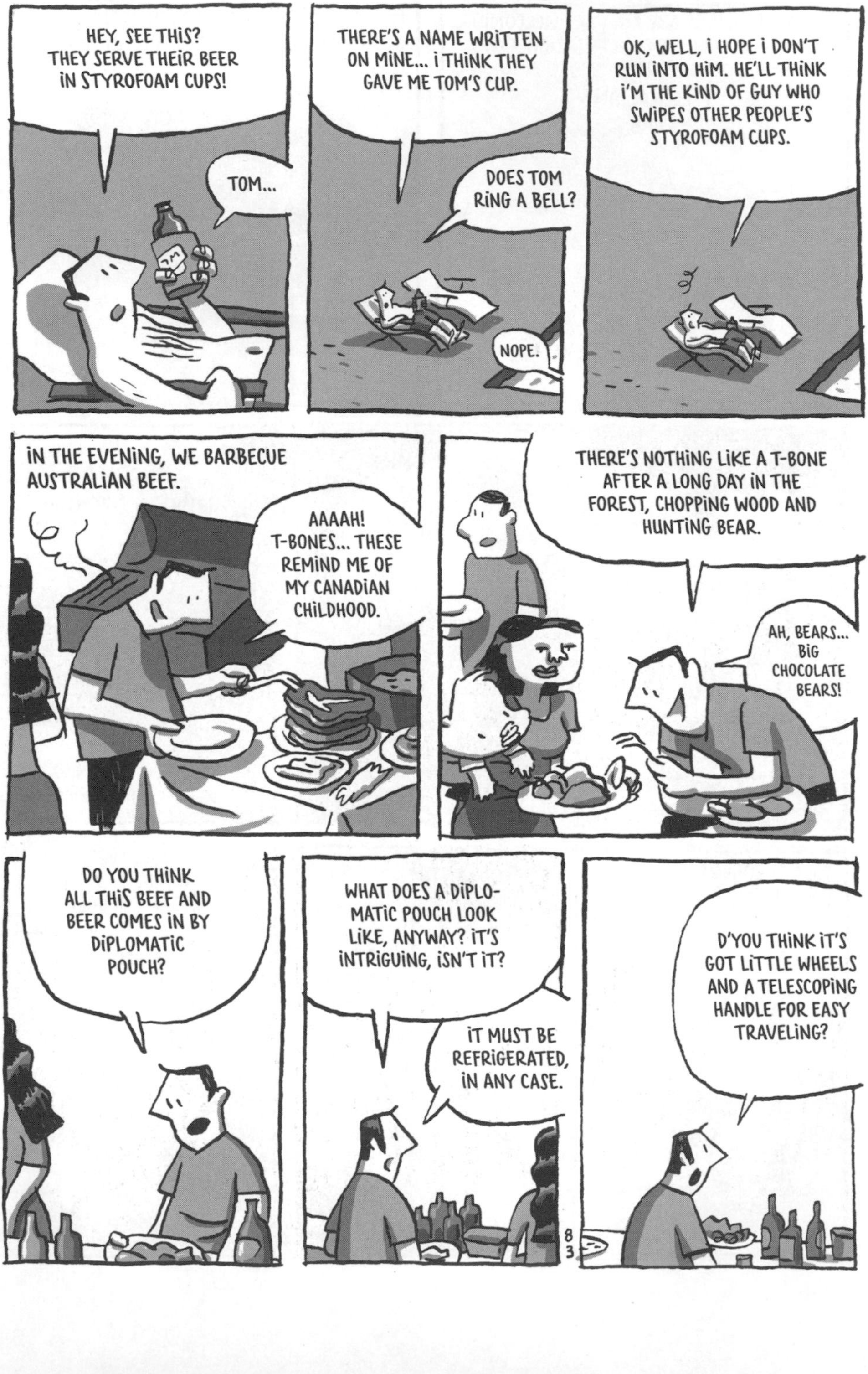
HEY, SEE THIS? THEY SERVE THEIR BEER IN STYROFOAM CUPS!
TOM...
THERE'S A NAME WRITTEN ON MINE... I THINK THEY GAVE ME TOM'S CUP.
DOES TOM RING A BELL?
NOPE.
OK, WELL, I HOPE I DON'T RUN INTO HIM. HE'LL THINK I'M THE KIND OF GUY WHO SWIPES OTHER PEOPLE'S STYROFOAM CUPS.
IN THE EVENING, WE BARBECUE AUSTRALIAN BEEF.
AAAAH! T-BONES... THESE REMIND ME OF MY CANADIAN CHILDHOOD.
THERE'S NOTHING LIKE A T-BONE AFTER A LONG DAY IN THE FOREST, CHOPPING WOOD AND HUNTING BEAR.
AH, BEARS... BIG CHOCOLATE BEARS!
DO YOU THINK ALL THIS BEEF AND BEER COMES IN BY DIPLOMATIC POUCH?
WHAT DOES A DIPLOMATIC POUCH LOOK LIKE, ANYWAY? IT'S INTRIGUING, ISN'T IT?
IT MUST BE REFRIGERATED, IN ANY CASE.
D'YOU THINK IT'S GOT LITTLE WHEELS AND A TELESCOPING HANDLE FOR EASY TRAVELING?

THE AUSTRALIANS ARE ALL VERY WELCOMING. i TRY TO FOLLOW THE CONVERSATION, BUT THEIR ACCENT MAKES iT DIFFICULT.

SORRY?

HEY? DiD YOU KNOW THAT A BOMB EXPLODED BY THE TRAIN STATION YESTERDAY?

YES, i HEARD ABOUT iT AT WORK.

HUH. NOBODY EVER TELLS ME ANYTHING.

TO BECOME A MEMBER, YOU NEED TO BE SPONSORED BY SOMEBODY FROM THE EMBASSY.

AH!

OH WELL, WE'LL GO TO THE NEIGHBORHOOD POOL INSTEAD. iT'S NICE TOO.

← MEN
WOMAN →

8
4

LOOK AT MY HAND! THE SKiN LOOKS SWOLLEN! i DON'T KNOW WHAT KiND OF PRODUCT THEY USE HERE, BUT i THINK i'M ALLERGIC.

OH RIGHT, iT SEEMS A BiT WHITE, HUH?

SURE YOU DON'T KNOW ANYONE AT THE AUSTRALIAN EMBASSY?

PC

i THOUGHT i COULD DO WiTHOUT, BUT i'VE DECiDED TO BUY A COMPUTER AFTER ALL. iNTERNET CAFES ARE RARE, AND i'LL NEED TO BE iN DAiLY CONTACT WiTH THE COLORiST FOR MY NEXT BOOK.

i GET A LiFT WHEN THE MSF DRiVER HAS A FREE MOMENT. i'D RATHER NOT TAKE A CAB BECAUSE i'M CARRYiNG CASH.

i NEED TO MAKE A STOP ON THE WAY.

"A STOP ON THE WAY" MEANS WE'LL SPEND HALF THE DAY SORTiNG OUT HiS PAPERWORK. i'M iN NO HURRY, SO iT'S FiNE BY ME.

NO PROBLEM, PAO!

AND WHEN iT'S NOT TOO HOT, THE LiTTLE DOWNTOWN STREETS ARE A PLEASURE TO DRiVE THROUGH.

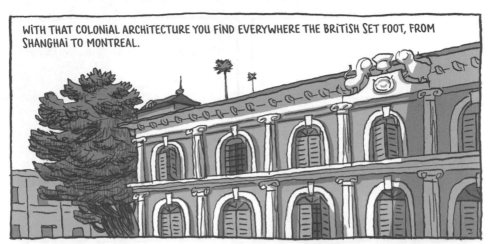

WITH THAT COLONIAL ARCHITECTURE YOU FIND EVERYWHERE THE BRITISH SET FOOT, FROM SHANGHAI TO MONTREAL.

BUT WITH FACADES MOTTLED BY COUNTLESS MONSOONS, AND ELECTRICAL CONNECTIONS WORTHY OF SOME MAD GENIUS.

WE STOP TO PAY THE POWER BILL IN A BUILDING THAT IS PLUNGED INTO DARKNESS.

NEXT STOP: THE BANK.
THERE ARE NO COMPUTERS IN SIGHT, JUST PILES OF MASSIVE LEDGERS.

86

AND THE PC?

NEXT, WE STOP AT WHAT LOOKS LIKE A WAREHOUSE.

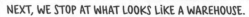

i WAIT AT THE DOOR WHILE PAO TALKS TO SOMEONE iNSIDE.

SUDDENLY A MAN COMES FOR ME. HE iNSiSTS THAT i GO iN AND HAVE A SEAT.

WiTHOUT KNOWiNG WHY, i FiND MYSELF iN THE MANAGER'S OFFiCE.

NiCE TO MEET YOU AFTER ALL THiS TiME...

i GLANCE OVER AT PAO FOR SOME KiND OF CLUE, BUT HE JUST SEEMS ROOTED TO THE SPOT.

HEH...

87

A BIZARRE CONVERSATION ENSUES.

YOU KNOW ABOUT THE IMPORT REGULATIONS?

AH YES, THE REGULATIONS... OF COURSE.

AND WHAT KIND OF MEDICATION ARE YOU BRINGING IN?

UH...

THE KIND THAT TREATS...

...THAT TREATS MALARIA.

YES, UH...MAINLY MALARIA.

...AND A FEW OTHERS AS WELL.

I PULL IT OFF AND GET A NICE STAMPED DOCUMENT FOR MY TROUBLES.

WE END THE DAY AT THE COMPUTER STORE. A PC DOESN'T COST MUCH IN BURMA, BUT SINCE THE LARGEST CURRENCY NOTE IS WORTH ONLY ONE EURO, IT TAKES FOUR BIG STACKS TO PAY FOR MY PURCHASE.

THERE.

THREE CLERKS SIT DOWN FOR A RECOUNT BEFORE LETTING ME GO.

ALRIGHT, CAN I LEAVE NOW?

JEEZUS, I MIGHT AS WELL BE SMUGGLING HEROIN.

DEMONETIZATION

i GOT RIPPED OFF TODAY. AFTER MAKING A PURCHASE, i WAS SLIPPED A BILL THAT ISN'T LEGAL TENDER ANYMORE. BUT i'M PRETTY PLEASED, i'VE NEVER SEEN ONE OF THESE.

OH!

IT'S AN OLD 5 KYAT NOTE WITH A PORTRAIT OF AUNG SAN ON IT. BURMA'S GREAT HERO OF INDEPENDENCE.

THE FATHER ON BANKNOTES AND HIS DAUGHTER UNDER HOUSE ARREST. STRANGE COUNTRY.

HE WAS A GOOD-LOOKING GUY. HIS DAUGHTER LOOKS A LOT LIKE HIM, IN FACT. AND THAT'S OFTEN ALL PEOPLE KNOW ABOUT HER: THAT SHE'S THE PRETTIEST NOBEL PRIZE WINNER.

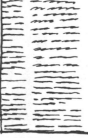

ON THE NEW BILLS, THE HERO HAS BEEN REPLACED BY THE MYTHICAL LEOGRYPH.

GRR...

ALSO, OUT OF SUPERSTITION, THE LAST DICTATOR ISSUED BILLS IN DENOMINATIONS OF 15, 45 AND 90 KYATS. NICE WAY TO DRIVE PEOPLE NUTS OR MAKE THEM MATH WIZARDS.

15   45   90

AH, NO: 217, THAT'S 2 X 90, 2 X 15, 1 X 5 AND 2 X 1...

DIDN'T i GIVE YOU MORE?

IT ALL ADDS UP.

89

BABY
GROUP

EVERY WEDNESDAY AFTERNOON, A GROUP OF PARENTS GET TOGETHER TO HAVE THEIR KIDS PLAY TOGETHER.

BEE-GOO

BABY GROUP.

A BIT OF SOCIALIZATION WON'T HURT LOUIS.

AND WHO KNOWS, MAYBE I'LL MEET AN AUSTRALIAN TO GET ME INTO THE CLUB.

THE HOUSE IS HUGE.

WOW!

TAXI

I'M THE ONLY DAD IN THE GROUP. THERE'S A SMALL POOL AND A SWING SET, CANAPÉS AND WHITE WINE.

AND BOXES FILLED WITH TOYS.

(REFLEX OF THE GUY WHO CAME TO BURMA CARRYING A BACKPACK.)

GOOD GOD. THAT STUFF MUST WEIGH A TON.

THE GROUP OF MOMS ARE ON ONE SIDE...

...THE NANNIES AND BABIES ON THE OTHER.

I TRY GOING BACK AND FORTH, BUT LOUIS DOESN'T SEE IT THAT WAY.

I DRAW COMICS.

AH, LOVELY...

...WHAT A NICE HOBBY.

IT'S NOT A HOBBY. IT'S WHAT I DO FOR A LIVING.

HOW ABOUT YOU? WHAT DO YOU DO?

WE WORK AT THE U.N.

"WE"?

MY HUSBAND.

AH, I SEE.

AND DOES ANYBODY HERE HAVE A HUSBAND AT THE AUSTRALIAN EMBASSY?

THE AFTERNOON WINDS DOWN AND PEOPLE GO HOME.

CHAUFFEUR-DRIVEN 4X4S COME TO PICK UP NANNIES AND BABIES.

NEW MODEL 4X4S!

JEEZUS, THE TAXES YOU'D PAY TO BRING A CAR LIKE THAT INTO THE COUNTRY.

i GET OFFERED A LIFT.

AFTER HAVING GONE TO THE BABY GROUP REGULARLY, i GOT TO KNOW MANY OF THE MOMS. MOST HAD CHOSEN TO TAKE A BREAK IN A DIPLOMATIC, HUMANITARIAN OR INTERNATIONAL CIVIL SERVICE CAREER TO TAKE CARE OF THEIR KIDS.

BUT iT'S NOT JUST A HOBBY, iT'S MY JOB.

GONE MISSING

THERE, THAT'S ONE MORE PAGE. FIVE TO GO AND THE BOOK IS DONE.

YOO HOO!

NOBODY IN THE KITCHEN, NOBODY IN THE GARDEN. WHAT'S GOING ON HERE? I SURE WOULDN'T MIND KNOWING WHERE LOUIS IS.

A HALF HOUR LATER, MAUNG AYE COMES BACK WITH LOUIS IN HIS ARMS.

NOT A MOMENT TOO SOON.

HE EXPLAINS WHERE HE WENT, BUT I DON'T UNDER-STAND A THING HE'S SAYING.

BED... OLD LADY...

NEXT TIME, I WANT TO SEE WHERE YOU GO.

TWO DAYS LATER, HE WANTS TO RETURN.

OK, BUT I'M COMING ALONG THIS TIME.

HEY, WAIT!

A BLOCK LATER, MAUNG AYE DISAPPEARS THROUGH A GATE.

IT'S DARK IN THE HOUSE, AN ACTION MOVIE SOUNDTRACK IS PLAYING DOWN THE HALL AND KIDS ARE CHASING EACH OTHER FROM ROOM TO ROOM.

IN THE MIDST OF IT ALL, TWO GIRLS (ONE LOOKS LIKE SHE MIGHT HAVE DOWN SYNDROME) ARE FIGHTING OVER LOUIS.

ODDLY ENOUGH, HE DOESN'T SEEM TO MIND. NO ONE PAYS ATTENTION TO ME.

MAUNG AYE, ALL SMILES, INVITES ME INTO THE NEXT ROOM.

94

AN ELDERLY WOMAN MOTIONS FOR ME TO SIT. SHE IS LYING ON A BED. A FAN BY HER HEAD NOISILY BLOWS AIR HER WAY.

WHAT A HORRIBLE COUNTRY THIS IS.

THE FRANKNESS SURPRISES ME, COMING FROM A STRANGER.

IN MY STATE, I'VE GOT NO ONE TO FEAR. I CAN SPEAK MY MIND.

WE TALK, AND I FIND OUT THAT SHE HAS BEEN BEDRIDDEN SINCE AN ACCIDENT 13 LONG YEARS AGO.

AFTER OPENING FIRE ON THE STUDENTS IN '88, THEY SHUT THE UNIVERSITIES. THE LEVEL OF EDUCATION IS DEPLORABLE. YOUNG PEOPLE CAN'T EVEN SPEAK ENGLISH.

SHE'S PLEASED TO HAVE SENT HER TWO DAUGHTERS TO STUDY ABROAD.

THE ONE THING I HOPE IS THAT THEY NEVER COME BACK...

...NOT LIKE DAW AUNG SAN SUU KYI.

(WHO ORIGINALLY RETURNED TO BURMA TO CARE FOR HER SICK MOTHER.)

SHE TALKS TO ME ABOUT THE PAST, HER YOUTH, RANGOON IN ITS GOLDEN DAYS. IT SOUNDS LIKE IT MUST HAVE BEEN A GREAT PLACE TO LIVE.

IT'S GETTING LATE, I HAVE TO GO.

SORRY TO BE RECEIVING YOU IN SUCH A RUN-DOWN COUNTRY.

YOU'RE ALWAYS WELCOME IN MY HOME.

REBEL REBEL

IT ISN'T EASY BEING A YOUNG REBEL IN MYANMAR. THE MILITARY JUNTA THAT'S OPPRESSING THE POPULATION DOESN'T LEAVE MUCH ROOM FOR MISBEHAVIOR.

BUT YOUTH WILL BE YOUTH, AND THAT'S WHY, IN A BIG CITY LIKE RANGOON, THERE ARE SHOPS FOR THOSE DETERMINED TO MAKE A FASHION STATEMENT.

THERE'S LOTS OF VARIETY.

AZURFA

LINKIN PARK

CHE GUEVARA

MARIJUANA LEAF

KORN

SO YOU CAN FIND MARILYN MANSON T-SHIRTS, BUT YOU NEED TO GO TO THAILAND TO HEAR HIS MUSIC. THERE'S NOTHING HERE BUT LOCAL BANDS, ABBA AND CELINE DION.

SONIC YOUTH! I DEFY ANYONE TO FIND A SINGLE SONIC YOUTH ALBUM IN BURMA.

97

THEN THERE ARE THE GUYS DRESSED IN GULF WAR-STYLE FATIGUES.

AZUREA

SHIT, LIKE THERE AREN'T ENOUGH SOLDIERS IN THE STREETS?

GIVEN THE PRICE OF THE T-SHIRTS, I DON'T SEE WHO CAN AFFORD THEM OTHER THAN THE SONS OF MILITARY PERSONNEL.

THE ONES THAT REALLY GET TO ME, THOUGH, ARE THOSE WITH THE SWASTIKAS.

OH HELL...

NOW THERE'S A GREAT IDEA! WHY NOT TOPPLE THE JUNTA TO MAKE ROOM FOR THE THIRD REICH? THAT WOULD BE A REAL IMPROVEMENT.

PFFF...

I TELL YA...

CHE GUEVERA AND SWASTIKAS, SAME STRUGGLE?

WHAT A DOWNER.

SOMEBODY'S GOTTA BE SPINNING IN HIS GRAVE.

98

DAMN! WHERE'D THE SUN GO?

SENIOR MONK

THIS MORNING, WE'RE GOING TO THE TEMPLE. NADÈGE'S ASSISTANT MANAGER IS CELEBRATING HIS NEW APPOINTMENT. U TOE WIN IS A DEVOUT BUDDHIST AND HE HAS JUST REACHED THE RANK OF SENIOR MONK.

HE'S A MARRIED MAN WITH CHILDREN AND GRANDCHILDREN. SO IN THERAVADA BUDDHISM, YOU CAN BE BOTH A LAYMAN AND A MONK AT THE SAME TIME.

DID YOU KNOW THAT?

NOPE.

WE LEFT HIM FRIDAY NIGHT, BURIED DEEP IN HIS LEDGERS...

ONLY TO FIND HIM THE NEXT DAY WITH A SHAVED HEAD, GLOWING WITH WISDOM IN THE LIGHT OF A THOUSAND TINY BLINKING LIGHT BULBS.

WE BROUGHT HIM A LITTLE SOMETHING.

IT'S NOT EASY FINDING A GIFT FOR A MONK.

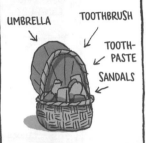

LUCKILY, THERE ARE READY-MADE KITS SPECIALLY PRE-PARED FOR ALL THE CIRCUMSTANCES IN A MONK'S LIFE.

UMBRELLA

TOOTHBRUSH

TOOTH-PASTE

SANDALS

GIVEN ALL THE GUESTS TODAY, U TOE WIN SHOULD HAVE ENOUGH TOOTHPASTE TO LAST HIM A LIFETIME.

FOOD IS SERVED IN THE MEDITATION HALL.

IT SUITS HIM BETTER, DON'T YOU THINK?

THE ONLY THING THAT KIND OF BUGS ME ARE THE GLASSES.

ACTUALLY, THE DALAI LAMA WEARS THE SAME ONES! I WONDER IF THEY'RE PART OF THE PERFECT-LITTLE-MONK OUTFIT.

100

THAT'S WHEN SOMEBODY INTRODUCES US TO THE HEAD OF THE MONASTERY.

NEWS FROM
THE FRONT

NADÈGE IS GOING BACK OUT INTO THE FIELD. WE'VE BEEN HERE ALMOST 6 MONTHS, AND I STILL HAVEN'T VISITED THE PROJECT.

HOW COME I CAN'T GO?

TRAVEL PERMITS FOR SENSITIVE ZONES ARE INCREDIBLY HARD TO COME BY THESE DAYS. THE GOVERNMENT IS MAKING IT DIFFICULT FOR US...

AND WE DON'T KNOW WHY.

LOOKS PACKED TONIGHT.

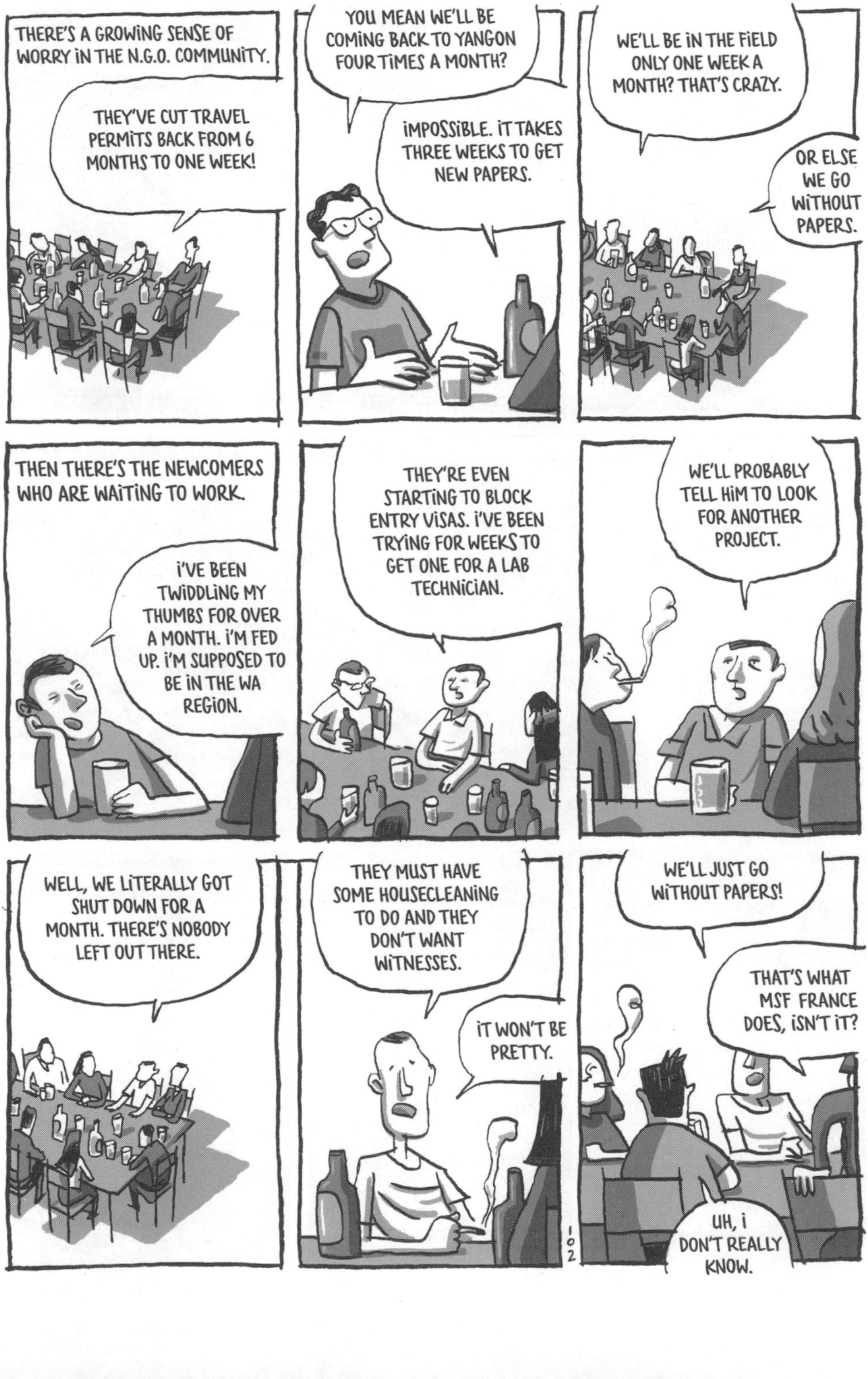
THERE'S A GROWING SENSE OF WORRY IN THE N.G.O. COMMUNITY.
THEY'VE CUT TRAVEL PERMITS BACK FROM 6 MONTHS TO ONE WEEK!
YOU MEAN WE'LL BE COMING BACK TO YANGON FOUR TIMES A MONTH?
IMPOSSIBLE. IT TAKES THREE WEEKS TO GET NEW PAPERS.
WE'LL BE IN THE FIELD ONLY ONE WEEK A MONTH? THAT'S CRAZY.
OR ELSE WE GO WITHOUT PAPERS.
THEN THERE'S THE NEWCOMERS WHO ARE WAITING TO WORK.
I'VE BEEN TWIDDLING MY THUMBS FOR OVER A MONTH. I'M FED UP. I'M SUPPOSED TO BE IN THE WA REGION.
THEY'RE EVEN STARTING TO BLOCK ENTRY VISAS. I'VE BEEN TRYING FOR WEEKS TO GET ONE FOR A LAB TECHNICIAN.
WE'LL PROBABLY TELL HIM TO LOOK FOR ANOTHER PROJECT.
WELL, WE LITERALLY GOT SHUT DOWN FOR A MONTH. THERE'S NOBODY LEFT OUT THERE.
THEY MUST HAVE SOME HOUSECLEANING TO DO AND THEY DON'T WANT WITNESSES.
IT WON'T BE PRETTY.
WE'LL JUST GO WITHOUT PAPERS!
THAT'S WHAT MSF FRANCE DOES, ISN'T IT?
UH, I DON'T REALLY KNOW.

SHORTLY AFTER MIDNIGHT.

SEE YOU! AND GOOD LUCK WITH EVERY-THING!

JEEZ, THERE ARE STILL CHAUFFEURS WAITING.

GOOD NIGHT, GUYS!

OH BOY, AM I LOOPED!

AT NIGHT, PACKS OF STRAY DOGS RULE RANGOON.

THERE'S ONE CORNER IN PARTICULAR WHERE THEY TEND TO GATHER.

GRRR!

GET LOST, YOU FUCKING MUTTS!

WOOF!

OH SHIT, THEY'RE AFTER ME!

THANK GOD I GOT VACCINATED AGAINST RABIES BEFORE COMING HERE.

SIX MONTHS EARLIER, AT THE PASTEUR INSTITUTE IN PARIS.

...DT POLIO, HEPATITIS A AND B, JAPANESE ENCEPHALITIS, AND i SUGGEST RABIES AS WELL, WHILE YOU'RE AT IT.

PFF... RABIES. OBVIOUSLY, SINCE THEY INVENTED THE VACCINE, THEY HAVE TO PRESCRIBE iT TO EVERYONE.

ALRIGHT, IT'S ALL IN THERE. YOU'LL NEED TO TAKE iT ALONG AND CONTINUE THE TREATMENT. BE SURE TO KEEP iT COOL.

PADDED ENVELOPE WITH AN ICE PACK INSIDE AND ELASTICS TO KEEP iT SHUT.

HOTEL

SUBWAY

TRAIN

AiRPORT

PLANE

TRANSiT

PLANE

TAXi

COOL? ALL THE WAY TO BURMA?

THAT'S RIGHT.

My dear sir, I am not in the habit of arguing with puppies. Get out! At once!... I have to be at the Central Station in fifteen minutes.

And I must get to the hospital urgently...

... as I've just been bitten by this mad dog!

GOOD OLD TiNTIN! THAT GUY IS EVERYWHERE!

104

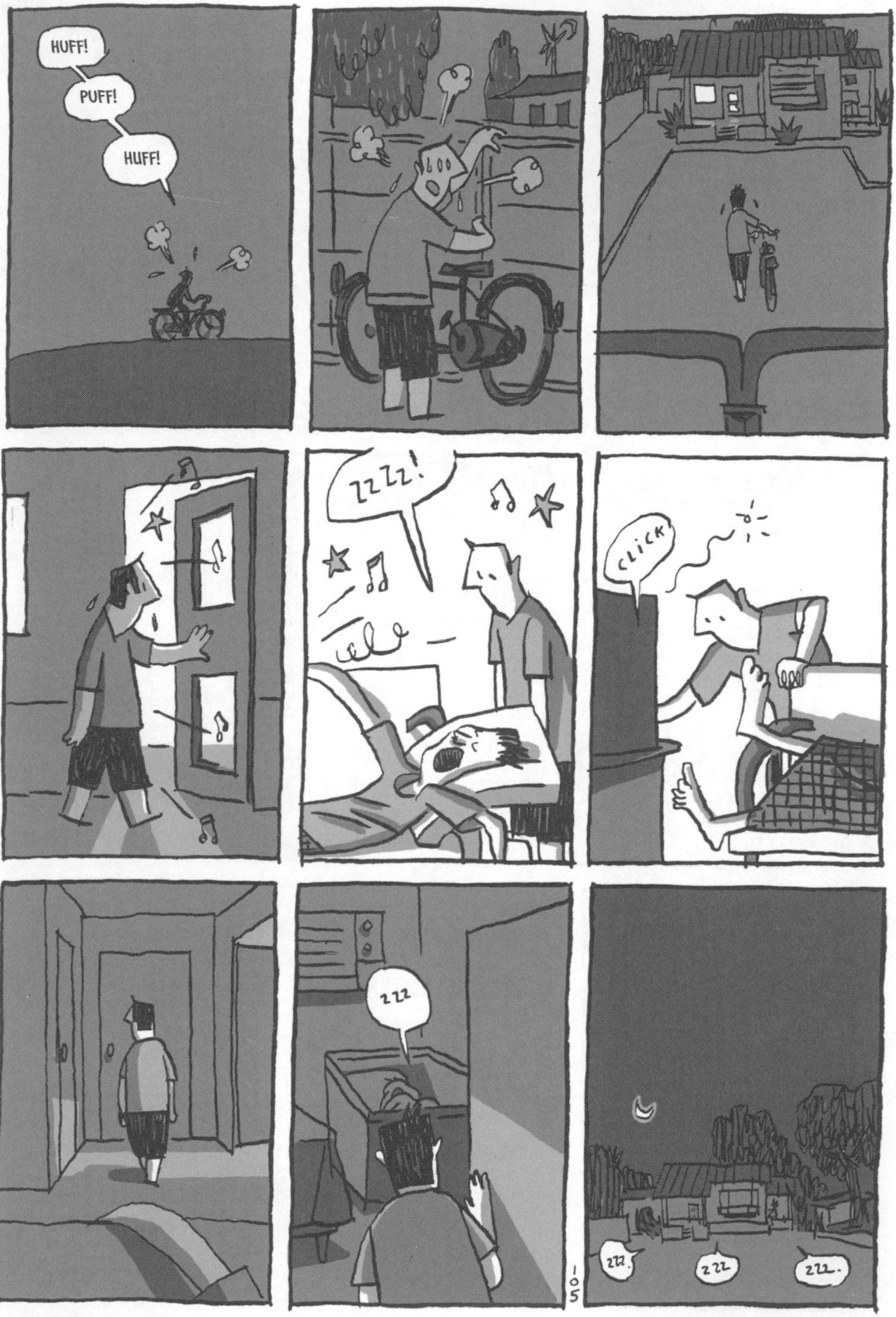
HUFF!
PUFF!
HUFF!
ZZZZ!
CLICK
ZZZ
ZZZ.
ZZZ
ZZZ.

GENERATOR

KIPLING, SOMERSET MAUGHAM AND JOSEPH KESSEL ALL CAME TO THE STRAND IN THE DAYS OF COLONIAL RANGOON.

THE FABLED HOTEL IS WHERE I'M CELEBRATING THE DUTCH QUEEN'S BIRTHDAY. IT'S A NATIONAL HOLIDAY IN THE NETHERLANDS.

I TALK COMICS WITH A DIPLOMAT WHO'S FRESH IN FROM BRUSSELS. I TELL HIM ABOUT MY BACKGROUND IN ANIMATION.

DURING THE WEEK, A MERCEDES PULLS UP AND THE CHAUFFEUR DELIVERS AN INVITATION TO HAVE LUNCH THE NEXT DAY.

THERE, I GET TO KNOW A BURMESE GRAPHIC ARTIST WHO HAS ALWAYS WANTED TO LEARN ANIMATION.

I SET UP A LITTLE ANIMATION WORKSHOP WITH HIM AND A FEW OF HIS FRIENDS. WE MEET SUNDAY MORNINGS AT ONE OF THEIR HOMES.

AND SO I FIND MYSELF EXPLAINING THE BASIC PRINCIPALS OF MOTION, AS I'VE DONE MANY TIMES BEFORE, USING THE BOUNCING BALL EXERCISE.

THIS IS NO GOOD.

IT'S LIMP.

IT'S GOT NO WEIGHT.

WE NEED TO ADD FRAMES UP HERE.

AND USE JUST ONE FOR THE MOMENT OF CONTACT, OR ELSE IT LOOKS LIKE THE BALL IS GLUED TO THE GROUND.

FOR TECHNICAL REASONS, WE DON'T GET VERY FAR. WE'RE IN A WORKING CLASS NEIGHBORHOOD AND THESE DAYS, THEY GET ONLY 4 HOURS OF POWER A DAY. JUST ENOUGH TO RECHARGE THE BATTERY, BUT SINCE IT'S NOT EXACTLY NEW ANYMORE, IT DOESN'T HOLD ITS CHARGE FOR LONG.

AT ONE OF OUR MEETINGS, I FOUND OUT ABOUT THE VIP DISTRICTS. THE CITY'S OTHER SECTORS SHARE THE LEFTOVERS.

HOW ABOUT WE MEET AT MY PLACE NEXT WEEK?

NO THANKS.

TOO KIND.

LET'S GO HAVE A DRINK.

WE'D BE A BOTHER.

107

A CHORUS OF GENERATORS GREETS US IN THE STREET. THE NOISE IS DEAFENING.

WE TALK ABOUT THIS AND THAT. COMPUTERS, THE INTERNET...

IT ALL GOES THROUGH THE ARMY'S PROVIDER. THEY HAVE POWERFUL FILTERS THAT BLOCK MANY SITES AND THE TRANSMISSION RATES ARE TOO SLOW.

THE CONVERSATION STRAYS TO POLITICS, AND I'M SURPRISED AT HOW OPENLY THEY TALK ABOUT THINGS.

SO, IF I INVITE YOU TO SLEEP AT MY PLACE, I NEED TO TELL THE OFFICIALS IN MY NEIGHBORHOOD.

WHY? BECAUSE I'M A FOREIGNER?

NO, IT'S THE SAME FOR BURMESE, TOO.

ONE OF THEM LOOKS JUST LIKE PETER LORRE. IT'S DISCONCERTING. I KEEP STARING AT HIM AND MISS HALF THE CONVERSATION.

I WONDER IF EVERY COUNTRY HAS ITS OWN PETER LORRE.

I INSIST A BIT MORE, AND THEY FINALLY AGREE TO COME TO MY PLACE NEXT TIME.

SEE YOU.

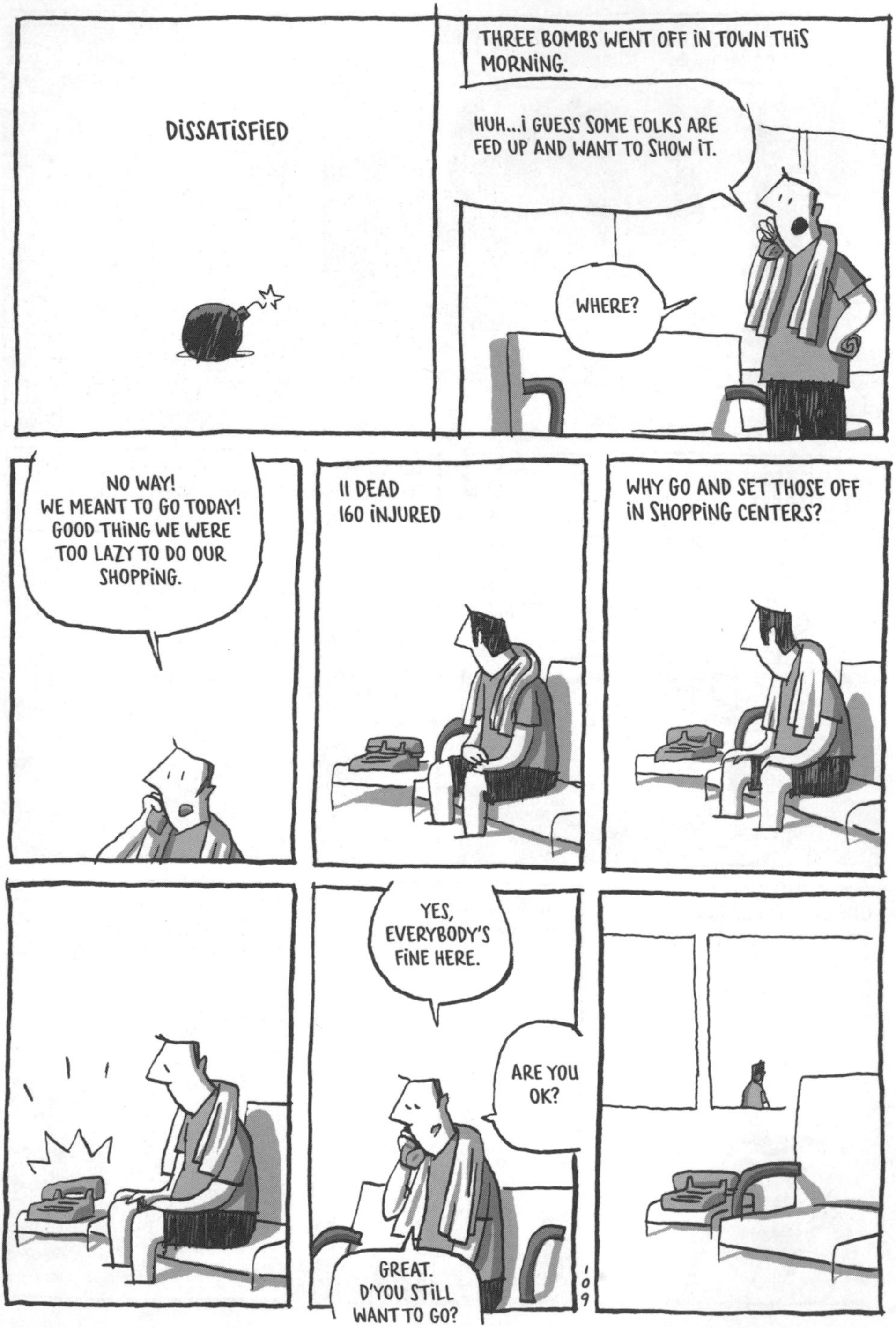

DISSATISFIED
THREE BOMBS WENT OFF IN TOWN THIS MORNING.
HUH...I GUESS SOME FOLKS ARE FED UP AND WANT TO SHOW IT.
WHERE?
NO WAY! WE MEANT TO GO TODAY! GOOD THING WE WERE TOO LAZY TO DO OUR SHOPPING.
11 DEAD
160 INJURED
WHY GO AND SET THOSE OFF IN SHOPPING CENTERS?
YES, EVERYBODY'S FINE HERE.
ARE YOU OK?
GREAT. D'YOU STILL WANT TO GO?

SO, YOU FINALLY GOT A CARD?
YUP. I TAPPED INTO A COUPLE OF GOOD CONNECTIONS.
BABY GROUP CONNECTIONS?
YOU BET. BEING A DAD CHANGES EVERYTHING, YOU KNOW.
AUSTRALIAN CLUB →
IYS →
ACF
AND THAT MEANS YOU GET TO BE MY GUEST TODAY.
TOO COOL.
SQUASH
TENNIS
I THINK THE BOMBS WERE SET BY THE MONS.
NO, THE SHANS.
NO, THE KARENS.
THE WAS.
THE NAGAS.
THE ROHINGYAS.
THE RAKHINES.
THE MILITARY.
THE KACHINS.

OUCH! I THINK I MIGHT HAVE OVERDONE IT FIRST TIME AROUND.

NEXT DAY.

AAARGHH, SHEEE-IT!

THIS IS CRAZY, I CAN HARDLY INK THE PAGE. JEEZ, I CAN'T STOP NOW— I'VE GOT JUST 4 MORE TO GO.

I SCREWED UP MY ELBOW.

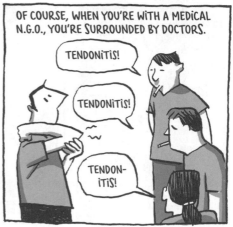

OF COURSE, WHEN YOU'RE WITH A MEDICAL N.G.O., YOU'RE SURROUNDED BY DOCTORS.

TENDONITIS!

TENDONITIS!

TENDON-ITIS!

BUT I'VE GOT 4 MORE PAGES TO GO.

ANTI-INFLAMMA-TORIES.

ANTI-INFLAMMA-TORIES.

ANTI-INFLAMMATORIES

HERE WE GO AGAIN.

EXCEPT FOR THE BELLYACHE, I'M OK.

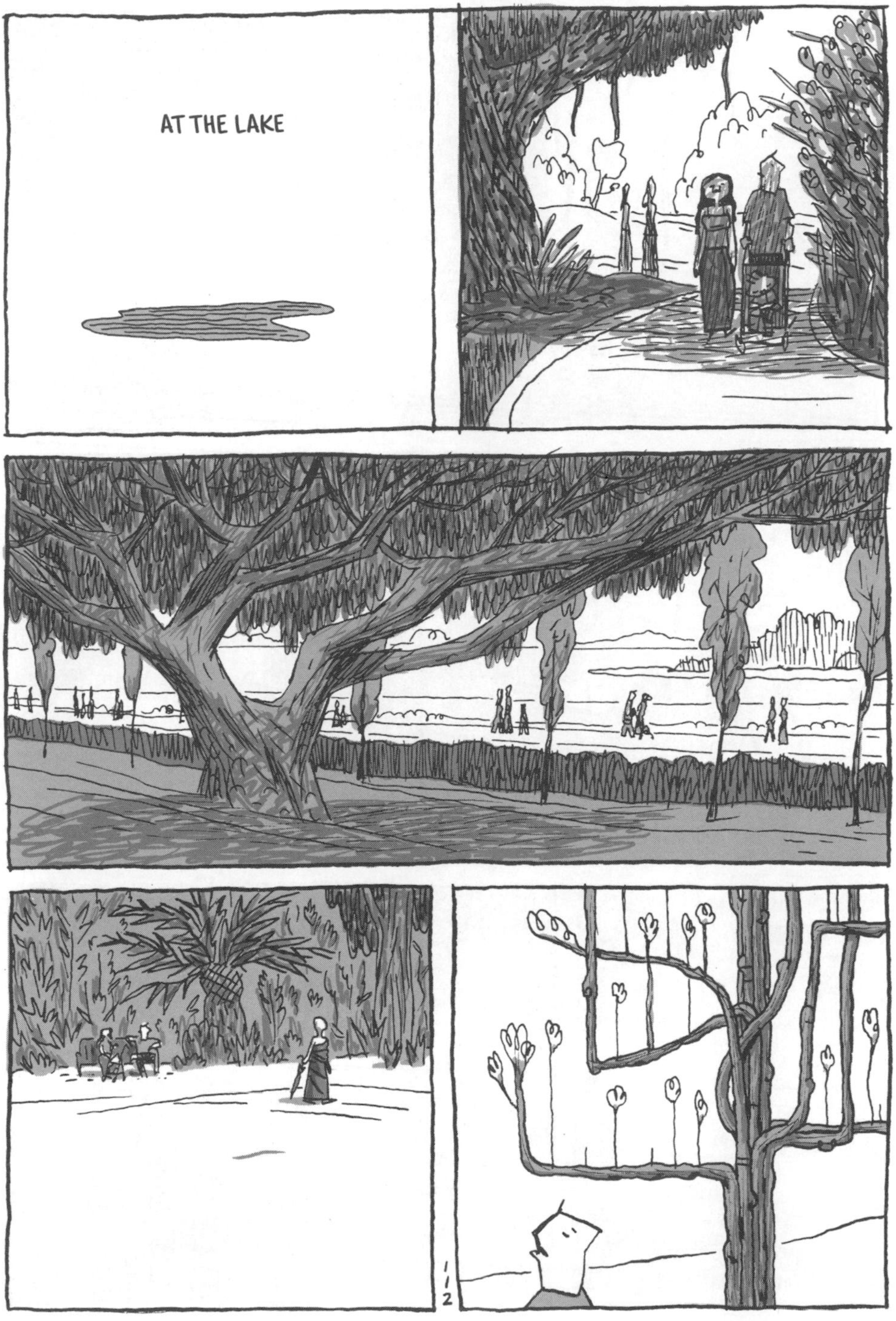
AT THE LAKE

LITTLE
PRAYERS.

3 MONTHS LATER.

6 MONTHS LATER.

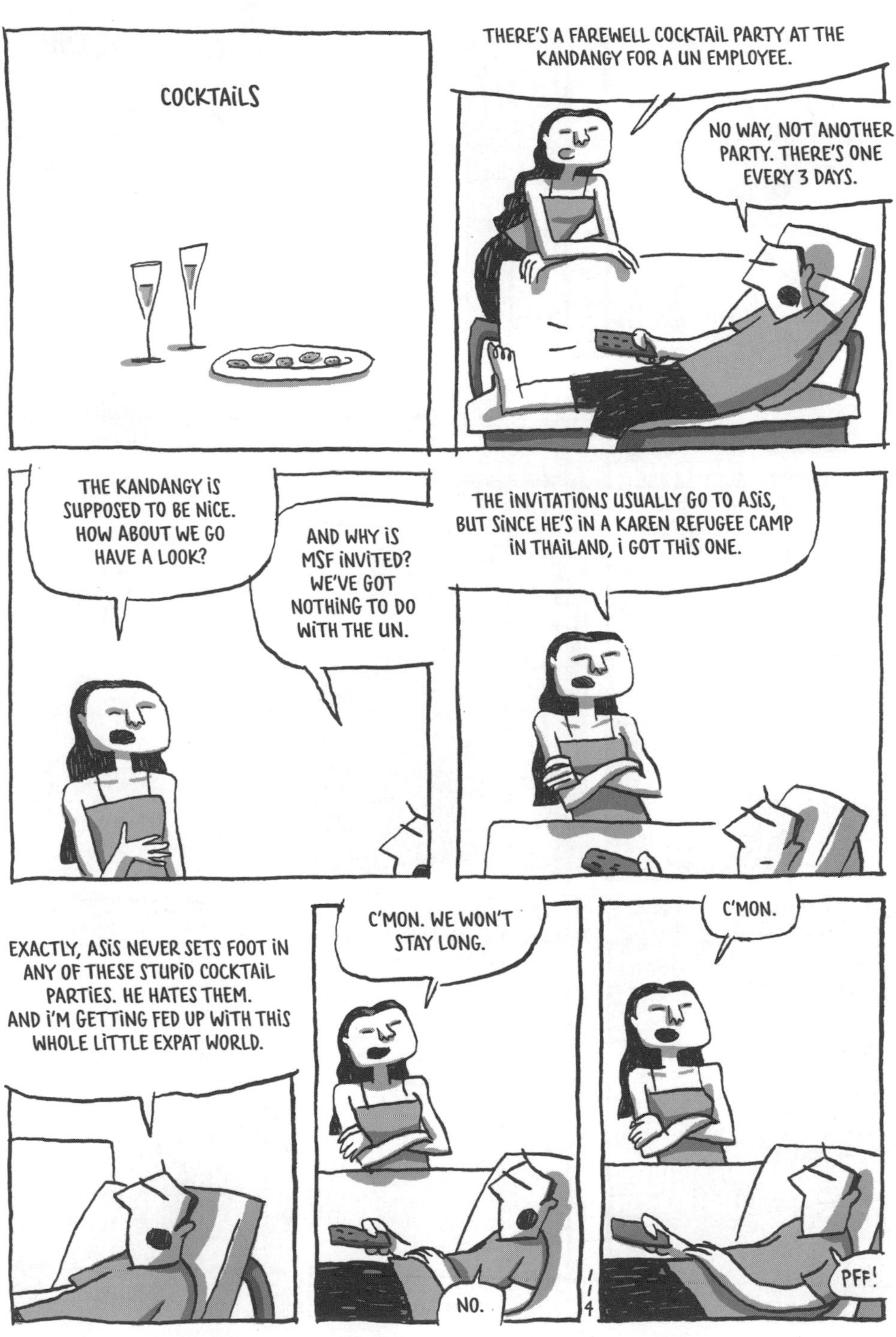
COCKTAILS
THERE'S A FAREWELL COCKTAIL PARTY AT THE KANDANGY FOR A UN EMPLOYEE.
NO WAY, NOT ANOTHER PARTY. THERE'S ONE EVERY 3 DAYS.
THE KANDANGY IS SUPPOSED TO BE NICE. HOW ABOUT WE GO HAVE A LOOK?
AND WHY IS MSF INVITED? WE'VE GOT NOTHING TO DO WITH THE UN.
THE INVITATIONS USUALLY GO TO ASIS, BUT SINCE HE'S IN A KAREN REFUGEE CAMP IN THAILAND, I GOT THIS ONE.
EXACTLY, ASIS NEVER SETS FOOT IN ANY OF THESE STUPID COCKTAIL PARTIES. HE HATES THEM. AND I'M GETTING FED UP WITH THIS WHOLE LITTLE EXPAT WORLD.
C'MON. WE WON'T STAY LONG.
NO.
C'MON.
PFF!

THIS IS IT, RIGHT?

OH, LOOK HOW NICE IT IS. THERE'S A DINOSAUR.

PFF...A DINOSAUR!

THERE YOU GO. AVERAGE AGE IS TWICE MINE. NOT A SINGLE FAMILIAR FACE. THE PERFECT EVENING FROM HELL.

IS THIS WINE CORKED?

OH MAN, NO WAY.

EXCUSE ME, ARE YOU THE FRIEND OF NADÈGE'S WHO DRAWS COMICS?

HELP.

IN PERSON.

...AND WHEN HE TRIES TO GET THROUGH CUSTOMS WITH HIS BABY PASSPORT. HA HA HA !

AND I LOVE IT WHEN LOUIS GOES...

"OH, FOR CRYING OUT LOUD. YES. THERE. YES, I AM A SEDUCTIVE MALE."

HA! HA!

"LOUIS ROMAN-CIER, PARANOIAC IN THE PARISIAN PUBLIC HOSPITAL SYSTEM, MILD CASES."

HA! HA! HA!

GOOSSENS* IS SUCH A GENIUS.

APOPO 200 FEET!

*DANIEL GOOSSENS, FRENCH COMIC BOOK AUTHOR

PSST! C'MON, LET'S GO!

ALREADY?

WATER
FESTIVAL

BEFORE THE RAINY SEASON, WHEN THE HEAT BECOMES UNBEARABLE, THE BURMESE CELEBRATE THE WATER FESTIVAL, WHICH MARKS THE BUDDHIST NEW YEAR.

TRADITIONALLY, YOU WASH AWAY YOUR MISDEEDS BY LETTING OTHERS POUR WATER OVER YOUR BACK.

AT OUR NEIGHBORS'

THE FESTIVITIES GO ON FOR 4 DAYS.

DAY 1

TRUCK

WATER TANK WITH BLOCK OF ICE INSIDE

AND WATER PISTOLS

THESE DAYS, YOU GET SPRAYED BY FIRE HOSES.

116

CARS TAKE A SPECIAL ROUTE TO GET REALLY DOUSED.

THEY PASS BY OUR HOUSE AND THEN TURN ONTO THE MAIN ROAD, WHERE GUYS ON SPECIALLY BUILT STAGES SPRAY AS MUCH WATER AS THEY CAN PUMP FROM THE LAKE.

SHWE DAGON CENTER

BY EARLY AFTERNOON, TRAFFIC COMES TO A FULL STOP. TOTAL GRIDLOCK.

I GET OUT OF THE CAR AND CONTINUE ON FOOT.

ARGH! IT'S FREEZING!

IN PRINCIPLE, YOU'RE NOT SUPPOSED TO SPRAY MONKS AND COPS.

OOOH! THAT FELT GREAT!

IT'S A FREE FOR ALL! THIS IS ONE OF THE FEW TIMES A YEAR WHEN THE BURMESE ARE ALLOWED TO GATHER IN GROUPS AND CELEBRATE.

I SUDDENLY REALIZE "THE LADY"* LIVES NEARBY. WITH ALL THE DECIBELS STREAMING OUT OF THE LOUDSPEAKERS, SHE MUST BE ABLE TO HEAR US. ALONE IN HER HOME...

*AUNG SAN SUU KYI

DAY 2 — i DECIDE TO PASS ON GETTING SOAKED AND BECOME A SOAKER INSTEAD.

iT'S PRETTY GOOD, TOO.

ROASTED GRASSHOPPERS.

HEY!

i HAD PROMISED MYSELF TO TRY THEM AT LEAST ONCE DURING MY STAY.

YOU HAVE TO REMOVE THE STINGER.

CRUNCH CRUNCH

HMM... NOT SO GREAT.

A BiT GROSS, ACTUALLY.

WANT TO TRY ONE? HERE YOU GO.

SO, WHAT DO YOU TH....

DAMN! A DRY T-SHiRT!

DAY 3

I'LL BE RIGHT BACK.

HA HA HA HA HA

I RIDE MY BIKE THROUGH NEIGHBORHOODS THAT GET LESS TRAFFIC.

OH! A FOREIGNER!

THEY'RE MUCH CALMER. FAMILIES WAIT IN FRONT OF THEIR HOMES. THEY ASK ME TO STOP SO THEY DON'T MISS ME.

BACK HOME, THE GATE IS SHUT AND OUR GUARD IS BESIDE HIMSELF.

SOMEONE WAS STABBED IN FRONT OF OUR HOUSE. THE POLICE CAUGHT THE ASSAILANT, AND THE VICTIM WAS A TRANSVESTITE.

YOU'RE KIDDING.

119

DAY 4

I'D BE HAPPY TO STAY HOME AND DRY TODAY, BUT I NEED TO GO TO THE M.S.F. OFFICE TO SEE IF THEIR INTERNET IS WORKING.

MINE IS DOWN AND I'M EXPECTING AN IMPORTANT EMAIL.

GOOD AND
LOYAL SERVICE

I'VE FINISHED THE CHILDREN'S BOOK I HAD BEGUN BEFORE LEAVING.

DESPITE ALL THE ANTI-INFLAMMATORIES, MY ARM IS STILL A WRECK.

I DECIDE TO AUTHORIZE A LITTLE SICK LEAVE FOR MYSELF.

IN OTHER WORDS: GET INSPIRED...

...GET BETTER

...AND CATCH UP ON MY READING.

IN AN OUTLYING NEIGHBORHOOD, I COME ACROSS A REAL FIND. A HUGE, HALF-RUSTED DAIMLER STANDS PARKED IN FRONT OF AN OLD HOTEL, LOOKING AS THOUGH IT'S BEEN WAITING SINCE INDEPENDENCE FOR THE RETURN OF ITS OWNER.

I DO SOME RESEARCH: TURNS OUT IT'S A 1968 DAIMLER DS 420 LIMOUSINE.

I CUT BACK ON MY REHAB PROGRAM. I SWIM A FEW LENGTHS, BUT MY HEART ISN'T IN IT.

NEARBY, A GROUP OF WORKERS REPAIR THE DAMAGE CAUSED BY A FALLEN PALM TREE.

"AND LIFE TOOK ROOT, SETTLED IN, SLIPPED INTO A ROUTINE, AMID THE BACKDROPS AND CHARACTERS OF A DREAM."

JOSEPH KESSEL IN BURMA, FROM MOGOK, THE VALLEY OF RUBIES, 1955

DOCTORS
WITH BORDERS

ASIS IS BACK. HE MET WITH A REPRESENT-
ATIVE OF THE KNU (KAREN NATIONAL UNION)
TO DISCUSS MSF'S PLANS FOR THE KAREN
REGION.

HERE, SOME
FRESH NEWS.

SUPER.

THE BANGKOK POST SAYS THERE WERE 4,
NOT 3, EXPLOSIONS IN RANGOON, AND AN
EYE WITNESS MENTIONED AT LEAST 40
VICTIMS AT JUST ONE SITE, NOT THE TOTAL
OF 11 REPORTED BY BURMESE AUTHORITIES.

HMPF!

NO ONE WILL
EVER KNOW
WHO DID IT.

SO, HOW WAS THE TRIP
TO THAILAND?

MISSION ACCOM-
PLISHED. THEY'RE
GOING TO LET US
INTO THE REGIONS
THEY CONTROL.

NICE.

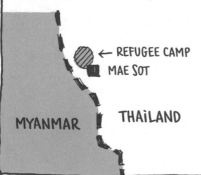

IN THAILAND, AN MSF TEAM HAS BEEN
WORKING SINCE 1983 AT A KAREN REFUGEE
CAMP THAT HOUSES SOME 40,000 PEOPLE.

← REFUGEE CAMP
MAE SOT

THAILAND

MYANMAR

DURING ITS EXTERNAL CONSULTATIONS, THE
MSF MEDICAL TEAM REGULARLY SLIPS
ACROSS THE BORDER TO HELP THE BURMESE
ON THE OTHER SIDE.

THE DECISION TO OPEN A PROGRAM IN BURMA CAME IN RESPONSE TO THE URGENT NEEDS OF THESE GROUPS AND THE DIFFICULTY INVOLVED IN CROSSING THE BORDER ON A REGULAR BASIS.

THAIL
THAILA
RANGOON
RANGOON
PLAN A
PLAN B

REALLY? THAT'S HOW YOU ENDED UP HERE?

IT IS, EXCEPT WE STILL HAVEN'T GOT TO WHERE WE WANTED TO GO...

ARE YOU TAKING YOUR ANTI-INFLAMMATORIES?

YES. I'VE EVEN STOPPED DRAWING.

THINK YOU COULD HAVE A LOOK AT OUR COMPUTER? IT'S BEEN ACTING UP.

SURE, OF COURSE. WHAT'S GOING ON?

OVER THE PAST FEW DAYS, ALL OUR EMAILS TO MSF PARIS HAVE BOUNCED BACK. THE OTHER ADDRESSES WORK FINE, JUST THAT ONE DOESN'T. THEY HAVEN'T CHANGED THEIR ADDRESS— I CHECKED...
THINK IT'S A VIRUS?

NO, VIRUSES BEHAVE DIFFERENTLY.

IT SOUNDS A BIT SUSPICIOUS. I'LL GIVE IT A TRY AT THE INTERNET CAFE TO SEE IF IT GOES THROUGH OVER THERE.

THIS NEEDS TO GET FIXED QUICKLY. WE'VE GOT DOCUMENTS TO SEND THEM.

124

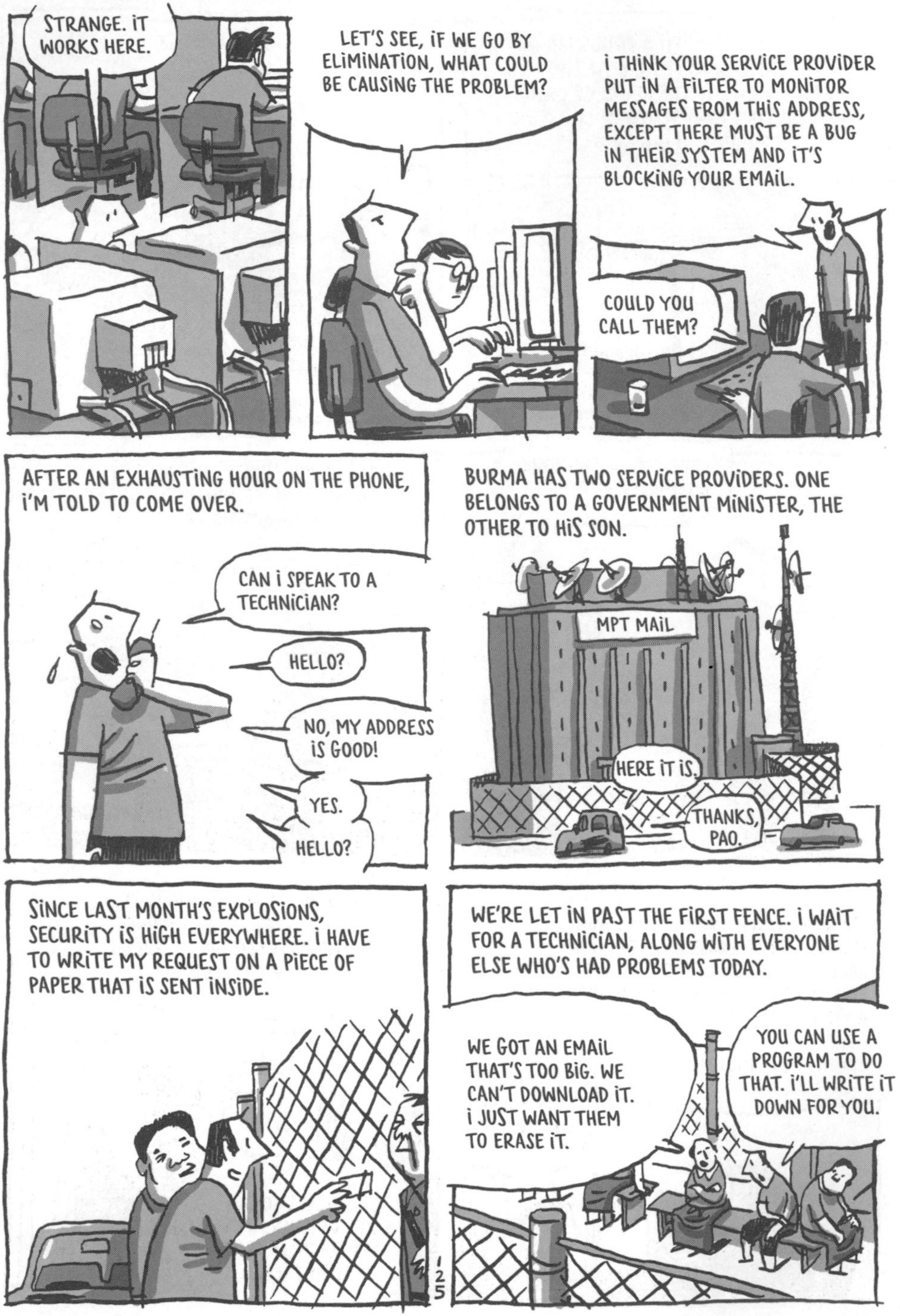
STRANGE. IT WORKS HERE.
LET'S SEE, IF WE GO BY ELIMINATION, WHAT COULD BE CAUSING THE PROBLEM?
I THINK YOUR SERVICE PROVIDER PUT IN A FILTER TO MONITOR MESSAGES FROM THIS ADDRESS, EXCEPT THERE MUST BE A BUG IN THEIR SYSTEM AND IT'S BLOCKING YOUR EMAIL.
COULD YOU CALL THEM?
AFTER AN EXHAUSTING HOUR ON THE PHONE, I'M TOLD TO COME OVER.
CAN I SPEAK TO A TECHNICIAN?
HELLO?
NO, MY ADDRESS IS GOOD!
YES.
HELLO?
BURMA HAS TWO SERVICE PROVIDERS. ONE BELONGS TO A GOVERNMENT MINISTER, THE OTHER TO HIS SON.
MPT MAIL
HERE IT IS.
THANKS, PAO.
SINCE LAST MONTH'S EXPLOSIONS, SECURITY IS HIGH EVERYWHERE. I HAVE TO WRITE MY REQUEST ON A PIECE OF PAPER THAT IS SENT INSIDE.
WE'RE LET IN PAST THE FIRST FENCE. I WAIT FOR A TECHNICIAN, ALONG WITH EVERYONE ELSE WHO'S HAD PROBLEMS TODAY.
WE GOT AN EMAIL THAT'S TOO BIG. WE CAN'T DOWNLOAD IT. I JUST WANT THEM TO ERASE IT.
YOU CAN USE A PROGRAM TO DO THAT. I'LL WRITE IT DOWN FOR YOU.

MY SUPER TECHNICIAN COMES OUT BUT DOESN'T UNDERSTAND.

SEE, ALL THE EMAILS WE TRY TO SEND TO ONE SPECIFIC ADDRESS COME BACK TO US.

HE DOESN'T REACT UNTIL I SAY:

BASICALLY, I THINK YOUR FILTER IS SCREWED.

THAT DOES IT. OPEN SESAME, WE'RE INVITED INTO THE INTERNET FORTRESS.

I MEET WITH A TECHNICIAN. SHE NOTES THE DEFECTIVE ADDRESS AND THE PROBLEM IS SOLVED.

MPT MA

WE OFTEN GET OUR EMAILS A WEEK LATE. NOW I KNOW WHY.

126

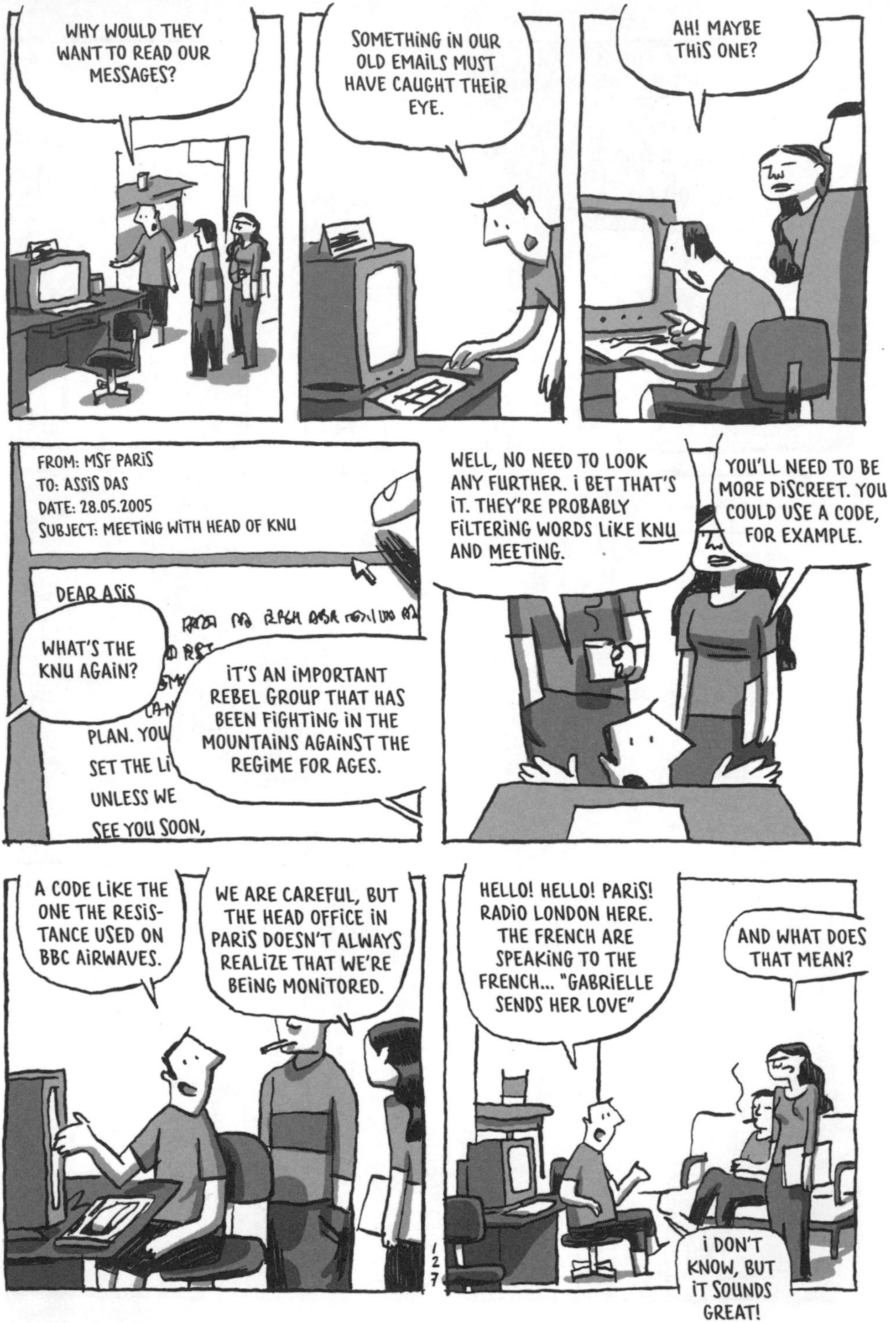
WHY WOULD THEY WANT TO READ OUR MESSAGES?
SOMETHING IN OUR OLD EMAILS MUST HAVE CAUGHT THEIR EYE.
AH! MAYBE THIS ONE?
FROM: MSF PARIS
TO: ASSIS DAS
DATE: 28.05.2005
SUBJECT: MEETING WITH HEAD OF KNU
DEAR ASIS
PLAN. YOU
SET THE LI
UNLESS WE
SEE YOU SOON,
WHAT'S THE KNU AGAIN?
IT'S AN IMPORTANT REBEL GROUP THAT HAS BEEN FIGHTING IN THE MOUNTAINS AGAINST THE REGIME FOR AGES.
WELL, NO NEED TO LOOK ANY FURTHER. I BET THAT'S IT. THEY'RE PROBABLY FILTERING WORDS LIKE KNU AND MEETING.
YOU'LL NEED TO BE MORE DISCREET. YOU COULD USE A CODE, FOR EXAMPLE.
A CODE LIKE THE ONE THE RESISTANCE USED ON BBC AIRWAVES.
WE ARE CAREFUL, BUT THE HEAD OFFICE IN PARIS DOESN'T ALWAYS REALIZE THAT WE'RE BEING MONITORED.
HELLO! HELLO! PARIS! RADIO LONDON HERE. THE FRENCH ARE SPEAKING TO THE FRENCH... "GABRIELLE SENDS HER LOVE"
AND WHAT DOES THAT MEAN?
I DON'T KNOW, BUT IT SOUNDS GREAT!

THE RAINY
SEASON BEGAN
SUDDENLY.

THE BIRDS

I'VE ALWAYS ASSOCIATED CROWS WITH NORTHERN CLIMATES, BUT I WAS WRONG. BURMA IS FULL OF THEM.

THERE'S ONE.

AND THERE'S ANOTHER.

KA-WO.

IT'S NO WONDER THERE ARE SO MANY. THEY'RE REAL TRASH PICKERS.

THAT'S IT, WE'VE THROWN THEM ALL OUR STALE BREAD.

LET'S GO GET READY FOR SCHOOL NOW.

SA-KUL

TA-KSI.

TODAY, YES.

OH, LOOK, IT'S GARBAGE DAY TODAY.

ONCE A WEEK, A TRUCK PICKS UP THE GARBAGE. ALL OUR NEIGHBORS TURN OUT.

THEY THROW AWAY ANYTHING THEY CAN'T BURN AND THAT THE CROWS AND DOGS DON'T WANT.

ACTUALLY, SOME PEOPLE MUST NOT RECYCLE MUCH, BECAUSE THE STENCH IS UNBELIEVABLE.

OH MAN...IN THIS HEAT, STUFF MUST FERMENT THE MOMENT IT DROPS IN THERE... MMM.

UGH! THE POOR GUYS WHO WADE THROUGH THAT SLUDGE ALL DAY. HOW CAN THEY STAND THE SMELL?

REALLY, OF THE FIVE SENSES, ONLY THE EYES GET AN OCCASIONAL REST THANKS TO THEIR LIDS. THE OTHERS ARE ALWAYS ON THE ALERT.

IT'S A LOUSY SYSTEM.

TAK-SI!

TO THE RIGHT

RITEE RITEE

WE'VE GOT LOUIS SIGNED UP IN A LITTLE FRENCH NURSERY SCHOOL. HE'S A BIT YOUNG, BUT HE LOVES IT.

WHOA!

HEY! WASN'T THERE
A HITCHCOCK FILM
LIKE THIS THAT
ENDED BADLY?

HMM...
SHOULD
I RUN?

FIRST
FIELD
VISIT

I'M FINALLY GOING INTO THE FIELD FOR A FIRST-HAND LOOK AT THE MISSIONS I'VE BEEN HEARING ABOUT SINCE MY ARRIVAL.

SOCKS?

YES.

HAT?

NAH...DON'T HAVE ONE. SHOULD I?

THE GOVERNMENT SEEMS TO HAVE RELAXED ITS RESTRICTIONS, AND SINCE I'VE BEEN WANTING TO GO, IT'S NOW OR NEVER.

HO HO! ADVENTURE, HERE WE COME!

I HAVE NO TRAVEL PERMIT, BUT THAT'S NOT A PROBLEM FOR THE FIRST PART OF THE TRIP, SINCE MOULMEIN IS A TOURIST DESTINATION. THE REST OF THE WAY, I'LL TRAVEL IN THE MSF CAR, WHICH IS RARELY CHECKED BY THE AUTHORITIES.

THAILAN

YANGOUN

MOULMEIN

KAWKA REIK

MUDON

WE'LL GET THERE EARLY, AFTER A NIGHT ON THE BUS.

THE FIRST CHECKPOINT IS RIGHT OUTSIDE THE CITY.

A FEW HOURS LATER, THERE'S ANOTHER, THEN ANOTHER, AND SO ON THROUGH THE NIGHT. SOMETIMES WE HAVE TO GET OFF THE BUS.

NO WAY! I'M FED UP. LET'EM COME GET ME HERE.

ZZZZ

AT ONE CHECKPOINT, A PASSENGER IS HELD BACK. HIS SON STAYS ON THE BUS WITH SOMEONE WHO SEEMS TO BE FAMILY. YOU CAN SEE THE WORRY ON THEIR FACES WHEN THE BUS PULLS OUT.

133

THE TRIP WOULD TAKE ROUGHLY HALF AS LONG WITHOUT ALL THE CHECKPOINTS.

i END UP WISHING i'D BROUGHT A HAT. THE AC IS SET ON MAX FOR THE WHOLE RIDE.

SOME PEOPLE SLEEP IN SHORT SLEEVES ANYWAY.

THAT'S INCREDIBLE.

BESIDES THE POLAR AMBIANCE, THERE'S THE TV, SERVING UP LOCAL NEWS AND EQUALLY LOCAL VIDEOS FOR THOSE WHO CAN'T SLEEP. WITH THE VOLUME CRANKED ALL THE WAY UP, OF COURSE.

MOULMEIN.

HOW'S THE GREAT EXPLORER?

F-F-F-FRESH AS A ROSE.

COMING INTO THE CITY, VISITORS CAN ADMIRE AN UGLY MONUMENT THAT DATES BACK TO THE COUNTRY'S "SOCIALIST" PERIOD.

IT'S GOT FIVE MEN, HAND IN HAND. A WORKER WITH HIS HAMMER ON ONE SIDE, AND A PEASANT WITH HIS SICKLE ON THE OTHER.

THE THREE IN THE MIDDLE ARE ARMED. A SOLDIER, A COP, AND ONE MORE SOLDIER, TO PLAY IT SAFE. ALL FIVE ARE SMILING.

3 SOLDIERS TO 2 CIVILIANS. EXCEPT FOR THE TWO SMILING GUYS AT EITHER END, IT SEEMS LIKE A FAIRLY ACCURATE REPRESENTATION OF HOW THIS COUNTRY OPERATES.

I DON'T GET IT, THEY SHOULD BE HERE BY NOW. THEY WERE SUPPOSED TO PICK US UP... OK, WELL, WE'LL HAVE TO TAKE THE LOCAL BUS AND HOPE YOU DON'T GET CHECKED.

ALL RIGHT.

I TRY TO IMAGINE GEORGE ORWELL, POSTED HERE AT 19 AS AN OFFICER IN THE IMPERIAL POLICE FORCE. DISGUSTED BY COLONIALISM, HE DESERTED WHILE ON LEAVE IN EUROPE.

IF I WASN'T SO EXHAUSTED, I'D TRY TO MAKE OUT A HOUSE FROM 1903 TO TELL MYSELF THAT HE MUST HAVE WALKED BY IT, JUST LIKE ME NOW.

HEAD HURTS.

WE FINALLY MANAGE TO FIND A BUS THAT WILL GET US TO MUDON.

MUDON?

MUDON?

MUDON?

THE DRIVE IS SUPPOSED TO BE BEAUTIFUL, BUT UNFORTUNATELY I DON'T GET TO APPRECIATE IT.

OW!

YOU OK?

FIRST OFF, BECAUSE THESE MINI-BUSES ARE COVERED BY A TARP THAT PREVENTS YOU FROM SEEING ANYTHING.

SECOND, I GET A SPECK OF DUST IN MY EYE BEFORE GETTING ON. THE SLIGHTEST EYEBALL MOVEMENT HURTS LIKE HELL. I SPEND THE TRIP WITH MY HEAD IN MY HANDS, TRYING TO MAKE IT SEEM LIKE I'M JUST TIRED.

AFTER WHAT FEELS LIKE 3 HOURS, WE GET TO OUR DESTINATION.

DAMN.

IT'S RIGHT THERE

HEY! WAIT UP!

MSF RENTS A MAGNIFICENT TEAK HOUSE. IT BELONGED TO THE ENGLISH BACK WHEN LOWER BURMA WAS ANNEXED TO INDIA. LATER, IT WAS REQUISITIONED BY THE JAPANESE DURING THE OCCUPATION.

THEY CARRIED OUT INTERROGATIONS HERE, AND NOT ALL PRISONERS CAME OUT ALIVE. LOCALS SAY THE PLACE IS TEEMING WITH GHOSTS, WHICH IS WHY THEY HESITATE TO COME HERE TO BE TREATED.

KENTARO, THE JAPANESE PHYSICIAN POSTED IN MUDON, HAS A LOOK AT MY EYE AND GIVES ME A SALVE.

WHEW! THANKS! TRAVELING WITH MSF IS GREAT. IMAGINE THE SHAPE I'D BE IN IF I WAS TRAVELING WITH CLOWNS WITHOUT BORDERS.

HA HA HA!

NOT TOO FUNNY, HUH? OK, FORGET IT.

I LEAVE NADÈGE TO HER WORK AND FIND A BIKE TO EXPLORE THE SURROUNDINGS.

I COME ACROSS A CUTE VILLAGE, WITH A FENCED GARDEN IN FRONT OF EVERY HOUSE.

REAL LITTLE ENGLISH COTTAGES.

THE PEOPLE HERE HAVE GOT AN INGENIOUS SYSTEM FOR BUILDING RAINPROOF ROOFS.

THEY PUT OUT LARGE LEAVES TO DRY...

THEN ATTACH THEM TO A WOOD FRAME...

JUST LIKE TILES ARE PLACED ON OLD ROOFS IN EUROPE.

WE EAT IN ONE OF THE TOWN'S FOUR RESTAURANTS. THERE'S ANOTHER BEHIND AN OLD COLONIAL HOUSE THAT ALSO DOUBLES AS A BAR AT NIGHT, WITH A LOCAL WHISKY THAT DOESN'T COST A LOT BUT GIVES YOU ONE HELL OF A HEADACHE. OH MAN!

ORDERING IS A BREEZE: BEEF, CHICKEN OR FISH.

I'LL HAVE THAT.

IT'S NOT GREAT.

NO, IT REALLY ISN'T.

HAVE YOU BEEN HERE LONG?

ALMOST A YEAR.

WOW, BRAVO!

CONGRATU-LATIONS.

NEXT, WE HEAD OVER TO THE SECOND MOST POPULAR PLACE IN TOWN: THE PUBLIC PHONE.

MSF RENTS A LINE IN THE BACK OF THE SHOP TO PICK UP ITS EMAIL.

IT'S THE INTERNET CAFÉ, BUT YOU NEED TO BRING YOUR OWN COMPUTER?

LATER, THEY LEAVE ME TO GO DO THE ROUNDS OF THE NEARBY MOBILE CLINICS.

CAN I COME TOO?

NO. YOU DON'T HAVE A TRAVEL VISA. IT'S TOO RISKY.

PFF.

HEY, LOOKS LIKE SCOOTERS ARE ALLOWED HERE.

140

IN THE EVENING, KENTARO COOKS A JAPANESE MEAL WITH INGREDIENTS HE BROUGHT BACK FROM HIS LAST TRIP HOME.

IT'S A FEAST. AT THE END OF THE MEAL, I POLISH OFF THE LEFTOVERS, INCLUDING SOME FISH EGGS WITH SEAWEED THAT I WON'T FORGET ANYTIME SOON.

AAAAH-RI-GA-TO!

UNLIKE THE CAPITAL, THIS IS AN INTENSE MALARIA ZONE. THERE ARE MOSQUITO NETS IN EVERY ROOM...

PSSHT PSSHT PSSHT

STOP. I CAN'T BREATHE

BUT SINCE I CAN'T STAND BEING SHUT IN WHEN I SLEEP, I TAKE A FEW PRECAUTIONS.

YOU KNOW YOU'RE NOT FOLLOWING MSF PROTOCOL?

OH REALLY?

THE NEXT MORNING, WE RIDE AROUND A LAKE WITH A MONASTERY ON ITS SHORES. ONLY MEN CAN SWIM HERE. I DON'T KNOW WHY EXACTLY, BUT I KNOW THE MONASTERY HAS SOMETHING TO DO WITH IT.

SEE? EVEN THESE NICE BUDDHISTS THINK WOMEN ARE IMPURE.

IT'S PRETTY HOT TODAY, HUH?

IN ONE OF THE SMALL FOOD SHACKS JUTTING OVER THE LAKE, WE'RE SERVED THE BEST "MOTEE" (TRADITIONAL BREAKFAST) I'VE HAD. THE PLACE IS EMPTY, THERE'S NOT A TOURIST IN SIGHT. I FIGURE THAT MUST BE THE ONE UPSIDE OF LIVING IN A MILITARY ZONE.

WE HIT THE ROAD AGAIN, DESTINATION KAWKAREIK, A FEW HOURS AHEAD TOWARD THE THAI BORDER.

THE SIGHTSEEING IS A WRITE-OFF AGAIN. I'M IN BACK, SQUEEZED INTO THE MIDDLE.

BUT AS WE PULL INTO THE TOWN, I GET A GLIMPSE OF SOMETHING THAT LOOKS LIKE A FIRE STATION. AND I THINK I SEE FIRE TRUCKS DATING BACK TO WWII.

KAWKAREIK IS EVEN SMALLER THAN MUDON. IT'S STARTING TO FEEL LIKE THE WILD WEST OUT HERE.

THIS TIME, WE'RE GREETED BY A PERSIAN PHYSICIAN, BABAK, WHO HAS BEEN POSTED HERE WITH HIS WIFE FOR A FEW MONTHS.

IN KAWKAREIK, POWER IS HARD TO COME BY. THE COMPUTERS RUN OFF A GENERATOR.

THE FRIDGE WORKS THE OLD FASHIONED WAY, WITH ICE THAT NEEDS REPLACING EVERY 2 DAYS.

THANKS.

SOME JUICE?

INSULATING PLASTIC

AND THE CLEANING LADY HAS TO PUT CHARCOAL INTO THE CLOTHES IRON.

TO THINK MY MOTHER USED ONE LIKE THAT IN HER GASPESIAN YOUTH.

SHIT, I DON'T FEEL TOO GOOD.

I SPEND THE DAY AND NIGHT GOING BACK AND FORTH BETWEEN THE BED AND BATHROOM.

THE AUTHORITIES ARE NUTS. I CAN'T RUN THE CLINIC IF I NEED TO SPEND HALF MY TIME IN THE CAPITAL. THEY SHOULD...

THANK GOD IT'S NOT A SQUAT TOILET.

...AND I CAN'T ALWAYS BE ASKING THE LOCAL EMPLOYEES TO GO OUT TO THE SENSITIVE ZONES WITHOUT US. IT'S THE....

WHOA!

YOU'RE WHITE AS A SHEET.

THANKS.

DOCTOR BABAK PRESCRIBES ALL THE SALINE WATER I CAN DRINK AND PARACETAMOL.

WHEN I GET THE SWEATS AND SHAKES THE NEXT DAY, THE OTHERS START GETTING WORRIED.

IS IT SERIOUS, DOC?

THEY CONDUCT A "PARACHECK", A QUICK TEST FOR MALARIA.

144

GOOD NEWS: THE PARACHECK IS NEGATIVE. THAT MEANS I DON'T HAVE MALARIA, OR AT LEAST NOT ITS MOST VIRULENT FORM, FALCIPARUM, WHICH IS ALL THE KIT CAN TEST FOR.

HURRAY.

A LAB TECHNICIAN IS SENT IN TO COMPLETE THE DIAGNOSIS (IN A WHITE GOWN AND GLOVES).

MINGALABA.

LOOKING FOR A WEAPON OF MASS DESTRUCTION?

MSF BDR

HEY! DID YOU KNOW THAT THE WORD MALARIA COMES FROM BAD (MAL) AND AIR (ARIA)? PEOPLE THOUGHT THAT FOUL SWAMP ODORS CAUSED THE DISEASE.

MSF

THAT'S FASCINATING.

IN THE END, IT'S NOTHING SERIOUS. FOR THE FIRST TIME IN MY LIFE, I'M ALMOST HAPPY TO HAVE HAD JUST DIARRHEA.

WHAT A GREAT WEEKEND.

BEFORE WE GO, I MANAGE TO PULL MYSELF OUT OF BED FOR A QUICK TOUR OF THE TOWN.

MSF

OUCH, MY BUTTHOLE IS BURNING, BUT I REALLY NEED TO HAVE A LOOK AT THAT FIRE STATION.

IT'S WORTH THE
TROUBLE.

ISUZU

TOYOTA

THE JAPANESE MUST HAVE SHIPPED
THEM OVER DURING THEIR BRIEF
OCCUPATION, FROM 1943 TO 1945.

LATER, WE TAKE THE
BUS BACK TO RANGOON.
I DON'T SLEEP A WINK
ALL NIGHT.

JULY 1

A PARTY HAS BEEN ORGANIZED TO CELEBRATE CANADA DAY.

IT TAKES BEING ON THE OTHER SIDE OF THE PLANET FOR ME TO GO TO A CANADA DAY PARTY.

THEY HAD THE STRANGE IDEA OF SERVING CANADIAN SPECIALTIES.

IT'S CRAZY HOW MANY CANADIANS THERE ARE HERE.

WHAT'S THIS?

EVERYTHING IS JUST ABOUT INEDIBLE, WITH HONORABLE MENTION FOR SOMETHING BEING PASSED OFF AS POUTINE.

YUCK! IT'S PRETTY LOUSY TO BEGIN WITH.

THE TROPICAL VERSION MUST BE SOMETHING ELSE.

THIS EVENING, DURING WHICH I TALK WITH A WHO* EMPLOYEE ABOUT BIRD FLU, MARKS THE START OF A CREEPING PANIC THAT HAUNTS ME FOR THE NEXT TWO MONTHS.

IT'S AN IMMINENT THREAT

*WORLD HEALTH ORGANISATION

THE H5N1 VIRUS IS MUTATING. IT'S JUST A MATTER OF TIME.

AND WHEN THE EPIDEMIC HITS, NO OTHER COUNTRIES WILL LET US BACK IN.

THE WAY THEY CENSOR INFORMATION HERE, WE WON'T KNOW WHAT'S GOING ON BEFORE IT'S TOO LATE.

WE'LL BE QUARANTINED.

TRAPPED!

INDONESIA, HONG KONG, VIETNAM. IT'S CLOSING IN AT FULL SPEED.

OVER AT THE UN, THEY'VE ALREADY STOCKPILED TAMIFLU FOR THEIR EMPLOYEES.

IF I WERE YOU, I'D TRY TO GET MY HANDS ON SOME BEFORE PANIC HITS.

TAMIFLU! WE NEED TAMIFLU! ASAP!

GUY, THIS IS MR. WINKEL. HE REPRESENTS THE EUROPEAN COMMUNITY IN BURMA.

HEY, HOW'S IT GOING?

DO YOU KNOW WHETHER MSF HAS ORDERED TAMIFLU FOR ITS EMPLOYEES? NO? WE NEED TO WRITE TO PARIS AND HAVE THEM SEND IT IMMEDIATELY!

FOR THE NEXT MONTH, IT'S ALL I TALK ABOUT.

THE EPIDEMIC IS COMING!

HUH?

I ASK MY EMBASSY ABOUT ITS MEDICAL EVACUATION PROCEDURE.

WHAT? WE'D BE EVACUATED BY THE AMERICANS?

HOW HUMILIATING.

I PRESSURE NADÈGE INTO ALERTING MSF ABOUT OUR SITUATION.

HAVE YOU ASKED PARIS ABOUT THE TAMIFLU?

IT'S DONE.

I SPEND MY DAYS ON THE INTERNET, TRACKING THE LATEST BIRD FLU DEVELOPMENTS.

I TRY TO GET THE MEDICATION THROUGH FRIENDS WHO ARE GOING TO HONG KONG.

BUT THE PHARMACIES THERE ARE ALREADY SOLD OUT.

THE TV COVERAGE DOESN'T HELP.

...EXPECTED TO BE WORSE THAN THE SPANISH FLU, WHICH TOOK 40 MILLION LIVES.

MSF FINALLY SENDS ALL ASIAN SECTIONS SUPPLIES TO TREAT ITS EMPLOYEES.

VICTORY.

SURE, BUT THERE'S NO PROOF THAT IT WORKS. IT'S ALL HYPOTHETICAL. ORIGINALLY, IT WAS PRESCRIBED TO TREAT SEASONAL FLU. WHO KNOWS? MAYBE THE ALARM ABOUT TAMIFLU WAS TRIGGERED BY THE PRODUCING LAB ITSELF, SEEING THAT IT'S THE ONLY SUPPLIER.

YOU'RE BETTER OFF WEARING A LITTLE CLOTH FACE MASK FOR PROTECTION.

149

RAINY SEASON
II

AUSTRALIAN
CLUB

150

ART CLASS GET-TOGETHERS

Since I can't draw, I wind up with lots of free time. I learn to use the mouse with my left hand and I throw together a few exercises for my animation class.

This Sunday, we meet at the home of my youngest student. He's a civil servant, so he gets the perk of a well-located apartment with enough electricity for me to get through my lesson uninterrupted.

Today, they were all sitting on the ground with note pads in hand. It was very sweet, but I had them make adjustments.

DID YOU FINISH LAST WEEK'S EXERCISES?

NO.

NO TIME.

NO.

The joys of teaching are the same everywhere.

GREAT.

SO, WHAT'LL WE DO? WANT TO SEE WHAT I DID?

YES.

YES.

AFTER AGREEING TO MEET AGAIN NEXT SUNDAY, WE GO OUT FOR COFFEE.

AND THIS TIME YOU'LL DO THE EXERCISES.

YES.

OF COURSE.

YES.

FOR SURE.

ONE OF THEM WORKS AS A CARTOONIST FOR A COMPANY THAT EMPLOYS 300 ARTISTS TO CHURN OUT KOREAN MANGAS.

COULD i VISIT?

i DOUBT iT. THE 2ND FLOOR PEOPLE CAN'T EVEN GO SEE THOSE ON THE 3RD. iT'S ALL TOP SECRET OVER THERE.

TOO BAD.

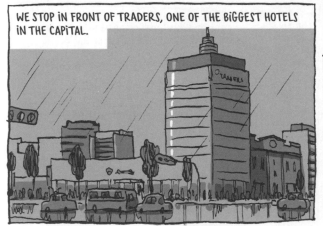

WE STOP IN FRONT OF TRADERS, ONE OF THE BiGGEST HOTELS iN THE CAPITAL.

BUiLT BY KHUN SA, THE FORMER OPiUM BARON.

KHUN WHO?

SA, KHUN SA. FROM THE SHAN REGION. HE STOOD UP TO THE REGiME FOR AGES WITH A MiLITiA OF 800 SOLDiERS.

BUT THEN THE AMERICANS PUT A $2 MiLLiON BOUNTY ON HiS HEAD. SO HE DECIDED TO TURN HiMSELF IN AND NEGOTiATE WiTH HiS OLD ENEMiES, THE ARMY. SINCE THEN, HE'S BEEN LiViNG THE GOOD LiFE iN RANGOON.

AND THIS CHAIN OF COFFEE SHOPS BELONGED TO THE SON OF THE PRIME MINISTER WHO WAS JAILED LAST DECEMBER. THEY CLOSED FOR A WHILE, BUT NOW THE CHAIN'S BEEN TAKEN OVER BY THE SON OF ANOTHER GENERAL.

ALTHOUGH THE NEWS IS CENSORED, THE BURMESE KNOW ALL ABOUT THE INTRIGUES AND SHADY DEALINGS GOING ON.

DO YOU COME HERE OFTEN?

THIS IS THE FIRST TIME.

AND SO HOW DO YOU GET YOUR HANDS ON THE LATEST VERSIONS OF ALL THE SOFTWARE ON YOUR COMPUTERS?

I GO HAVE A LOOK AFTER THE COFFEE.

THERE ARE HUNDREDS OF CDS, SORTED BY CATEGORY. ONLY PIRATED COPIES. ALL THE LATEST VERSIONS FOR THE PRICE OF A CUP OF COFFEE.

THAT STORE OVER THERE.

WHOA!

HERE'S SOME- THING TO FILL UP MY FREE TIME.

SUPER! I'LL BE ABLE POLISH UP MY ENGLISH OR LEARN HOW TO CREATE A WEB SITE OR EDIT A VIDEO... THERE SURE IS NO LACK OF CHOICES.

HEY, THERE'S A GAMES SECTION AS WELL.

NO WAY! NOT THE LATEST WARCRAFT!

WARCRAFT
III

OK, I'VE DECIDED TO BE PRODUCTIVE TODAY, EVEN THOUGH MY ELBOW STILL HURTS.

I'LL USE MY LEFT HAND TO DRAW.

TEXT IS OK, I MANAGE MORE OR LESS. WITH A BIT OF PRACTICE, I'LL BE FINE.

BUT DRAWING IS A WHOLE OTHER STORY. AND I CAN'T IMAGINE HOW MANY MONTHS IT WOULD TAKE TO GET IT RIGHT.

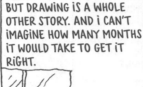

OK, I'VE DECIDED TO BE PRO-DUCTIVE TODAY, EVEN THOUGH MY ELBOW STILL HURTS.

I'LL JUST USE MY LEFT HAND ...

...TO ANNIHILATE THE ARMY OF THE ALLIANCE AND GET TO LEVEL 12 OF THE ORC CAMPAIGN.

I NEVER DID LEARN HOW TO DRAW WITH MY LEFT HAND, BUT I BECAME AMBIDEX-TROUS WITH THE MOUSE IN NO TIME.

154

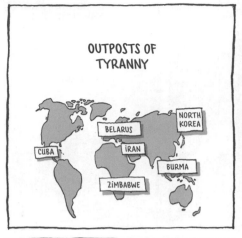

OUTPOSTS OF TYRANNY

A JOURNALIST FRIEND IS STAYING WITH US. HE'S WORKING ON AN ARTICLE ABOUT EACH OF THE "OUTPOSTS OF TYRANNY," AS DEFINED BY BUSH. HE'S STARTING WITH BURMA.

GETTING INTO NORTH KOREA COULD BE A REAL HEADACHE.

WE START WITH A NEIGHBORHOOD TOUR.

AND AUNG SAN SUU KYI LIVES JUST PAST THAT CHECKPOINT.

ACTUALLY, THE BURMESE DON'T REFER TO HER BY NAME. THEY JUST CALL HER "THE LADY." IT'S LIKE VOLDEMORT IN HARRY POTTER, "HE WHO MUST NOT BE NAMED."

EITHER WAY, WE CAN'T GET THROUGH. COMING?

I TAKE HIS COMPANY AS AN EXCUSE TO VISIT A FEW TOURIST ATTRACTIONS I HAVEN'T SEEN.

PAGODA-WISE, THIS IS AS BIG AS IT GETS.

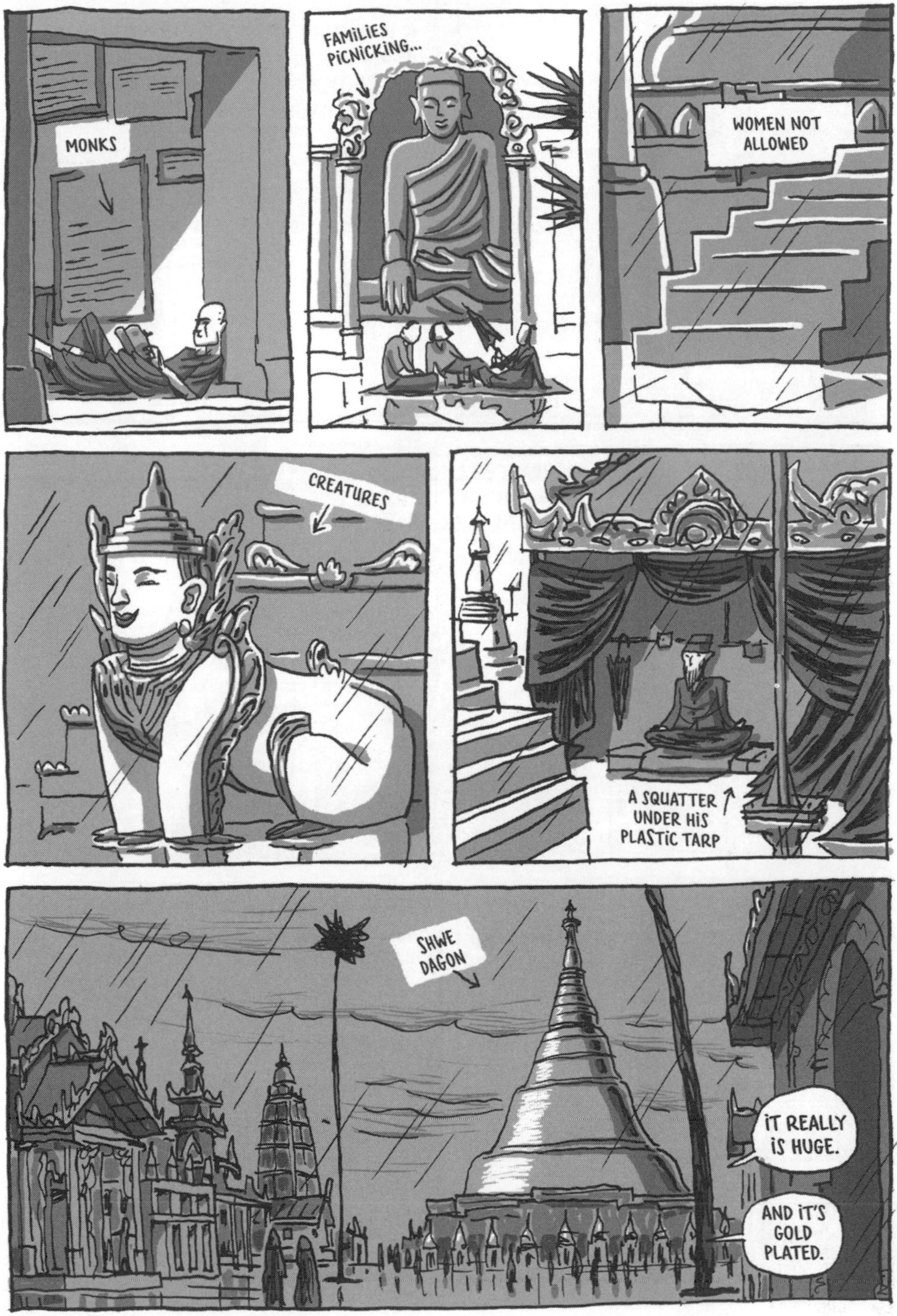
MONKS
FAMILIES PICNICKING...
WOMEN NOT ALLOWED
CREATURES
A SQUATTER UNDER HIS PLASTIC TARP
SHWE DAGON
IT REALLY IS HUGE.
AND IT'S GOLD PLATED.

NOTICE THE WAY THEY CARRY THEIR UMBRELLAS?

SOME SLIP IT IN BEHIND THEIR BACKS, NEXT TO THEIR WALLET.

AND STRANGER YET, SOME LET IT HANG OFF THEIR SHIRT COLLAR.

WE STOP FOR A BITE FURTHER ON.

IS YOURS ANY GOOD?

NO. YOURS?

NO.

WE PASS BY A FOREIGN MONK IN THE STREET. HE'S GIGANTIC. KIDS SKIP ALONG AFTER HIM.

MAN, WAS HE ODD-LOOKING.

I COVERTLY BUY A TIME MAGAZINE FROM A LITTLE BOY. I'M INTRIGUED: THE LADY IS ON THE COVER. IT'S AN OLD COPY FROM MAY 1990. I'VE BEEN HAD.

TIME

BUT IT'S FASCINATING ALL THE SAME. SHE HAD JUST WON THE ELECTIONS.

"WILL SHE BE ABLE TO LIFT THE COUNTRY OUT OF ITS ECONOMIC MORASS?" ASKED THE EDITORIAL.

SOON AFTER THAT ISSUE, THE JUNTA VOIDED THE VOTE AND ARRESTED HER FOR DISTURBING THE PEACE.

16 YEARS LATER, NOTHING'S CHANGED.

EELS

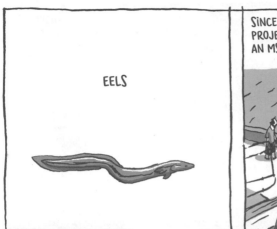

SINCE I STILL CAN'T GO SEE ANY MSF-FRANCE PROJECTS, I ASK FOR AUTHORIZATION TO VISIT AN MSF-HOLLAND CLINIC.

IT'S JUST NORTH OF THE CITY. WE'LL TAKE A TAXI.

THE CLINIC CATERS MOSTLY TO HIV POSITIVE PATIENTS.

IT'S NICE.

A DOCTOR FRIEND SHOWS US AROUND.

THIS IS THE RECEPTION AREA WHERE NEW PATIENTS REGISTER.

AT THE BACK OF THE ROOM, THERE'S A MOTHER WITH A BABY IN HER ARMS. IT'S SO SKINNY THAT I CAN'T STOP MYSELF FROM ASKING ABOUT ITS CHANCES OF SURVIVAL.

THAT ONE THERE?

158

WELL... THEY'VE BEEN HERE FOR A FEW DAYS AND THE BABY HASN'T PUT ON WEIGHT. THAT'S NOT A GOOD SIGN.

JEEZUS, I COULD NEVER DO THIS JOB.

SHALL WE MOVE ON ?

THE VISIT WAS FASCINATING. MSF-HOLLAND TREATS AN IMPRESSIVE NUMBER OF PATIENTS. THEY HAVE 3 CLINICS THIS SIZE IN RANGOON ALONE, AND MORE ELSEWHERE IN THE COUNTRY. IT'S ONE OF THE LARGEST AND OLDEST NGOS WORKING IN THE COUNTRY.

THEY EVEN HAVE A REINTEGRATION PROGRAM THAT HIRES FORMER PATIENTS TO PAINT HEALTH EDUCATION POSTERS.

THEY ALSO TREAT OPPORTUNISTIC INFECTIONS LIKE TUBERCULOSIS. IN FACT, I SAW ONE GUY PUKING HIS GUTS OUT WHEN I CAME OUT OF THE BATHROOM.

UGH!

REVOLTING!

HOW ABOUT A LITTLE WALK BEFORE WE GET BACK IN A TAXI?

HMM... I DUNNO...

HEY! HAVE YOU SEEN WHAT THEY USE TO CATCH EELS?

WE SPEND A LONG WHILE UNDER THIS TREE, WHEN A NEIGHBOR BRINGS US AN UMBRELLA...

FOLLOWED BY A SECOND SOON AFTER...

AND FINALLY INVITES US TO TAKE SHELTER IN HIS HOME.

160

WE MEET THE WHOLE FAMILY. SIX PEOPLE LIVE IN THERE!

WE'RE SERVED TEA AND, AFTER SOME POLITE CHITCHAT, SILENCE SETTLES IN. WE ALL LISTEN TO THE RAIN FALL.

THE SON LEAVES BY BIKE AND COMES BACK WITH SOMEONE WHO SPEAKS ENGLISH.

HOW ARE YOU!

ANOTHER MAN ARRIVES AND HAS OUR CONVERSATION TRANSLATED. THERE'S A PARTY OFFICIAL IN EVERY SECTOR TO KEEP AN EYE ON THINGS.

WE'RE VERY KINDLY ESCORTED TO A TAXI.

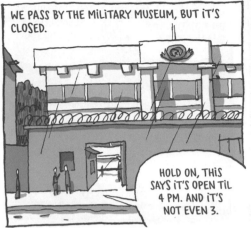

WE PASS BY THE MILITARY MUSEUM, BUT IT'S CLOSED.

HOLD ON, THIS SAYS IT'S OPEN TIL 4 PM. AND IT'S NOT EVEN 3.

TAKING A LOOK INTO THE SECURITY GUARD'S OFFICE, I SEE AN OBJECT I WOULD HAVE EXPECTED TO FIND IN THE MUSEUM INSTEAD.

MORSE CODE STRAIGHT KEY

IT LOOKS LIKE IT'S STILL IN USE, SEEING THAT THE CABLES ARE CONNECTED!

WE END THE DAY IN A RESTAURANT NEAR HOME.

OH, HEY, THEY SERVE EEL. WANT TO TRY IT?

WHY NOT.

MMM... NOT BAD.

SO, D'YOU LIKE IT?

DID YOU NOTICE THE MORSE CODE MACHINE ON THE SECURITY GUARD'S DESK?

YES, THE MILITARY GEAR HERE IS CUTTING EDGE.

YOU SHOULD SEE THEIR TRUCKS, TOO—THEY'RE FALLING APART!

WITH SUCH A DILAPI- DATED ARMY, YOU'VE GOT TO WONDER HOW THE JUNTA MANAGES TO HOLD ONTO POWER.

MAYBE IT'S THE TORTURE AND IMPRISONMENT THAT DO IT?

HM, YEAH...

MUST BE.

OVER THE FOLLOWING WEEK, I KEPT THINKING ABOUT THAT MOTHER AND HER EMACIATED BABY. NEXT TIME I MET THE DOCTOR, I ASKED HOW THEY WERE, BUT WITH ALL THE PATIENTS COMING AND GOING, SHE COULDN'T REMEMBER THEM.

PFF! I'M WIPED!

JULY 14*

*FRENCH NATIONAL HOLIDAY

THERE'S A PHOTO OF AN OIL PLATFORM ON ONE OF THE WALLS AT THE ENTRANCE TO THE EMBASSY.

HMM. VERY NICE.

IT'S EASY TO GUESS WHOSE IT IS, BUT THERE'S NO COMPANY NAME.

HMM...

THE CONSUL (OR MAYBE THE AMBASSADOR—I DIDN'T CATCH IT) AND HIS WIFE WELCOME US.

MINGALABA.

THE SPEECH →

m mm mmm m mmm mmm mmm mm mm mmm m mmm mm mmm mmm mm mmm mmm mm mm TO WELCOME THE FRENCH COLONY mmm m mm mm mm mm mm mmm

COLO

COLONY?

COLONY?

164

RED CROSS, UN, TOTAL, MSF: THERE'S A GENERAL RUSH FOR THE BUFFET.

'SCUSE ME

SALMON

DUCK TERRINE

BAGUETTES

PATÉ

PICKLES

SANDWICHES

THIS LOOKS GREAT!

PILOT

THERE'S ONE TRULY ODD COUPLE.

WOW

AND FOR THOSE WHO HAD PATÉ, THE FIREWORKS LASTED ALL NIGHT LONG.

YIKES.

THE GEM MUSEUM

i LEARNED A LOT ABOUT GEMS READING JOSEPH KESSEL'S "MOGOK, THE VALLEY OF RUBiES" (1955).

OUR HERO MAKES HiS WAY TO MOGOK, iN CENTRAL BURMA, TO SiT iN ON THE NEGOTiATiONS OF A JEWELER FRiEND.

THE MOST BEAUTiFUL RUBiES iN THE WORLD ARE FOUND iN BURMA.

THE REDDEST OF ALL ARE "PiGEON'S BLOOD" RED.

CAREFUL iNSPECTiON PRECEDES THE PURCHASE OF THE ROUGH STONE, WHiCH WiLL (AFTER CUTTiNG) PROVE TO BE EiTHER A TREASURE OR ENTiRELY WORTHLESS. THAT'S THE GAMBLE. ONLY A TRAiNED EYE CAN SORT OUT iMPERFECT OR CLOUDED SPECiMENS. iT'S A GAME OF HiGH STAKES POKER.

HEY, KNOW WHERE WE COULD GO TODAY?

GEM MUSEUM

GEM MUSEU

THAT'S iT!

EXCEPT FOR DiAMONDS, THEY'VE GOT EVERY PRECiOUS AND SEMi-PRECiOUS STONE iN THE SUBSOiL OF THiS COUNTRY.

SAPPHiRE   JADE   AMETHYST   EMERALD   AGATE

OH! HEY, LOOK! A RUBY iN THE ROUGH.

EACH DISPLAY CASE CONTAINS A FORTUNE IN PRECIOUS STONES.

WHICH DOESN'T KEEP THE MUSEUM FROM TREATING US TO NEON LIGHTING AND WIRING TAPED TO THE GROUND.

HA! THIS IS FANCY!

ON THE WAY OUT, WE PASS BY ROWS OF HUGE JADEITE BLOCKS, STRAIGHT FROM THE MINES UP NORTH.

THEY'RE LINED UP FOR ONE OF THE REGIME'S ANNUAL SALES.

BURMA HAS 90% OF THE WORLD'S JADE MINES. AN EXTREMELY PROFITABLE RESOURCE FOR THE RULING MILITARY OFFICIALS.

THEY DON'T EVEN BOTHER TO DO THE DIGGING. INSTEAD, THEY RENT THE CONCESSIONS TO PRIVATE AND FOREIGN COMPANIES THAT EXPLOIT LOCAL LABOR.

SAME THING GOES FOR TEAK.

167

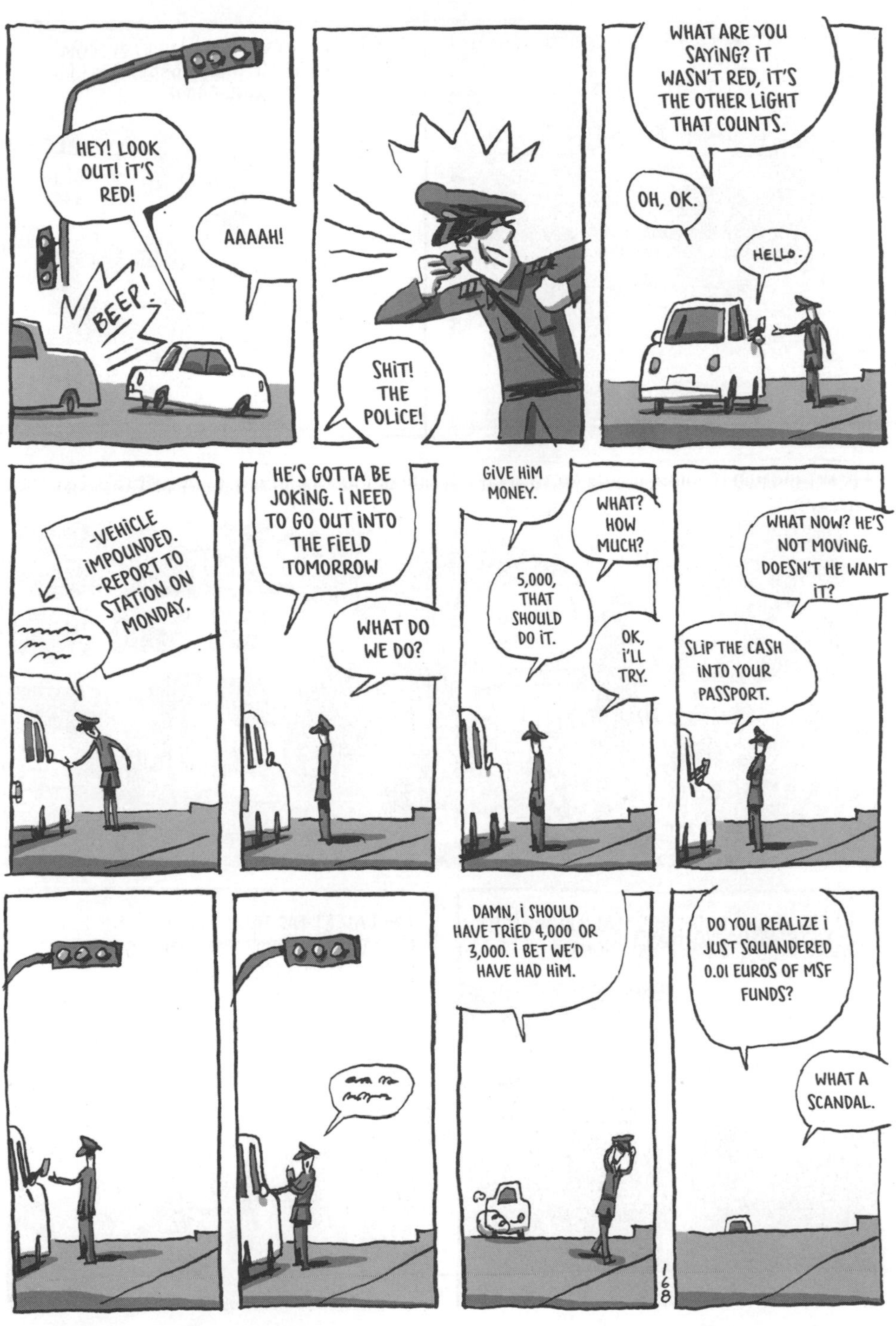
HEY! LOOK OUT! IT'S RED!
BEEP!
AAAAH!
SHIT! THE POLICE!
WHAT ARE YOU SAYING? IT WASN'T RED, IT'S THE OTHER LIGHT THAT COUNTS.
OH, OK.
HELLO.
-VEHICLE IMPOUNDED. -REPORT TO STATION ON MONDAY.
HE'S GOTTA BE JOKING. I NEED TO GO OUT INTO THE FIELD TOMORROW
WHAT DO WE DO?
GIVE HIM MONEY.
WHAT? HOW MUCH?
5,000, THAT SHOULD DO IT.
OK, I'LL TRY.
WHAT NOW? HE'S NOT MOVING. DOESN'T HE WANT IT?
SLIP THE CASH INTO YOUR PASSPORT.
DAMN, I SHOULD HAVE TRIED 4,000 OR 3,000. I BET WE'D HAVE HAD HIM.
DO YOU REALIZE I JUST SQUANDERED 0.01 EUROS OF MSF FUNDS?
WHAT A SCANDAL.

DERAILED

THE VISIT IS OVER, JULES LEFT THIS MORNING. TIME FOR ME TO GET BACK TO MY DESK AND START DRAWING AGAIN.

OUCH, EECH.

I DON'T OVERDO IT, THOUGH, AND GO TO A BABY GROUP ORGANIZED BY ONE OF THE MOTHERS AT THE DAYCARE.

NOT BAD!

IN THE LIVING ROOM ARE TWO MAGNIFICENT WOOD BUDDHAS (REPRODUCTIONS).

JEEZ, IF WE HADN'T COME WITH BACKPACKS, I'D BRING ONE HOME AS WELL.

THE LATEST FAD FROM BANGKOK: THE KIDS PLAY WITH A ROBOT THAT DOES SOME THIRTY MOVES. IT CAN EVEN DANCE.

OVER BY THE MOMS, TALK IS ABOUT SCHWEPPES TONIC, WHICH CAN'T BE FOUND ANYWHERE. FOLKS ARE MAKING DO WITH AN ERSATZ THAT ISN'T BAD, BUT JUST DOESN'T CUT IT FOR GIN TONICS.

THE DISCONNECTEDNESS FROM THE OUTSIDE WORLD SOMETIMES MAKES MY HEAD SPIN... OR MAYBE IT'S JUST THE ALCOHOL.

TALK ABOUT DISCONNECTED, SOME 14-YEAR OLD BURMESE KID HAS BEEN DRIVING HIS CONVERTIBLE MERCEDES TO SCHOOL. AT NIGHT, HE RACES THROUGH THE STREETS OF THE CAPITAL AND NOBODY DARES TO STOP HIM BECAUSE HE'S THE SON OF A LOCAL BIG SHOT.

I'VE PULLED MY SON OUT OF THAT SCHOOL. I PUT HIM IN A PUBLIC SCHOOL SO HE CAN LEARN BURMESE.

REALLY?

GOOD-BYE! AND THANKS!

170

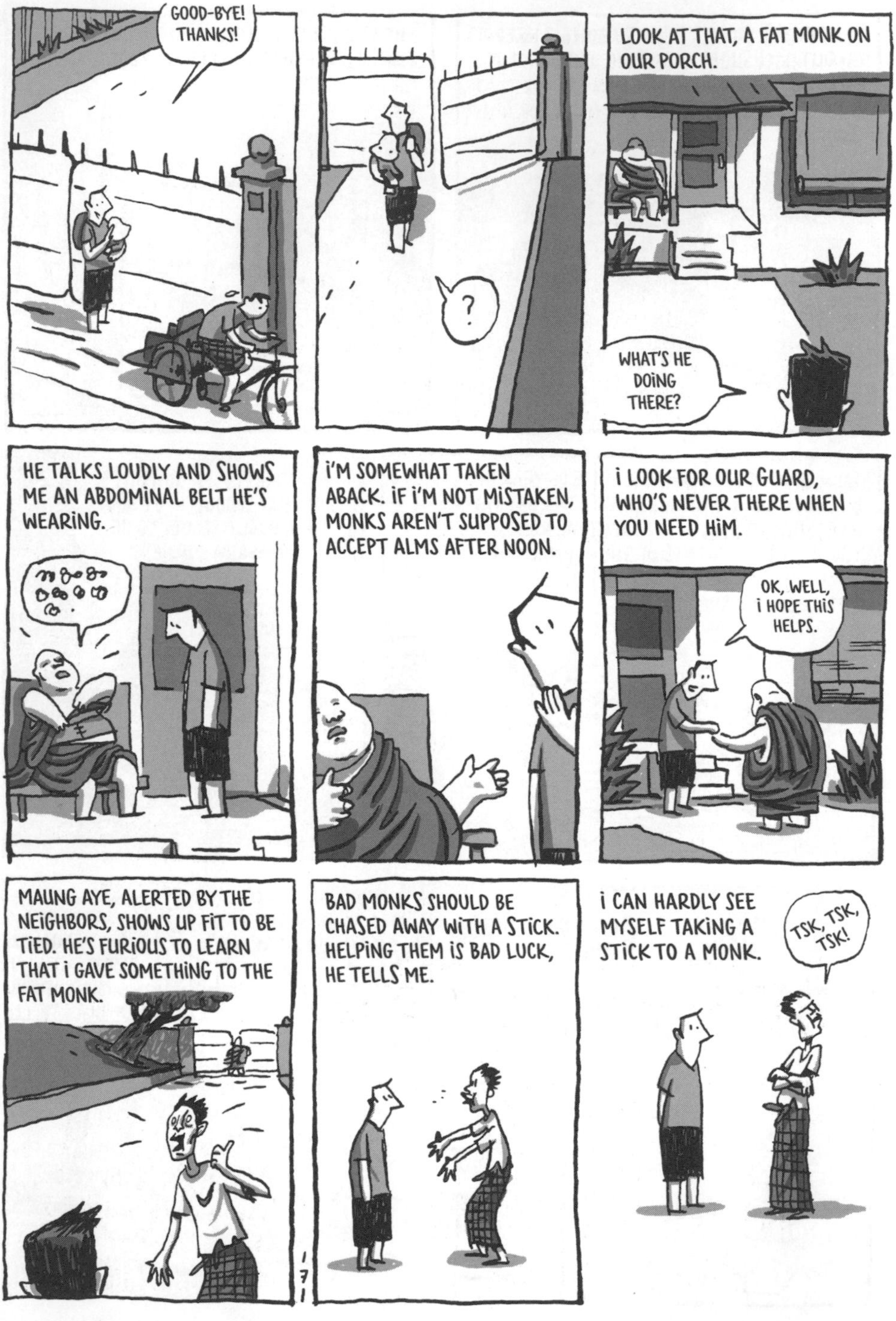
GOOD-BYE! THANKS!
?
LOOK AT THAT, A FAT MONK ON OUR PORCH.
WHAT'S HE DOING THERE?
HE TALKS LOUDLY AND SHOWS ME AN ABDOMINAL BELT HE'S WEARING.
I'M SOMEWHAT TAKEN ABACK. IF I'M NOT MISTAKEN, MONKS AREN'T SUPPOSED TO ACCEPT ALMS AFTER NOON.
I LOOK FOR OUR GUARD, WHO'S NEVER THERE WHEN YOU NEED HIM.
OK, WELL, I HOPE THIS HELPS.
MAUNG AYE, ALERTED BY THE NEIGHBORS, SHOWS UP FIT TO BE TIED. HE'S FURIOUS TO LEARN THAT I GAVE SOMETHING TO THE FAT MONK.
BAD MONKS SHOULD BE CHASED AWAY WITH A STICK. HELPING THEM IS BAD LUCK, HE TELLS ME.
I CAN HARDLY SEE MYSELF TAKING A STICK TO A MONK.
TSK, TSK, TSK!

THAT EVENING, HE'S STILL SULKING. I NEED TO GO OUT, SO I SUGGEST THAT HE MIGHT WANT TO COME BABYSIT AND WATCH TV.

HE LOOKS DELIGHTED. I THINK MANCHESTER UNITED IS PLAYING TONIGHT.

I SET OUT TO SEE THE NGOS. IT'S BEEN AGES SINCE I HAD A DRINK WITH THEM.

THE PLACE IS PACKED. NOT A GOOD SIGN.

INDEED →

GLOBAL FUND IS PULLING OUT OF BURMA.

OH REALLY. AND WHO'RE THEY?

THEY'RE THE ONES WHO PUT UP THE CASH FOR TB, AIDS AND MALARIA PROJECTS.

NO WONDER. IT'S BECOMING JUST ABOUT IMPOSSIBLE TO WORK HERE.

YOU CAN'T STAY IN THE FIELD FOR MORE THAN A WEEK AT A STRETCH. YOU'VE GOT TO COME BACK TO THE CAPITAL FOR A NEW VISA EACH TIME.

WE'VE GOT A PHYSICIAN WHO'S BEEN WAITING TWO MONTHS FOR AUTHORIZATION TO GO TO HIS MISSION.

THAT'S RIDICULOUS!

EVEN THE ICRC* IS GETTING HASSLED.

THEY'VE SHUT DOWN AN NGO UP NORTH FOR TWO MONTHS.

TIME TO DO SOME "CLEANSING"...

*INTERNATIONAL COMMITTEE OF THE RED CROSS

I HEAR MSF-FRANCE IS PLANNING TO IGNORE THE LATEST GOVERNMENT RULES.

SAME OLD SHIT-DISTURBERS EVERY TIME!

IS IT TRUE THAT NADÈGE AND ASIS LEFT WITHOUT THEIR TRAVEL PERMITS?

NO IDEA! NOBODY EVER TELLS ME ANYTHING!

I MEET A GERMAN WHO SPENT A LONG TIME IN NORTH KOREA. WE HIT IT OFF RIGHT AWAY.

LATER, I'D HAVE HIM READ PYONGYANG AND HE'D RECOGNIZE A FEW OF HIS BUDDIES.

WE END THE EVENING SWAPPING RUMORS. IN A COUNTRY WITHOUT JOURNALISTS, GOSSIP IS KING.

APPARENTLY THAN SHWE IS DEAD.

HA HA HA!

I HEAR THEY'RE GOING TO MOVE THE CAPITAL.

HA HA HA!

I'M BUSHED, SO I HEAD HOME. NGO NIGHTS EASILY GO ON TIL FOUR IN THE MORNING. I RARELY HOLD OUT THAT LONG.

TAKE CARE!

I'LL TRY!

173

EVEN THE DOGS ARE SLEEPING.

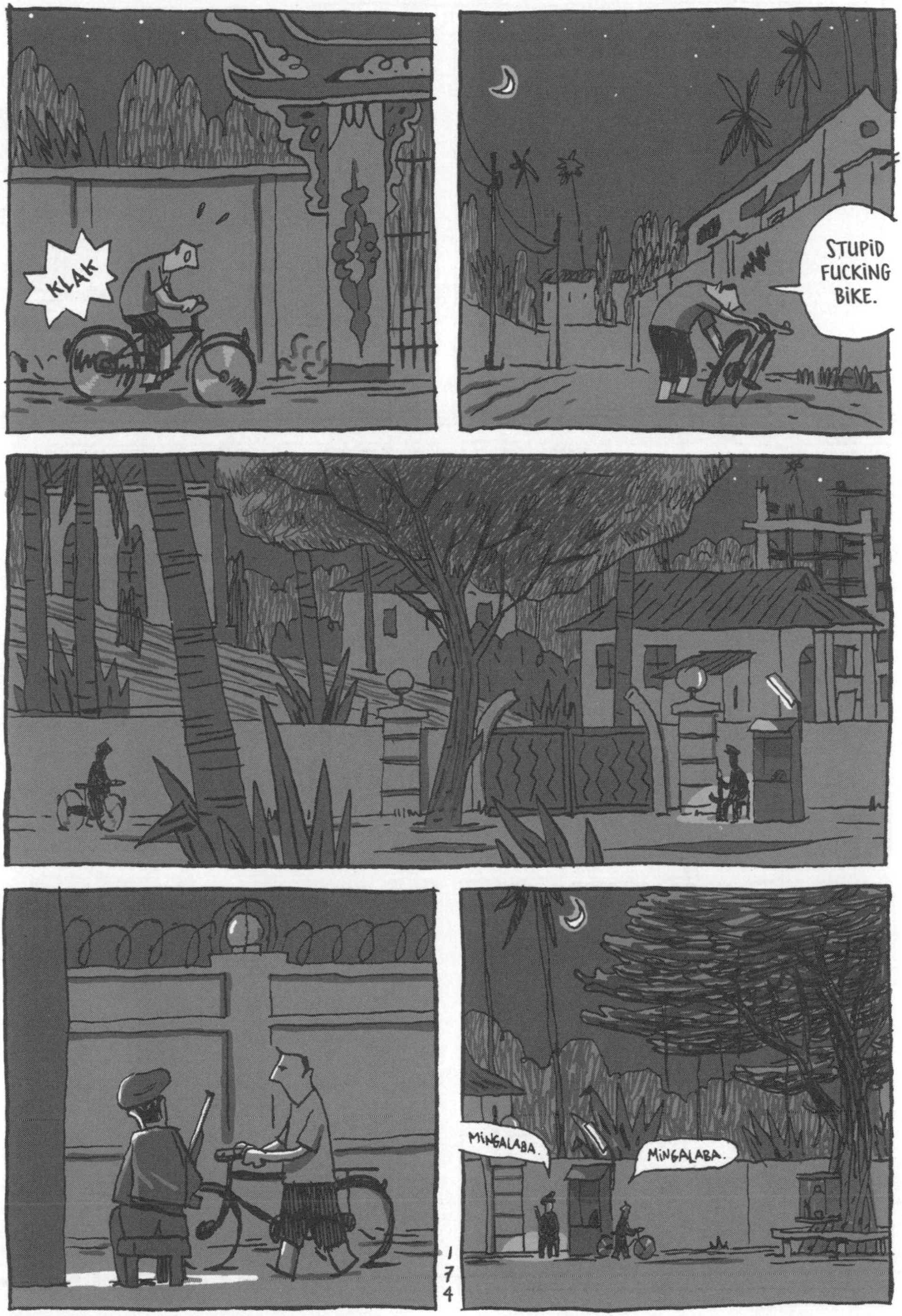
KLAK
STUPID FUCKING BIKE.
MINGALABA.
MINGALABA.

COMICS

i STOP BY A FEW BOOKSHOPS TO SEE WHAT'S GOING ON HERE iN THE WAY OF COMiCS.

THERE'S SOME STUFF FOR KiDS, BUT iT'S NOTHING GREAT.

SOMETIMES, THEY'LL REDRAW MiCKEY MOUSE OR CHARLIE BROWN.

↓

THERE ARE SOME GOOD iLLUSTRATORS iN THE WOMEN'S AND SPORTS MAGAZINES.

AND EVERY NOW AND THEN, YOU COME ACROSS A REAL GEM.

SUNDAY MORNING, I'M BACK WITH MY LITTLE GROUP OF ANIMATORS FOR A NEW SERIES OF EXERCISES.

I TAKE OUT A FRAME HERE...

AFTER CLASS, THEY INVITE ME TO JOIN THEM. THEY'RE VISITING AN ELDERLY ARTIST OUTSIDE THE CITY.

HMM... SURE, WHY NOT.

ON THE WAY, A STRANGE VEHICLE PASSES BY.

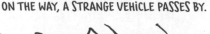

IT'S A FUNERAL.

BACK HOME, THEY TEND TO DRIVE SLOWER.

THEY MAKE LESS NOISE TOO.

HA HA! THEY'RE IN A HURRY TO CREMATE BECAUSE THEY'RE SCARED OF GHOSTS.

AND THEN THE FAMILY KEEPS THE ASHES?

NO, NO, NOT AT ALL.

REALLY? I THOUGHT THEY'D PUT THEM ON AN ALTAR AT HOME.

NO ASHES IN THE HOUSE, NO GHOSTS, HA HA!

OH. OK.

IT TURNS OUT HE USED TO WORK IN A CEMETERY AND A FRIEND RAN THE INCINERATOR.

HE'D FIRE IT UP AND THEN WHEN THE FAMILY LEFT, HE'D PUT IT OUT. HE'D STOCK UP CORPSES DURING THE DAY AND BURN THEM ALL AT NIGHT. MUCH CHEAPER THAT WAY.

NICE JOB!

THE OLD ARTIST USHERS US IN, HIS DAUGHTER GOES TO BUY DRINKS.

THE HOUSE HAS JUST ONE ROOM, WITH A PANEL TO SET OFF THE BEDROOM. IT'S UTTERLY DESTITUTE.

AFTER SOME LENGTHY CHITCHAT, HE BRINGS OUT THE ORIGINAL PAGES OF A COMIC PUBLISHED IN 1970.

YOU KNOW, HE WAS AN INSPIRATION FOR OUR ENTIRE GENERATION.

THE YOUNG GIRL COMES BACK WITH COCA COLA, WHICH I FEEL OBLIGED TO ACCEPT, EVEN THOUGH THE OTHERS TURN IT DOWN.

DAMN.

WITHOUT QUITE KNOWING WHY, I FEEL VERY MOVED TO BE HERE, AT THE OTHER ENDS OF THE EARTH, IN THE HOME OF THIS ELDERLY ARTIST, QUIETLY LEAFING THROUGH THE PAGES OF HIS COMIC BOOKS.

178

BETEL, APPLES AND COOKIES

THERE YOU GO! FABULOUS! THE INTERNET IS DOWN AGAIN AND I'M WAITING FOR PAGES FROM MY COLORIST.

WHAT A BUMMER!

I'LL GO TRY AT THE INTERNET CAFE.

PAIN IN THE ASS.

HEY, TAXI!

THE TAXIS HERE DON'T HAVE METERS. YOU NEED TO AGREE ON A PRICE BEFORE GETTING IN.

5,000
6,000
3,000
4,000
6,000

TAXI DRIVERS ARE BIG CONSUMERS OF BETEL.

OK.

THIS TIME, THOUGH, I THINK I'VE COME ACROSS THE KING OF QUID.

!

BECAUSE EVEN ON HIS LICENSE, HE'S POSING WITH BETEL IN HIS MOUTH.

OFFIC
N° 8 AT

WHAT A CHAMP.

179

SOME GUYS SPIT INTO PLASTIC BAGS AND THROW THEM OUT WHEN THEY'RE FULL. OTHERS DON'T BOTHER.

PTT

MMM... I'M HUNGRY.

IN FACT, CHEWING BETEL IS AN OLD AND NOBLE TRADITION.

"TO THE SOUND OF A DRUM ROLL, KING THIBAU APPEARED WITH A RETINUE OF HIGH DIGNITARIES. HE TOOK HIS SEAT, WHILE A PALACE LADY PLACED BEFORE HIM A GOLDEN BETEL BOX, A CUSPIDOR AND A BOWL OF WATER."

MAHE DE LA BOURDONNAIS
"A FRENCHMAN IN BURMA," 1880

CIAO AND THANKS.

AT THE INTERNET CAFÉ, YOU FIND ASIAN FOREIGNERS USING THE FREE VOIP AND THE LOCAL GILDED YOUTH SURFING THE NET OR PLAYING MULTIPLAYER WAR GAMES.

YOU ALSO FIND EMPLOYEES WHO KNOW THE NETWORK INSIDE OUT.

I CAN'T ACCESS MY MAILBOX. THE SITE IS BLOCKED.

LET'S HAVE A LOOK.

THE GREAT THING ABOUT THE INTERNET IS THAT THERE'S ALWAYS A WAY AROUND ANY OBSTACLE.

HEH HEH!

NICE COLORS. OK, APPROVED.

ALRIGHT, I'LL TAKE ADVANTAGE OF THIS GOOD CONNECTION TO SURF A BIT.

THE THING I GET A KICK OUT OF THESE DAYS IS BROWSING THROUGH THE SEARCHES OF PREVIOUS USERS.

YOU LEARN A LOT ABOUT THE HOPES AND FEARS OF A POPULATION BY PLAYING THIS LITTLE GAME.

GOOGLE

ANTI-VIRUS UPDATES
SEX BELGIUM
SEX AUSTRIA
SEX POLAND
SEX FRANCE
ENLARGE YOUR PENIS

WHOA! LOOKS LIKE SOMEBODY'S LONELY.

SINCE I'M HERE, I MIGHT AS WELL RUN SOME ERRANDS.
HEY, THIS IS THE EXACT SPOT WHERE THAT BOMB EXPLODED A WHILE BACK.
THEY'VE PUT GUARDS EVERY-WHERE SINCE THEN.
KAREN CARPENTER GOT TURFED, THANK GOD.
HERE, EXOTIC FRUIT IS THE OPPOSITE OF WHAT IT IS BACK HOME. THEY PRACTICALLY GIVE MANGOS AWAY, BUT A LOUSY APPLE CAN COST THREE TIMES THE PRICE OF A PINEAPPLE.
I'LL TAKE IT ANYWAY. I THINK I'VE OVERDOSED ON MANGOS AND PAPAYAS.
FOR A MONTH NOW, IT'S BEEN IMPOSSIBLE TO FIND UHT MILK.
HMPF... STILL NOTHING.
MILK TODAY, OATMEAL TOMORROW. THERE'S ALWAYS SOMETHING MISSING.
IN THE MEANTIME, YOU HAVE TO GO BACK EVERY TWO DAYS FOR FRESH MILK.
WHAT COULD PREVENT A COUNTRY FROM RECEIVING IMPORTED MILK? INTERNATIONAL ECONOMIC SANCTIONS?
WOW, A MONK IN THE COOKIE AISLE.

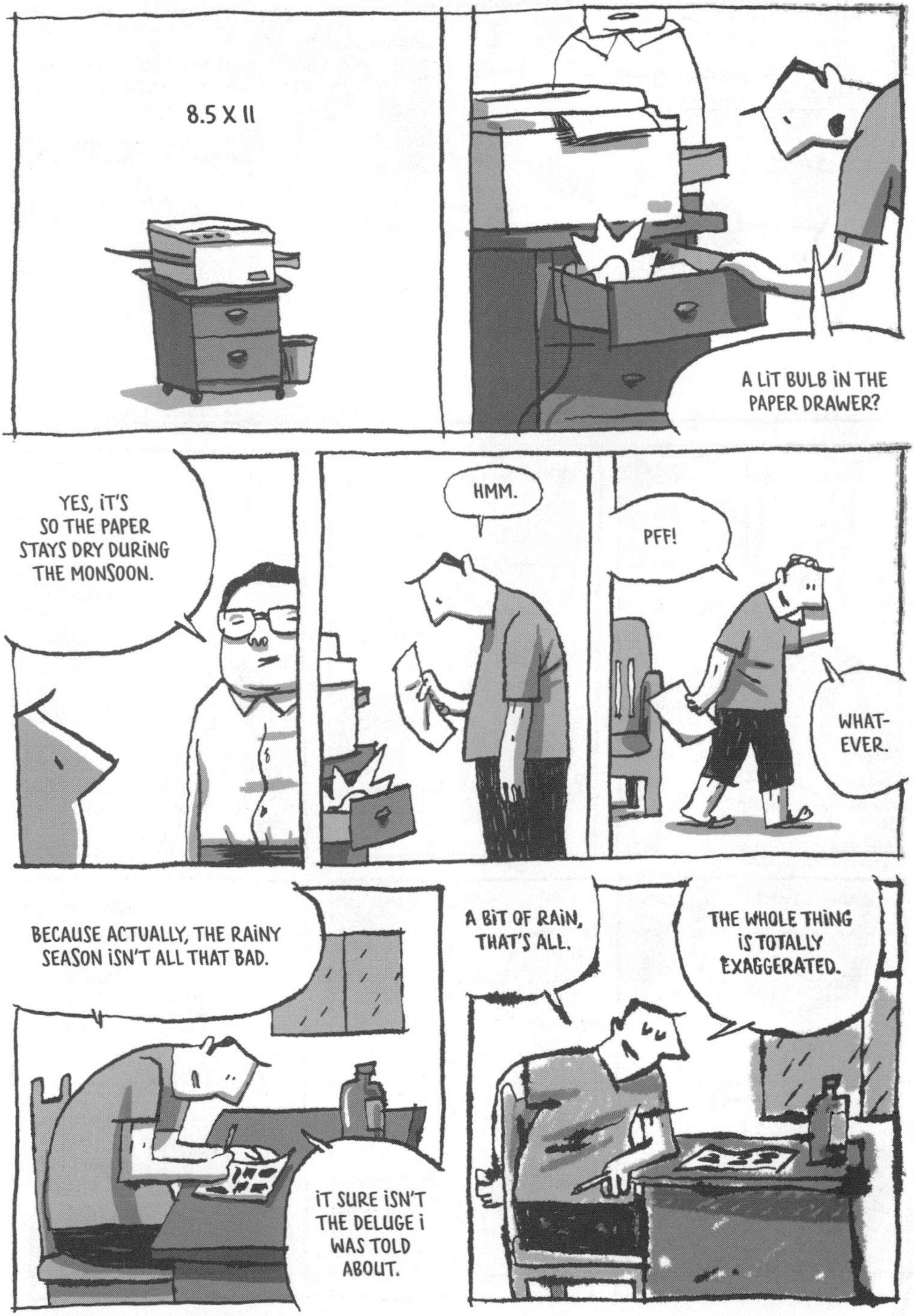
8.5 X 11
A LIT BULB IN THE PAPER DRAWER?
YES, IT'S SO THE PAPER STAYS DRY DURING THE MONSOON.
HMM.
PFF!
WHAT-EVER.
BECAUSE ACTUALLY, THE RAINY SEASON ISN'T ALL THAT BAD.
IT SURE ISN'T THE DELUGE I WAS TOLD ABOUT.
A BIT OF RAIN, THAT'S ALL.
THE WHOLE THING IS TOTALLY EXAGGERATED.

ADVENTURES
iN BURMA
III

AAAH!

NOTHING LIKE KICKING BACK AFTER A LONG DAY OF DOING NOTHING.

OH SHIT, i FORGOT MY TOWEL.

DAMN, WHAT DO i DO NOW?

i'M TOO FAR. IT'S NOT WORKING.

JEEZ, i JUST HOPE NOBODY COMES IN.

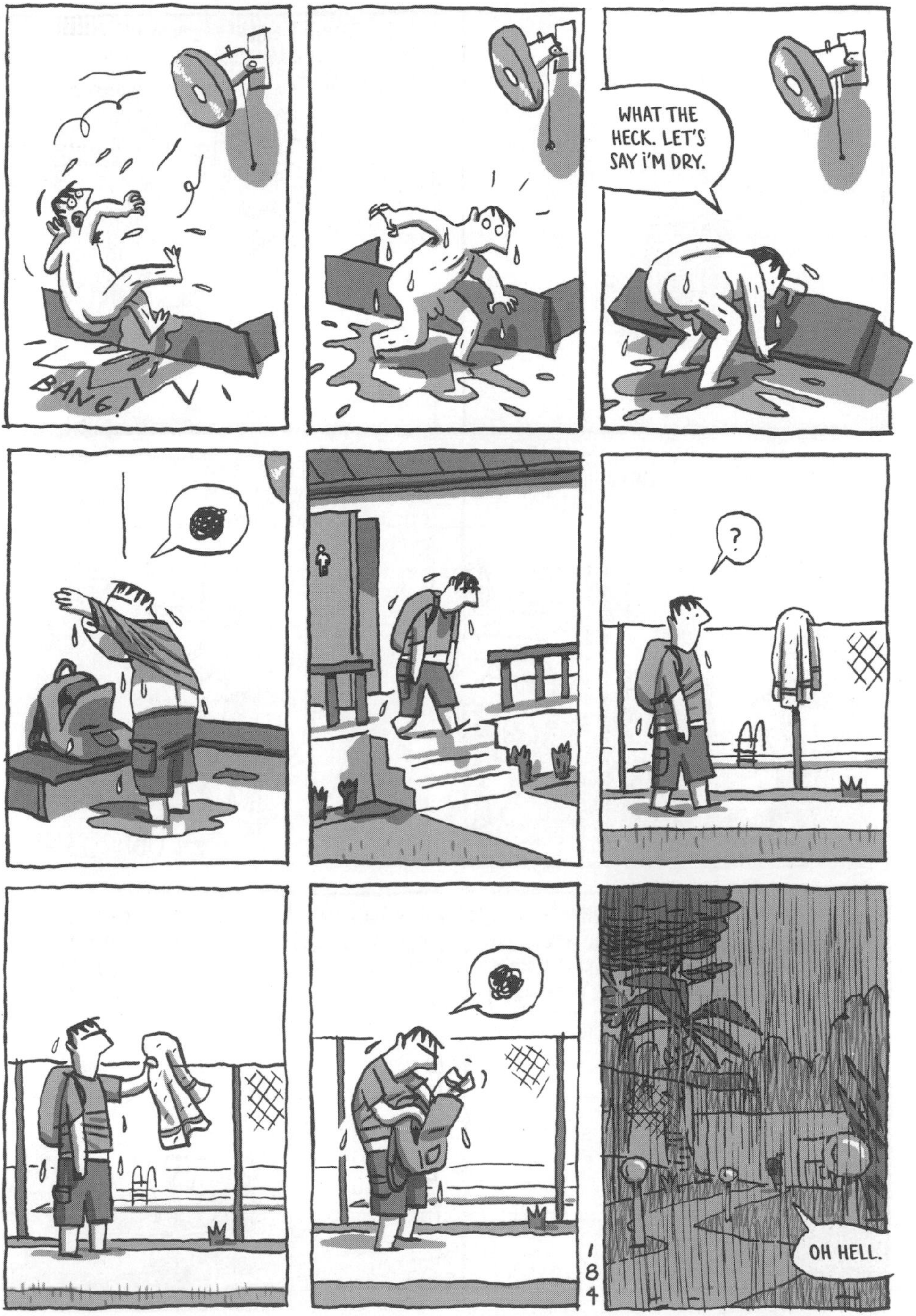
BANG!
WHAT THE HECK. LET'S SAY I'M DRY.
?
OH HELL.

POP TARTS AND
CHEEZ WHiZ

THiS MORNING, NADÈGE iS PLAYING iN THE FINALS OF THE AMERICAN CLUB'S MONSOON TOURNAMENT.

i'M HERE WiTH LOUiS TO CHEER ON HER TEAM, MADE UP MOSTLY OF MEMBERS OF THE VARiOUS FRENCH NGOS.

OH!

C'MON, GO FOR iT!

THE AMERICAN CLUB iS LOCATED ON THE NORTH SHORE OF THE LARGE iNYA LAKE. iT'S FAR BUT STiLL STRAIGHT ACROSS FROM AUNG SAN SUU KYi'S HOME.

THE
CLUB

THE LADY

AND EVERY YEAR, TO MARK HER BIRTHDAY, THEY RELEASE BALLOONS TO SEND HER A SiGN (THAT'S WHAT i HEAR, iN ANY CASE—i HAVEN'T SEEN iT). SHE WOULD NEED TO BE LOOKING THiS WAY AT THE RiGHT MOMENT, THOUGH.

YOO HOO!
AUNG SAN!

THE CLUB HAS EVERYTHING—A POOL, TENNIS COURTS, A WEIGHT ROOM...BUT iT'S ALL FAiRLY BARE AND EMPTY. YOU FIGURE THE PLACE HAS SEEN BETTER DAYS.

SINCE THE TIGHTENING OF ECONOMIC SANC-
TIONS IN 2003, AMERICAN FIRMS HAVE HAD
TO PULL OUT OF THE COUNTRY. ALL THAT'S
LEFT ARE A FEW GIs.

EVEN THE OIL COMPANIES HAVE CEASED
OPERATIONS. UNOCAL, FOR EXAMPLE, PLACED
ITS CONCESSION UNDER THE MANAGEMENT OF
THE FRENCH COMPANY TOTAL.

THERE'S STILL AN EMBASSY, BUT NO AMBASSADOR. THE US IS NOW REPRESENTED BY AN ATTACHÉ. THE
BUILDING, SITUATED DOWNTOWN, HAS TURNED INTO A BUNKER SINCE SEPTEMBER 11. THE STREET IS
BLOCKED TO TRAFFIC AND CAMERAS ARE PROHIBITED.

STRANGELY ENOUGH, THEY'VE BEGUN
BUILDING A NEW EMBASSY ON THE SOUTH
SIDE OF THE LAKE. AND NOT A LITTLE ONE
—WE'RE TALKING $50 MILLION.

IT'S ONE OF THE MYSTERIES OF AMERICAN
DIPLOMACY: WHY BUILD A GIGANTIC EMBASSY
IN A COUNTRY YOU DON'T RECOGNIZE AND
THAT YOU'VE PUT UNDER EMBARGO?

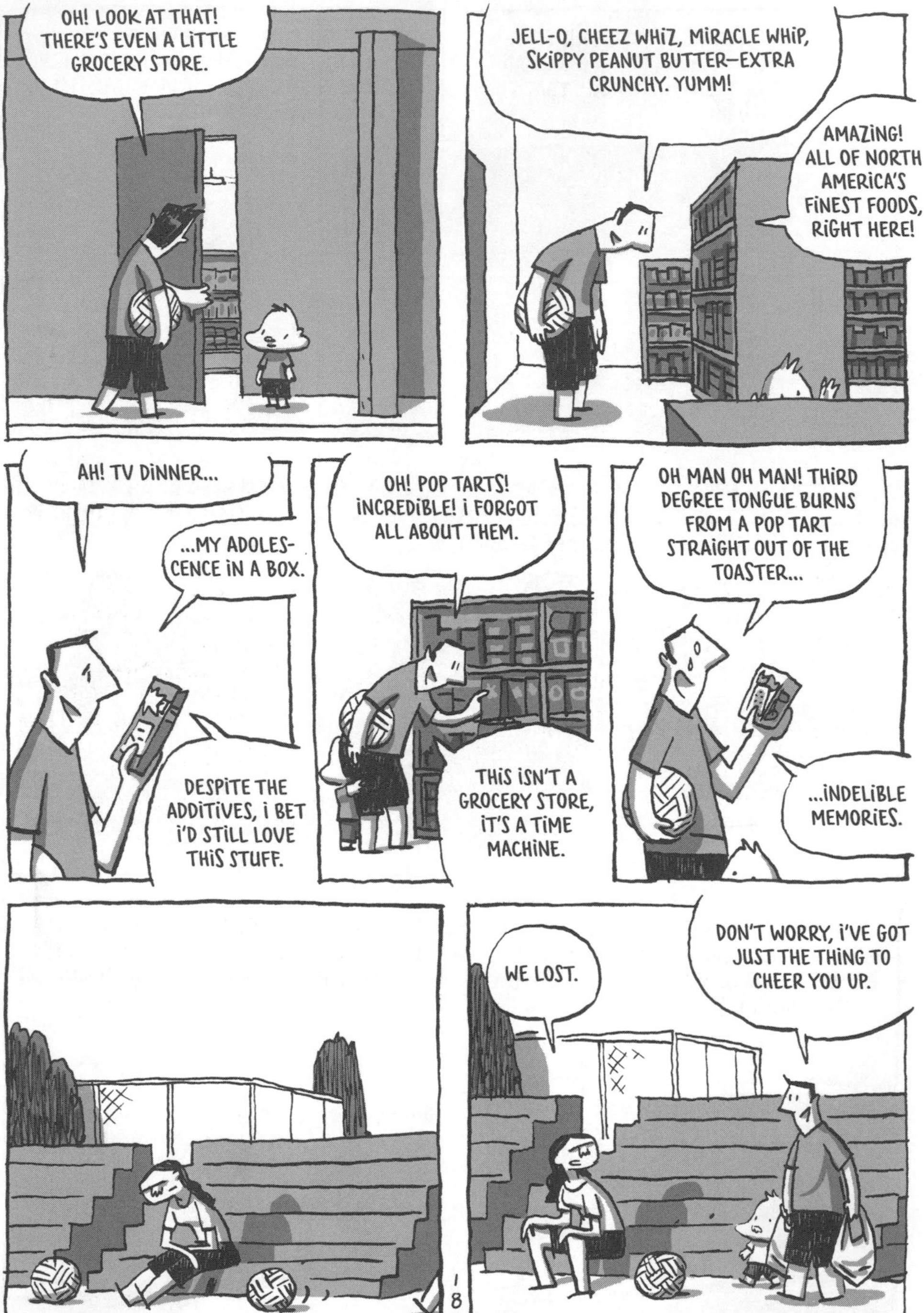

OH! LOOK AT THAT! THERE'S EVEN A LITTLE GROCERY STORE.
JELL-O, CHEEZ WHIZ, MIRACLE WHIP, SKIPPY PEANUT BUTTER—EXTRA CRUNCHY. YUMM!
AMAZING! ALL OF NORTH AMERICA'S FINEST FOODS, RIGHT HERE!
AH! TV DINNER...
...MY ADOLES-CENCE IN A BOX.
DESPITE THE ADDITIVES, I BET I'D STILL LOVE THIS STUFF.
OH! POP TARTS! INCREDIBLE! I FORGOT ALL ABOUT THEM.
THIS ISN'T A GROCERY STORE, IT'S A TIME MACHINE.
OH MAN OH MAN! THIRD DEGREE TONGUE BURNS FROM A POP TART STRAIGHT OUT OF THE TOASTER...
...INDELIBLE MEMORIES.
WE LOST.
DON'T WORRY, I'VE GOT JUST THE THING TO CHEER YOU UP.

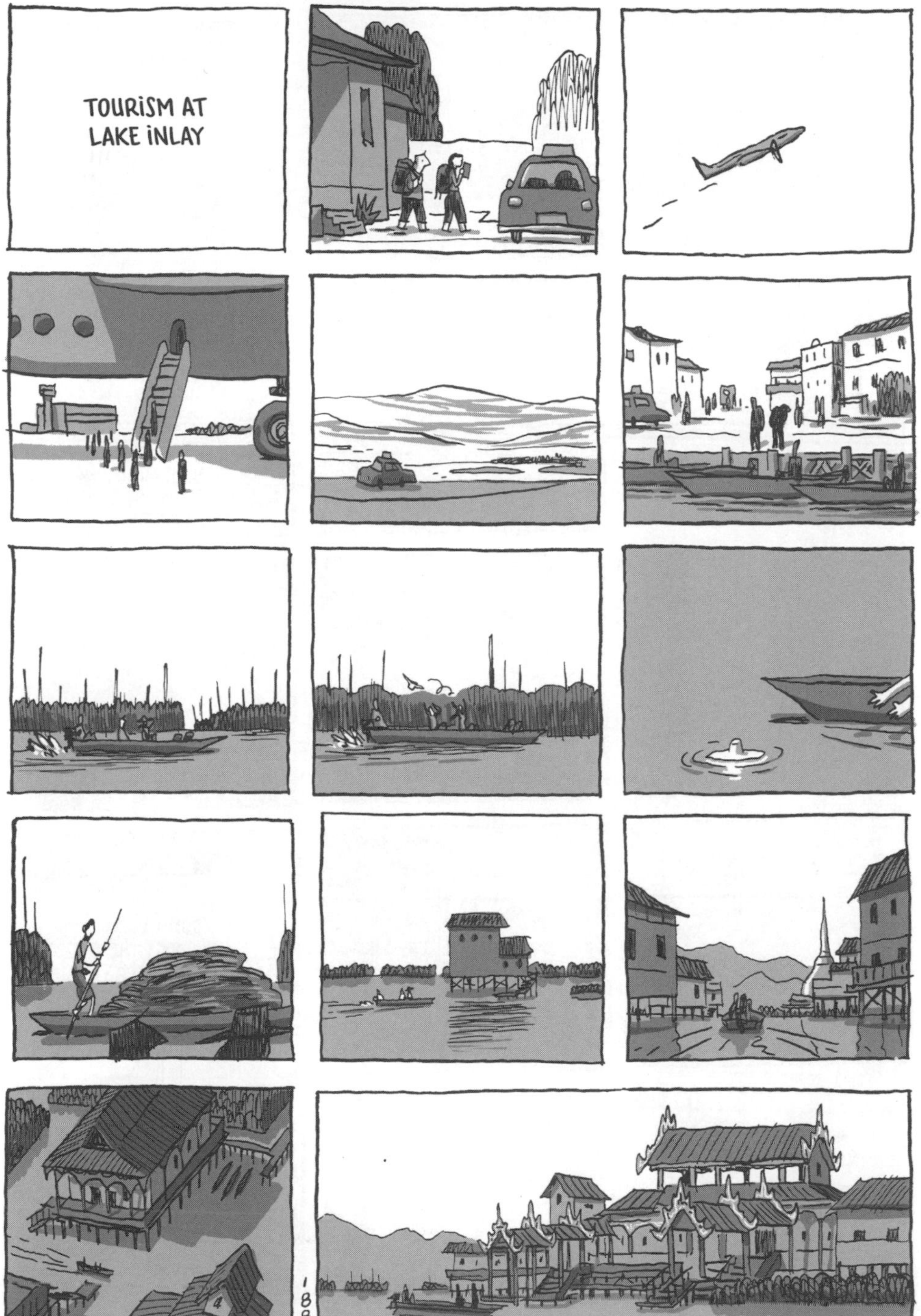
TOURISM AT
LAKE INLAY

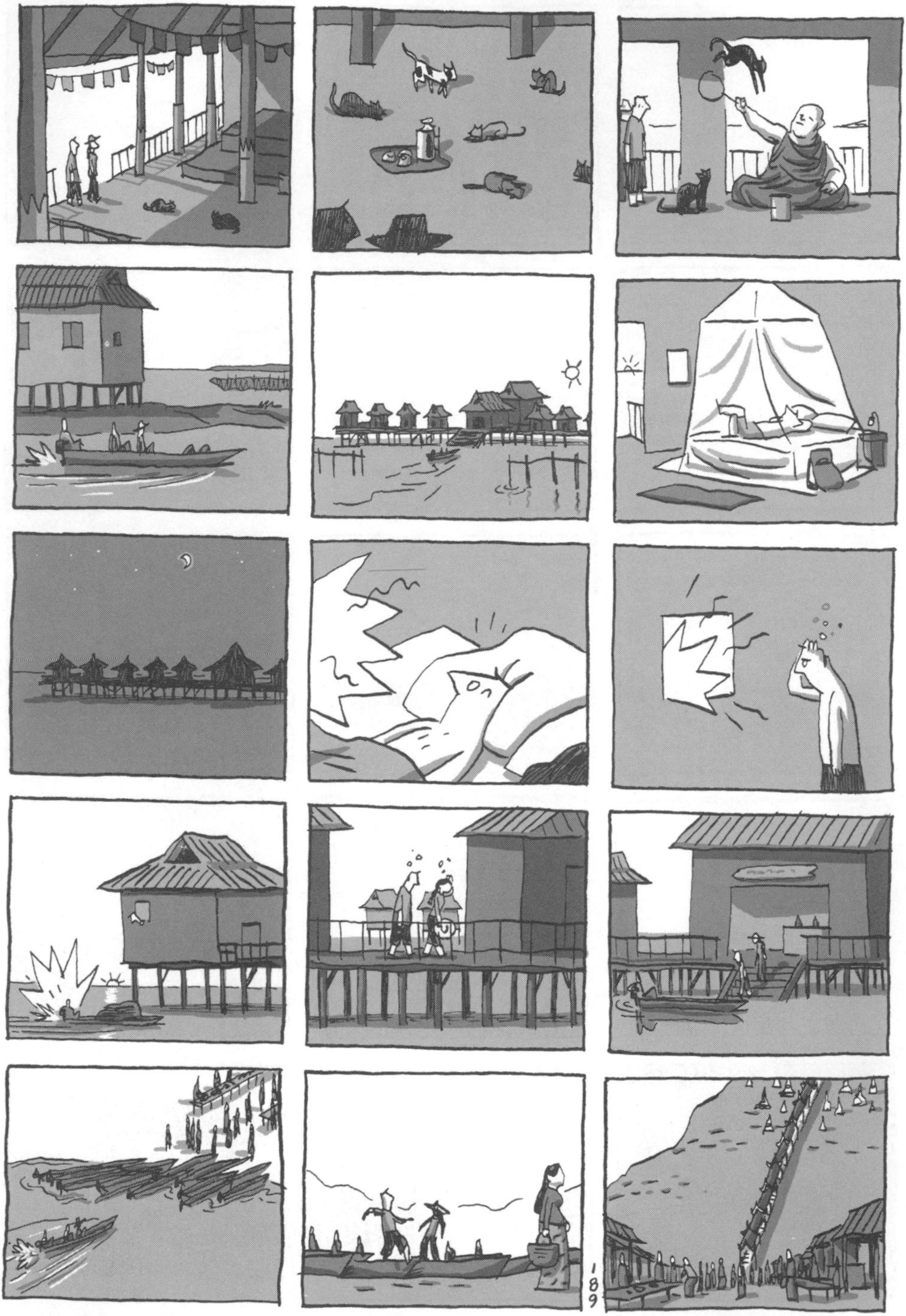

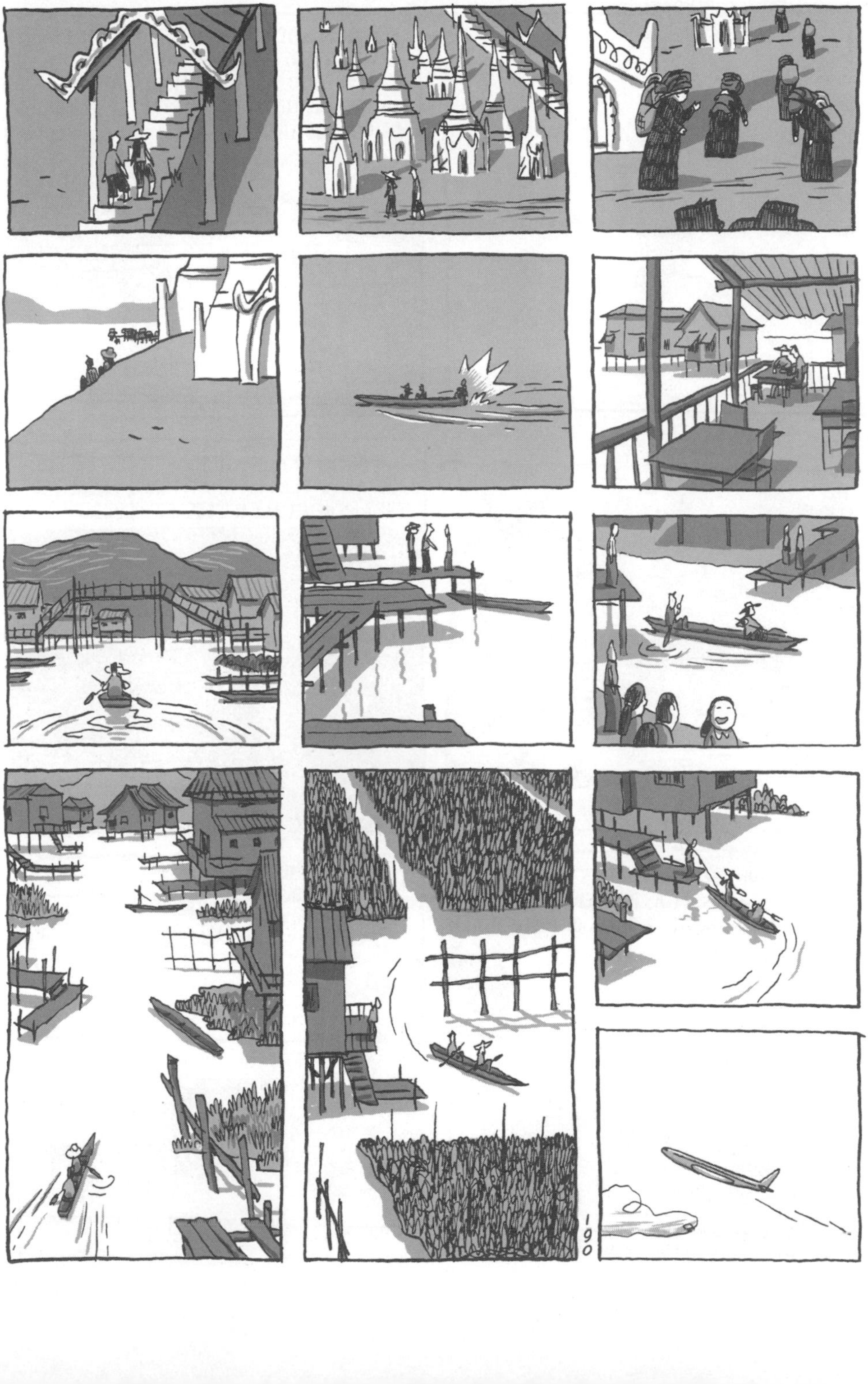

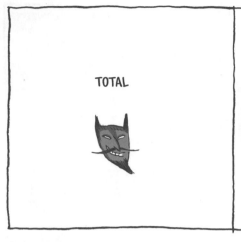

TOTAL

BEFORE I CAME TO BURMA, THINGS WERE SIMPLE. THERE WERE THE BAD GUYS ON ONE SIDE, WITH TOTAL GIVING MONEY TO THE JUNTA, AND NGOS LIKE MSF ON THE OTHER, CARING FOR THE SICK.

SO I WAS A BIT WARY AT FIRST.

HELLO.

NURSERY SCHOOL

TOTAL

HELLO.

BUT AFTER GETTING TO KNOW A FEW PEOPLE WHO WORK FOR MULTINATIONALS, I REALIZED THEY WEREN'T ALL NECESSARILY EVIL.

IN RANGOON, TOTAL SUBSIDIZES A FRENCH SCHOOL. ONE DAY, I WAS INVITED TO TEACH A COMICS WORKSHOP TO A CLASS OF HIGH SCHOOL STUDENTS.

THERE'S JUST 3 OF YOU?

YES, SIR.

JUNIOR HIGH'S GOT 7.

OF THE 3, 2 WERE FALLING ASLEEP.

TOTAL OIL EXTRACTS NATURAL GAS FROM OFF-SHORE FIELDS IN THE YADANA REGION, SELLING IT PRIMARILY TO THAILAND VIA A PIPELINE.

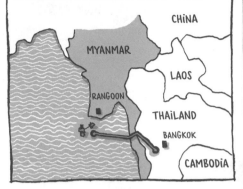

YOU CAN BET THAT ITS CONSTRUCTION INVOLVED THE DISPLACEMENT OF VILLAGES AND THE USE OF FORCED LABOR. THAT'S HOW THE ARMY WORKS, WHEREVER IT GOES. EVEN TODAY.

TO BLOCK OUT THAT EPISODE, TOTAL INVESTED IN A MAJOR SOCIAL PROGRAM.

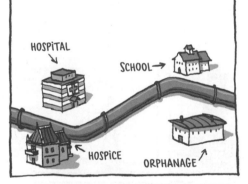

HOSPITAL

SCHOOL →

HOSPICE ←

ORPHANAGE ↗

WITH THE CURRENT OIL CRISIS, MANY COUNTRIES HAVE TURNED AN EAGER EYE TO BURMA'S ENERGY RESOURCES.

INDIA

CHINA

JAPAN

SOUTH KOREA

FOR EXAMPLE, WHEN ENGLAND'S PREMIER OIL PULLED OUT OF THE COUNTRY FOLLOWING PRESSURE AND SANCTIONS, MALAYSIA'S PETRONAS TOOK ITS PLACE.

DRILLING OPERATIONS DIDN'T STOP FOR A SINGLE MOMENT.

JOHN, A BRIT NOW WORKING FOR PETRONAS.
↓

THINGS ARE EASIER NOW WITH MALAYSIA. BEFORE, THERE WAS ALWAYS SOME PRESSURE GROUP STEPPING ON OUR TOES.

THEY KEPT ALL THE SAME EMPLOYEES?

PRETTY MUCH.

IT'S HARD TO IMAGINE HOW THINGS WOULD BE ANY BETTER IF, SAY, THE CHINESE TOOK OVER TOTAL'S ACTIVITIES.

WOULD THEY SPEND AS MUCH MONEY ON SOCIAL PROGRAMS? PROBABLY NOT.

YES, BUT TOTAL SHOULDN'T HAVE SET FOOT HERE IN THE FIRST PLACE.

SURE, BUT THEN SOME OTHER COMPANY WOULD HAVE COME.

HMM...

OBVIOUSLY, IN A PERFECT WORLD, ALL THE OIL COMPANIES WOULD AGREE TO BOYCOTT BURMA.

BUT THAT'S NOT THE CASE.

AND BESIDES, INTERNATIONAL PRESSURE HASN'T EVEN MANAGED TO ENFORCE WHALING MORATORIUMS.

193

WHAT DO WHALES HAVE TO DO WITH ANYTHING?

COLD SWEAT

VIA THE MSF MAILBAG, I GET A FEW COPIES OF THE NEWSPAPER IN WHICH JULES PUBLISHED HIS ARTICLE ON BURMA.

HEY, HE DREW ME.

RANGOON, NEAR THE HOUSE IN WHICH AUNG SAN SUU KYI IS BEING HELD: A CHECK POINT TURNS BACK CARS AND ACCESS IS STRICTLY FORBIDDEN. THE GAS STATION NEXT DOOR HAS CLOSED SHOP.

HERE, PEOPLE FEAST IN HONOR OF AUNG SAN SUU KYI ON HER BIRTHDAY...

SHE'S CALLED "THE LADY". NOBODY EVER SPEAKS HER NAME...LIKE THE BAD GUY IN HARRY POTTER.

ARTIST GUY DELISLE, WHO HAS BEEN LIVING IN BURMA FOR THE PAST 6 MONTHS...

A COUPLE OF DRAWINGS ILLUSTRATE THE ARTICLE. I GIVE MY ANIMATION STUDENTS A COPY AT OUR NEXT WEEKLY MEETING.

CLASS PROCEEDS AS USUAL.

HAVE YOU DONE YOUR EXERCISES?

UH...

OH, HEY, NOT BAD AT ALL.

THIS IS STARTING TO LOOK LIKE SOME-THING.

HELLO?

THE NEXT EVENING, I GET A CALL FROM ONE OF THEM. HE SOUNDS WORRIED AND WANTS TO COME SEE ME.

THERE'S A PROBLEM WITH THE NEWSPAPER YOU GAVE US.

YOUR FRIEND'S ARTICLE IS VERY CRITICAL OF BURMA, AND THERE'S A PICTURE OF YOU WITH YOUR NAME.

YOU'RE EASILY IDENTIFIABLE, WHICH COULD BE TROUBLE-SOME.

NORMALLY, IT WOULDN'T BE A BIG DEAL, BUT ONE OF US WORKS IN GOVERN-MENT, AND FOR HIM, JUST BEING ASSOCIATED WITH YOU IS DANGEROUS.

HE COULD LOSE HIS CAR, HIS APARTMENT... HE COULD EVEN FACE 10 YEARS IN JAIL.

HE CAN'T SLEEP ANYMORE.

BUT THAT'S AWFUL!

I...I...I'M SO SORRY!

THAT PAPER CAN'T FALL INTO THE WRONG HANDS. I HOPE YOU DIDN'T HAND OUT ANY OTHER COPIES?

NO, NO... THEY ALL STAYED RIGHT HERE. DON'T WORRY.

195

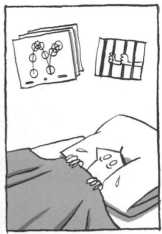

HELLO, REMEMBER THAT PAPER i GAVE YOU THE OTHER DAY? i NEED TO PiCK iT UP. i'LL EXPLAIN LATER.

CAN i COME OVER RiGHT NOW?

NEXT DAY, i PiCK UP THE 3 COPiES THAT WERE OUT AND ABOUT. EVEN THOUGH i KNOW THERE'D BE NO LEAKS, i'D RATHER REST EASY.

iN AN EXCESS OF ZEAL, i BURN EVERYTHiNG BEHiND THE HOUSE.

TO PREPARE FOR THE WORST, i DECIDE TO CONTACT THE MOST POLITICALLY iNFORMED PEOPLE i'VE MET HERE.

196

THE DIRECTOR OF AN NGO.

IF YOU ASK ME, YOUR FRIEND IS SCREWED. THERE ARE STAFF AT THE BURMESE EMBASSY IN FRANCE WHO READ AND REPORT ON EVERYTHING THAT GETS PUBLISHED.

AN ICRC REPRESENTATIVE WHO DOES REGULAR PRISON ROUNDS.

GIVE US HIS NAME AND WE'LL KEEP AN EYE OUT TO SEE WHICH PRISON THEY SEND HIM TO. OFTEN THE FAMILIES DON'T KNOW.

THAT'S REASSURING.

I EVEN MANAGE TO MEET AN AMBASSADOR (AND COMICS FAN).

SINCE THE PURGE LAST NOVEMBER, THE INTELLIGENCE SERVICES HAVE TAKEN A HIT.

IT'S HIGHLY UNLIKELY THAT ANYONE WOULD CARE ABOUT AN ARTICLE WITH SUCH A SMALL READERSHIP. PLUS I THINK THE BURMESE POSTED TO FRANCE DON'T SPEAK FRENCH. THE BENEFITS OF CORRUPTION, ONE MIGHT SAY.

THE NEXT WEEK, THERE'S ONE LESS STUDENT IN MY ANIMATION CLASS.

I TRY KEEP IT UPBEAT, BUT MY HEART ISN'T IN IT.

SO, HAVE YOU DONE YOUR EXERCISES?

FIRST AID

AND IF YOUR SON WAS BIT BY A SNAKE, WOULD YOU KNOW WHAT TO DO?

THERE ARE SOME HIGHLY VENOMOUS ONES AROUND.

AFTER HEARING THAT REMARK AT A BABY GROUP, I AGREE TO TAKE A FIRST AID COURSE AT THE OFFICES OF THE RED CROSS.

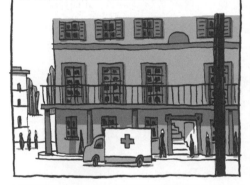

OUR INSTRUCTOR, A BURMESE ANGLOPHONE, USES A TEACHING METHOD WORTHY OF THE EARLY 1900S. HE READS TO US, SLOWLY, FROM THE MANUAL, WHILE WE FOLLOW ALONG ON PHOTOCOPIES.

IT'S A 4-DAY COURSE, BUT AFTER THE FIRST HALF HOUR I CAN'T TAKE IT ANYMORE. I TRY TO IMAGINE SOLUTIONS TO MAKE IT THROUGH TO LUNCH.

IT ALL TAKES ME BACK TO THE FEELING OF THOSE ENDLESS YEARS OF SCHOOL, SPENT WAITING IN A STATE OF NEAR LETHARGY FOR THE WHOLE ORDEAL TO END.

I DO LEARN A FEW THINGS, THOUGH, LIKE HOW TO PRESERVE A FRESHLY AMPUTATED PART FOR REIMPLANTATION.

AFTER LUNCH, I COME BACK ANYWAY FOR THE PRACTICAL EXERCISES.

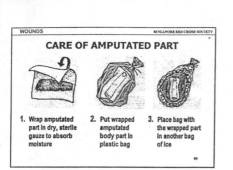

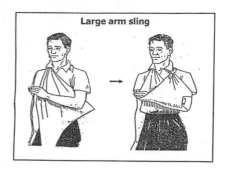

THE NEXT DAY, I GIVE IT ANOTHER TRY, BUT IT'S JUST TOO BORING. I SLIP AWAY AT NOON FOR A STROLL IN THE OLD TOWN AND HOPE THAT VENOMOUS SNAKES STAY AWAY FROM MY SON.

THE BIG MOVE

TO EVERYONE'S SURPRISE, THE REGIME HAS BEGUN MOVING THE CAPITAL THIS MORNING.

THE NEWS SPREADS QUICKLY AND IS GREETED WITH GENERAL AMAZEMENT AND DISBELIEF.

AW, I'LL BELIEVE IT WHEN I SEE IT.

BUT THE MOVING TRUCKS REALLY ARE OUT THERE IN FRONT OF THE GOVERNMENT BUILDINGS, AND THEY'RE EMPTYING THE OFFICES.

THE FIRST OFFICIALS TO GO WERE GIVEN 24 HOURS' NOTICE. THEY HAVE TO LEAVE THEIR FAMILIES BEHIND IN RANGOON, AND IF THEY REFUSE, THEY FACE JAIL TIME.

WITH ALL THE RUMORS AROUND, IT'S ODD THAT THE STRANGEST ONE IS COMING TRUE.

ACCORDING TO A HIGHLY UNOFFICIAL SOURCE, THE NEW CAPITAL WILL BE CENTRALLY LOCATED—A PURPOSE-BUILT CITY IN THE MIDDLE OF NOWHERE.

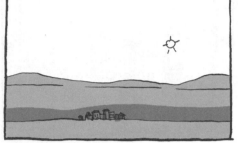

THE FIRST NEWS TO TRICKLE OUT ISN'T TOO GOOD. STAFF SLEEP IN THEIR OFFICES. THE HOUSES HAVE NO WATER AND NO POWER. THE HEAT IS STIFLING, THERE ARE SNAKES EVERYWHERE.

AN AMBASSADOR WHO ASKS A GOVERNMENT OFFICIAL ABOUT THE NAME OF THE NEW CAPITAL GETS THIS ANSWER.

DEFENSE SECRET.

IMAGINE THE DISMAY OF CERTAIN DELEGATIONS THAT HAVE JUST BUILT EMBASSIES IN WHAT THEY THOUGHT WAS THE CAPITAL.

NOT TO MENTION THOSE STILL UNDER CONSTRUCTION.

WE FOUND OUT LATER THAT IT WOULD BE CALLED PYINMAN. BUT THEN WE HEARD IT WOULD BE RENAMED NAY PYI DAW. CONFUSING, TO SAY THE LEAST.

PYIN MANA
NAY PYI DAW*

THE NGO COMMUNITY HAS ITS CONCERNS.

HOW IS THIS GOING TO WORK? DO I NEED TO GO MEET THE MINISTER OF HEALTH EVERY WEEK?

AND WILL WE HAVE TO GO THERE FOR OUR VISAS?

*"HOME OF KINGS"

MIND YOU, WITHOUT MAKING AN EFFORT, WE'LL HAVE LIVED IN BOTH THE CAPITAL AND THE METROPOLIS. THAT'S PRETTY COOL.

AMONG THE MANY HYPOTHESES TO EXPLAIN THE CHANGE, TWO SEEM ALMOST PLAUSIBLE.

THE MILITARY THEORY: RANGOON WOULD BE TOO VULNERABLE TO THE KIND OF ATTACK EXPERIENCED BY IRAQ.

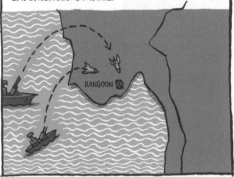

RANGOON

THE ESOTERIC THEORY: THAN SHWE'S ASTROLOGISTS APPARENTLY PREDICTED THE FALL OF RANGOON AS CAPITAL CITY. SO IT ONLY MADE SENSE TO GET AN EARLY START ON PACKING UP.

FOR THOSE WHO WANT TO BELIEVE IT, THE OFFICIAL VERSION:

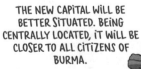

THE NEW CAPITAL WILL BE BETTER SITUATED. BEING CENTRALLY LOCATED, IT WILL BE CLOSER TO ALL CITIZENS OF BURMA.

AND THAT'S THAT, IN A COUNTRY RULED BY A JUNTA, NOBODY BOTHERS WITH EXPLANATIONS. IN ANY CASE, IT'S NOT LIKE ANYONE IS GOING TO ASK TOO MANY QUESTIONS OR WRITE WHAT THEY THINK.

NOBODY IS ANY LESS WORRIED WHEN WE LEAVE, LATE IN THE NIGHT.

HEY! CAREFUL ASIS! THERE MIGHT BE A SNAKE OVER THERE!

NO WORRIES.

IN BANGLADESH, THERE'S A SAYING THAT IF YOU GET KILLED BY A SNAKE, IT'S DESTINY...

I SEE.

BUT IF YOU GET KILLED BY A TIGER, IT'S JUST BAD LUCK.

HA HA HA!

HEY ASIS, AREN'T YOU WORRIED ABOUT THE CAPITAL MOVING?

NOT AT ALL, ACTUALLY. FOR THE SIMPLE REASON THAT WE'VE FINALLY DECIDED TO LEAVE THE COUNTRY. MSF-FRANCE IS PULLING OUT OF BURMA.

HA! THAT'S A GOOD ONE!

AND WILL I BE ABLE TO GO BACK IN THE FIELD BEFORE IT SHUTS DOWN?

RECESS

OK, I'M GOING. IT'S ALMOST TIME, I DON'T WANT TO MISS THIS OPPORTUNITY.

THE OFFICES OF THE AAH (ACTION AGAINST HUNGER) ARE NEXT TO LOUIS' SCHOOL.

ONE EVENING, AN AAH STAFFER TOLD ME:

YOU KNOW, WE CAN SEE THE KIDS AT RECESS FROM OUR BALCONY. I OFTEN TIME MY BREAK TO GO WATCH MY SON.

WANNA COME?

WHAT PARENT HASN'T DREAMED OF SEEING HOW THINGS REALLY ARE AT SCHOOL?

RIGHT ON TIME.

THERE HE IS! I SEE HIM!

WHAT THE HECK'S HE DOING?

HUH? ISN'T HE RUNNING WITH THE OTHERS?

THAT BIG KID KEEPS BUGGING HIM.

HEY, JERK! LAY OFF MY KID!

DAMN, ONE OF THEM SAW US.

HE'S TELLING YOUR SON TO LOOK THIS WAY.

LIE DOWN!

HEE HEE

CUT IT OUT! THEY'LL FIND US!

204

MINILE AND HER ANGELS

AT 80° F, MY NEIGHBOR WEARS A HAT.

MINGALABA!

OH, RIGHT, I FORGOT. I DON'T EXIST WITHOUT LOUIS.

YESTERDAY EVENING, ANOTHER BOMB WENT OFF DOWNTOWN. NO VICTIMS THIS TIME.

TAXI!

THERE WERE NO DEMANDS AND NO UPRISINGS EITHER. THINGS ARE ALWAYS VERY CALM HERE, THANKS TO A REGIME THAT CREATES PARALYSIS BY FOMENTING FEAR ON A DAILY BASIS.

EVEN LAST WEEK, WHEN AUNG SAN SUU KYI'S HOUSE ARREST WAS EXTENDED BY ANOTHER 6 MONTHS, THERE WASN'T THE SLIGHTEST SIGN OF DISCONTENT. IT SEEMS LIKE THE JUNTA STILL HAS A BRIGHT FUTURE TO LOOK FORWARD TO.

THIS MORNING, I HEAD OVER TO THE OFFICES OF MSF HOLLAND. THEY'VE CONVINCED ME TO WORK ON ILLUSTRATIONS FOR THEIR HEALTH EDUCATION PROGRAM.

HEY, AREN'T YOU THE "CARTOONIST"? HOW ABOUT DOING SOMETHING USEFUL FOR A CHANGE?

OH, SURE, WHEN YOU PUT IT THAT WAY...

THE IDEA IS TO PRODUCE A BOOK FOR YOUNG CHILDREN WITH HIV. WE NEED TO FIND A FUN WAY TO REMIND THEM TO TAKE THEIR MEDICATION TWICE A DAY.

A BOOK?

WOULDN'T IT BE BETTER TO WORK WITH LOCAL ILLUSTRATORS? I KNOW A FEW.

YES, WE OFTEN DO, BUT WE WANT TO TRY SOMETHING NEW.

OK, ALRIGHT.

I RECEIVE A TEXT WRITTEN BY A DOCTOR. I GET TO IT RIGHT AWAY.

LET'S SEE.

ALL CHILDREN ARE PROTECTED BY ANGELS THAT FIGHT AGAINST SICKNESSES.

BUT UNFORTUNATELY, THE EVIL ANGEL-SNATCHER (HIV) IS NEVER FAR AWAY.

POOR MINILE IS FEELING UNWELL.

THE DOCTOR ASKS TWO SUPERHEROES (ART*) TO HELP.

(ART*)

THEY CAPTURE THE EVIL THIEF AND FREE ALL THE LITTLE ANGELS.

THANKS TO HER ANGELS, MINILE IS BACK ON HER FEET IN NO TIME.

* ANTIRETROVIRALS

BUT IT'S IMPORTANT TO KEEP WATCH DAY AND NIGHT TO MAKE SURE THE ANGEL-SNATCHER DOESN'T GET AWAY.

AND IF MOM OR DAD FORGETS, YOU NEED TO REMIND THEM.

THAT'S WHY YOU NEED TO TAKE YOUR MEDICATION TWO TIMES A DAY.

BURMA IS ONE OF THE WORLD'S LARGEST OPIUM PRODUCERS. IN SOME PARTS OF THE COUNTRY, HEROIN CIRCULATES MORE OR LESS FREELY. LOTS OF JUNKIES, NOT MUCH HYGIENE. THE AIDS VIRUS IS SPREADING LIKE WILDFIRE. ADD TO THAT TRANSMISSION THROUGH PROSTITUTION.

THE MANY INFECTED PEOPLE ARE CARED FOR ONLY BY FOREIGN AID GROUPS. ANTI-RETROVIRALS ARE PURCHASED IN THAILAND, WHICH MANUFACTURES GENERICS. THE CUSTOMS FORMALITIES ARE SO COMPLEX THAT IT ISN'T UNUSUAL FOR DOCTORS TO DO ONE-DAY ROUND TRIPS TO BANGKOK TO RESTOCK ON MEDICATION.

DO I FEEL USEFUL WORKING ON THIS CHILDREN'S BOOK? NOT WHILE I'M AT IT, I DON'T. BUT JUST 3 WEEKS LATER, I'D HAVE THE OPPORTUNITY TO SEE THINGS DIFFERENTLY.

THERE! MY FIRST BOOK IN BURMESE.

A KIND OF "COLLECTOR'S" ITEM.

I SWEAR I'LL BE HUNG IF ANYBODY EVER SHOWS UP TO HAVE THIS ONE AUTOGRAPHED.

PFF!

THE BIG GATHERING

THERE'S NO ANIMATION CLASS AT MY PLACE TODAY. I'VE GOT ONLY 3 STUDENTS LEFT, AND THEY WANT US TO MEET AT ONE OF THEIR HOMES.

WHICH IS GREAT, BECAUSE IT LETS ME GET OUT OF THE HOUSE.

OOPS!

DAMN!

AFTER 30 MINUTES, THE POWER GOES OUT AND THE BATTERY DOESN'T HAVE ENOUGH JUICE TO RUN A COMPUTER.

THE CLASS IS CUT SHORT, BUT WE HAVE OTHER PLANS TODAY.

ARE YOU COMING?

I'D LOVE TO.

CAREFUL GOING DOWN THE STAIRS.

HIS DAUGHTER LIGHTS OUR WAY DOWN THE FIRST FLIGHT OF STAIRS, BUT AFTER THAT IT'S ALL PITCH BLACK.

THANKS.

HEY! I CAN'T SEE.

YOU NEED TO COUNT 8 STEPS FOR EACH FLOOR. I'M USED TO IT.

OK, FINE.

EXCEPT FOR THE LAST FLOOR. IT'S GOT 9 STEPS.

OH, THE ARCHITECT MADE A MISTAKE?

NO, IT'S A BURMESE TRADITION. ALL HOUSES NEED TO HAVE AN ODD NUMBER OF STEPS.

HUH!

...AND 9. IT'S TRUE.

FASCINATING COUNTRY.

THE CAR IS OVER THERE.

ONCE A YEAR, ALL OF BURMA'S CARTOONISTS GET TOGETHER TO HONOR ONE OF THEIR OWN. MY UNDERSTANDING IS THAT WE'RE GOING TO THE HOME OF THE ELDEST AMONG THEM, WHO IS QUITE ILL.

I CAN HARDLY BELIEVE MY EYES. ABOUT 150 CARTOONIST HAVE COME OUT FOR THE EVENT. I'M INTRODUCED TO PEOPLE, I SHAKE A LOT OF HANDS.

i MEET YOUNG ARTISTS, SOME OF WHOM i'D SEE AGAIN LATER FOR A LOOK AT THEIR WORK OR TO TALK ABOUT EUROPEAN COMICS.

i INVITED ONE OF THEM TO CONTRIBUTE TO MY BOOK. HE HAD SPENT HIS ADOLESCENCE IN BAGAN, THE MOST TOURISTIC TOWN IN BURMA.

ONE DAY IN MAY 1990, THE AUTHORITIES ORDERED VILLAGERS TO LEAVE THEIR HOMES AND MOVE TO "NEW BAGAN," A FEW MILES AWAY.

FIRST THEY CUT THE POWER, THEN THE WATER, AND IN THE END THEY BROUGHT IN THE BULLDOZERS.

i KNEW THE STORY AND WOULD HAVE LIKED A WITNESS OF THAT EXPROPRIATION TO TELL IT IN PICTURES.

HE SAID YES, BUT FOR SOME REASON, IT NEVER GOT DONE.

i ALSO MET A GUY WHOSE WORK WAS A BIT RISQUÉ.

TOO RISQUÉ, IN ANY CASE, TO BE PUBLISHED IN BURMA.

IN THE THICK OF THE GATHERING, THREE ARTISTS ARE SIGNING THEIR BOOKS.

CARICATURE PORTRAITS OF THEM DECORATE A BANNER STRUNG ACROSS THE BACK OF THE ROOM.

THERE ARE YOUNG ARTISTS DOING SKETCHES. THE ATMOSPHERE IS FAMILIAR, I FEEL ALMOST AT HOME HERE.

I'M TAKEN TO MEET THE PERSON FOR WHOM THIS CELEBRATION HAS BEEN ORGANIZED. HE IS LYING ON A BED, A WHEELCHAIR BY HIS SIDE.

NICE TO MEET YOU.

HE SPEAKS EXCELLENT ENGLISH AND APOLOGIZES FOR THE MISERABLE STATE OF THE COUNTRY.

THE WHOLE SCENE LEAVES ME WITH A DISTINCT FEELING OF DÉJÀ-VU.

HMM...

DURING THE CEREMONY, HE IS PLACED BETWEEN TWO OTHER VERY ELDERLY CARTOONISTS.

A SPEECH IS MADE IN HIS HONOR AS PEOPLE COME FORWARD WITH ENVELOPES OF MONEY.

AT ONE POINT, SOMETHING RATHER STRANGE HAPPENS. ONE OF THE OLD CARTOONISTS GETS UP AND BOWS DOWN BEFORE THE GUEST OF HONOR.

I MEET MY ANIMATOR FRIENDS ON THE WAY OUT. THEY WANT TO TALK TO ME, THEY LOOK SERIOUS. DAMN...DID I SCREW UP SOMEHOW?

THEY NEED TO STAY AND HELP, BUT THEY INSIST ON PAYING FOR MY TAXI HOME.

WHAT TO DO? MY INITIAL RESPONSE WOULD BE TO OBJECT, BUT GIVEN THE RESPECT THEY SHOW THEIR ELDERS AND TEACHERS, I DON'T WANT TO OFFEND THEM EITHER.

2/2

EVEN THOUGH I KNOW THAT A TAXI IS A HUGE EXPENSE FOR THEM.

WELL, UH...

SUNDAY EVENING

THE WEEKEND IS WINDING DOWN, YOU CAN SMELL IT. WHAT I MEAN IS, THE DISHES HAVE BEEN STACKING UP FOR TWO DAYS AND GIVEN THE HEAT, THERE'S A WEIRD SCENT SLOWLY MAKING ITS WAY TO THE LIVING ROOM.

IN THE BEGINNING, I'D PLAY MR. NICE GUY AND CLEAN THE KITCHEN ON SUNDAY EVENINGS SO THE NANNY WOULDN'T HAVE TO DO IT ON MONDAY. ALL TO HAVE A CLEAR CONSCIENCE, OF COURSE.

SINCE THEN, I'VE PUT THINGS INTO PERSPECTIVE. HOW MANY TIMES HAVE I SEEN EXPATS ASK ONE NANNY TO MAKE THEIR BRUNCH WHILE ANOTHER TAKES CARE OF THE KID?

"I KNOW, BUT WE PAY THEM EXTRA FOR COMING ON SUNDAYS."

PFF!

YEAH RIGHT, AS THOUGH THEY'RE IN ANY POSITION TO REFUSE.

LIKE, "NO, THANKS, BUT MY COLLECTIVE AGREEMENT ENTITLES ME TO AT LEAST ONE DAY OFF A WEEK SO I CAN SEE MY OWN KIDS AS WELL."

WEEKENDS ARE ALSO THE ONLY TIME I CAN WALK AROUND HALF NAKED. I SAY HALF, BECAUSE MAUNG AYE ALWAYS HANGS AROUND AND COMES TAPPING ON THE WINDOW TO ASK US QUESTIONS.

SOME PEOPLE DON'T MIND THAT KIND OF THING. BUT IT REALLY GETS ON MY NERVES AFTER A WHILE. I KNOW I SHOULD PLAY BOSS AND TELL HIM NOT TO DO THIS AND THAT, BUT IT'S JUST NOT IN ME, AND BESIDES, I FIGURE WE'LL BE LEAVING SOON ANYWAY.

YESS!

KNOCK KNOCK

WELL, WELL, SPEAK OF THE DEVIL!

MAUNG AYE IS ALL DRESSED UP TONIGHT. HE'S TRADED IN HIS TRADEMARK FADED MSF T-SHIRT FOR A WHITE SHIRT. AND, INCREDIBLE BUT TRUE, HE'S MANAGED TO GET THE THICK BLACK COATING OFF HIS TEETH.

I WONDER HOW MANY TOOTHBRUSHES THAT TOOK.

HE SHOWS ME A PHOTO OF HIMSELF WITH A GIRL. MY UNDERSTANDING IS THAT HE'S GOING TO MARRY HER. OR MAYBE HE ALREADY HAS. EITHER WAY, HE'S PLANNING TO MEET HER IN ANOTHER TOWN.

HE'S LIKE A DIFFERENT PERSON. HE LOOKS THINNER LIKE THIS.

LET'S SEE.

WHERE WAS I?

NADÈGE SHOWS UP LATER AND TELLS ME SHE'S HAD AN OFFER TO STAY ON, AND THAT IF I LIKE, WE COULD EXTEND BY 6 MONTHS.

UH...NOT REALLY.

A YEAR'S PLENTY, DON'T YOU THINK?

214

LATER THAT EVENING, I COME ACROSS A WELL-MADE SWISS DOCUMENTARY ABOUT THE SITUATION OF THE KAREN REBELS.

OH, HEY!

THEY USED TO GET HELP FROM THAILAND, BUT WITH THE THAI-BURMESE AGREEMENT TO BUILD A HYDROELECTRIC DAM, THEY'VE LOST THEIR ALLIES.

IT'S STRANGE HOW DISTANT IT ALL SEEMS ON TV, WHEN IN FACT IT'S RIGHT NEXT DOOR.

THE CHILDREN ARE THIN, THE ELDERLY SICK, SOLDIERS BURN DOWN THEIR VILLAGES ONE BY ONE, AND THEY HARDLY HAVE MUNITIONS FOR THEIR WEAPONS. IT'S A TRULY PITIFUL SITUATION.

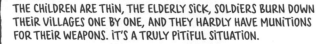

PFF!... TO THINK THAT MSF HAS BEEN TRYING TO GET TO THOSE REGIONS FOR YEARS.

AND NOW IT'S ALL OVER, WE'LL NEVER GO HELP THEM.

215

BANGKOK

GUEST HOUSE

BUY

-SANDALS FOR
 LOUIS

-CD BURNER FOR
 ASIS

2
1
6

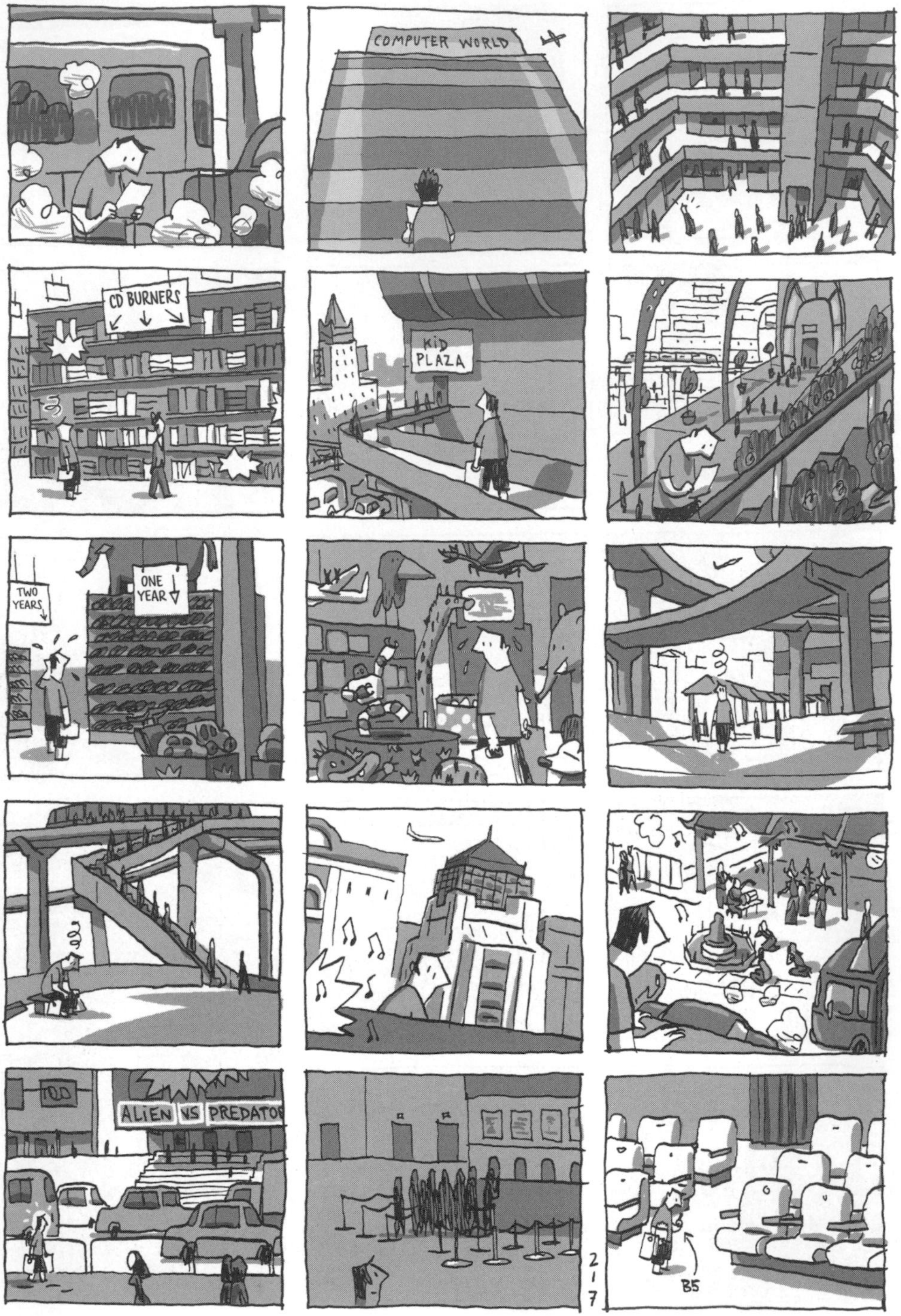
COMPUTER WORLD
CD BURNERS
KID PLAZA
TWO YEARS
ONE YEAR
ALIEN VS PREDATOR
B5

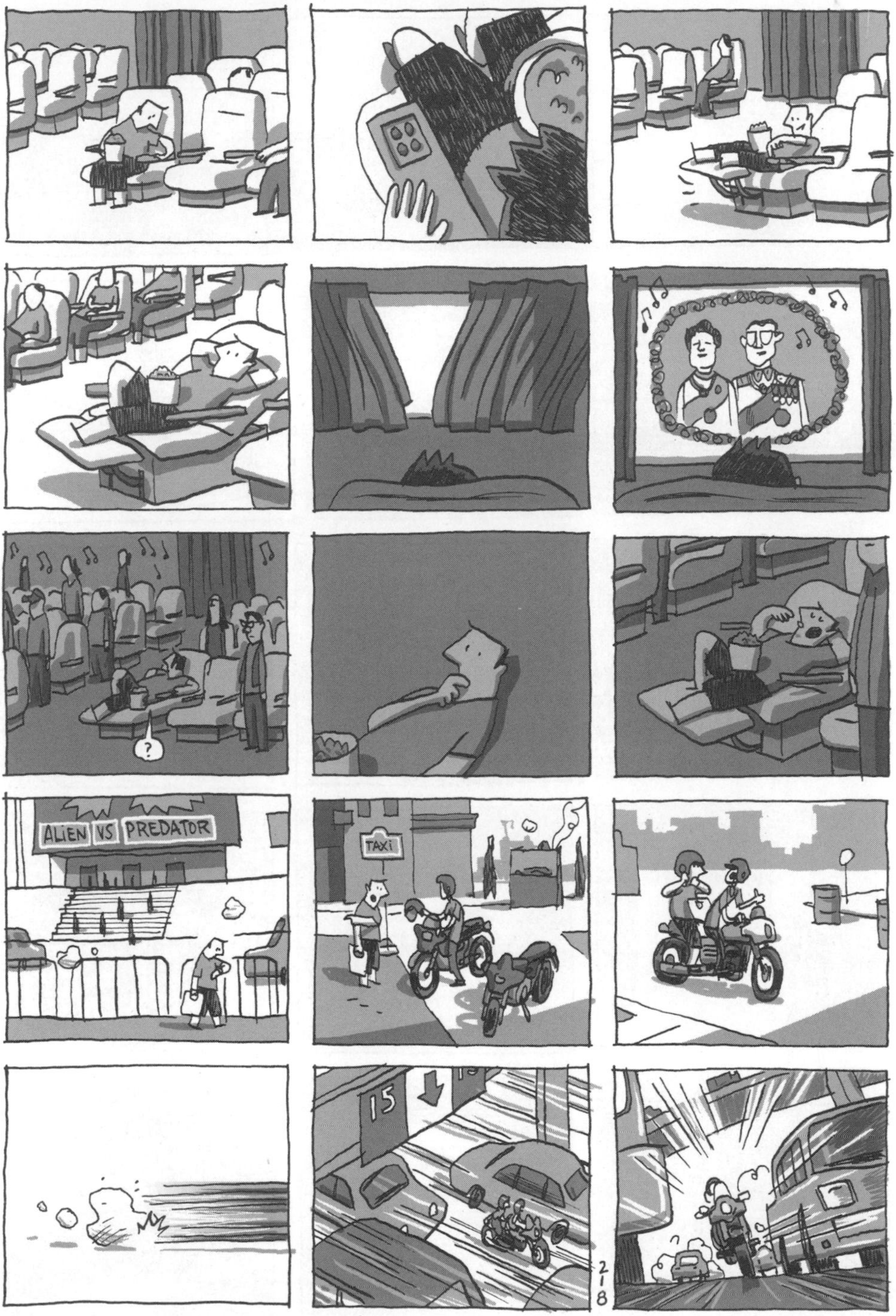
?
ALIEN VS PREDATOR
TAXI
15

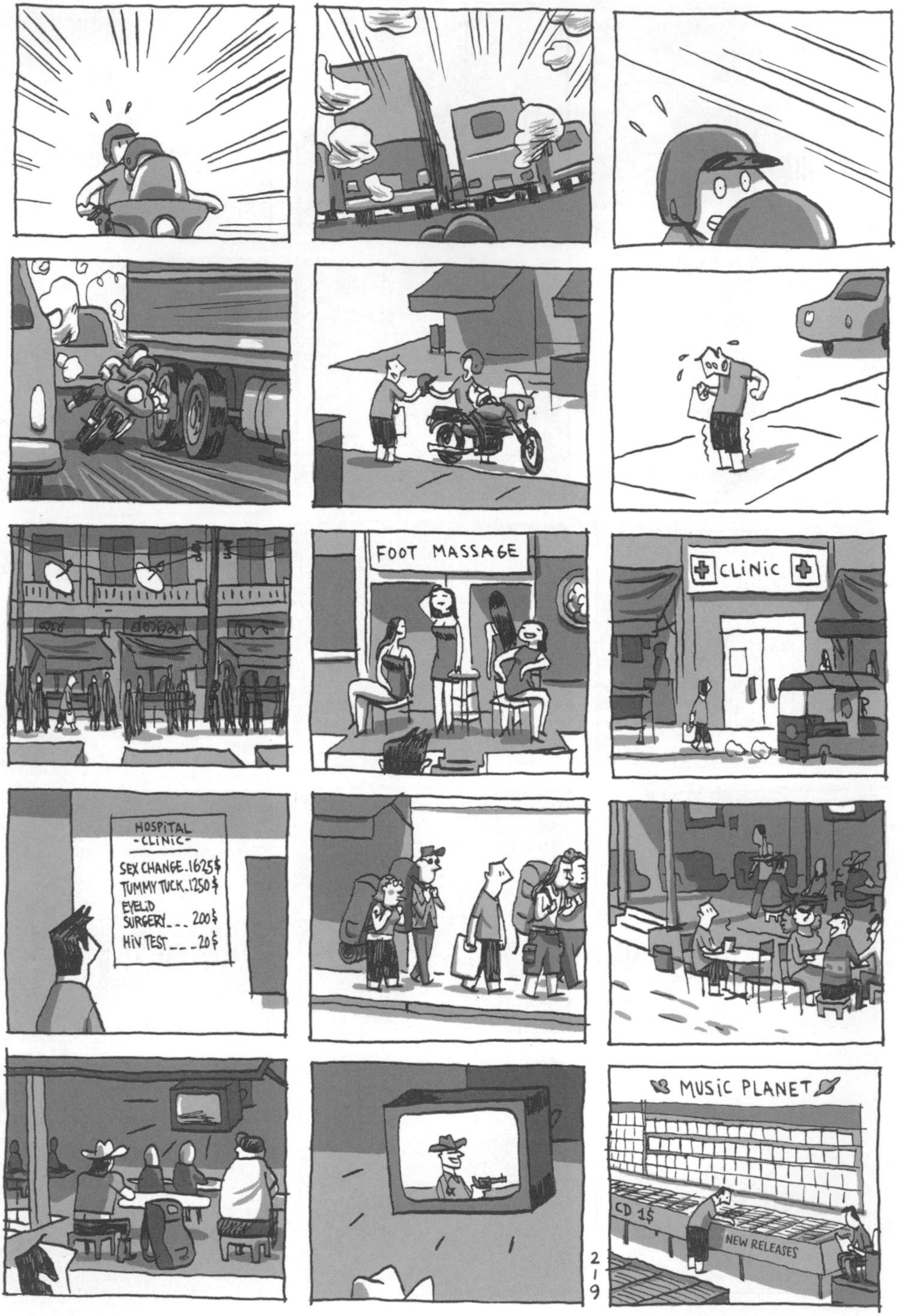
FOOT MASSAGE
CLINIC
HOSPITAL
-CLINIC-
SEX CHANGE. 1625$
TUMMY TUCK. 1250$
EYELID SURGERY___ 200$
HIV TEST___ 20$
MUSIC PLANET
CD 1$
NEW RELEASES

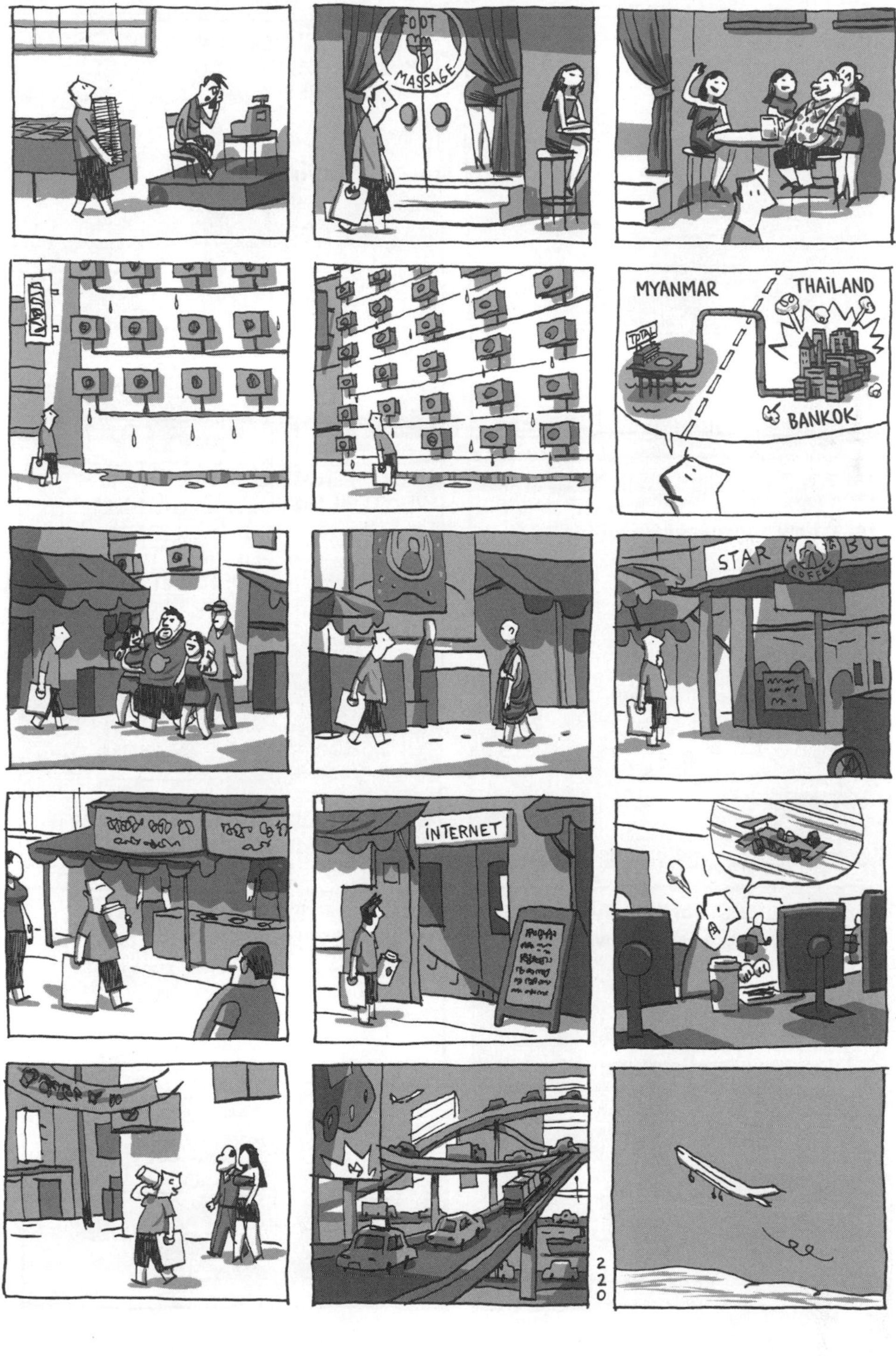
FOOT
MASSAGE
MYANMAR
THAILAND
TOTAL
BANKOK
STAR
BU
COFFEE
INTERNET

DRIVING

SINCE THE ANNOUNCEMENT OF THE MISSION'S CLOSURE, THE MOOD AT MSF HAS BEEN PRETTY LOW.

THE FEW EXPATS WHO WERE IN THE FIELD ARE LONG GONE AND WON'T BE REPLACED. AND THE LOCALS ARE LOOKING AT LOSING THEIR LIVELIHOODS.

GIVEN THE SITUATION, NADÈGE IS DOING EVERYTHING SHE CAN TO FIND NEW JOBS FOR THE STAFF.

YES, HELLO, I'M CALLING ABOUT THE SECURITY GUARD POSITION YOU HAVE ADVERTISED...

WHICH SHE MANAGES TO DO BY KEEPING AT IT TILL THE DAY BEFORE WE LEAVE.

THE GENERAL LAXITY OF THE SITUATION HAS ITS UPSIDE FOR ME: I GET TO DRIVE THE CAR.

AFTER A YEAR IN THE PASSENGER SEAT, I GET BEHIND THE WHEEL, WHICH IN THIS CASE IS ON THE RIGHT SIDE, AS FOR MOST CARS HERE.

IN WHAT'S SURELY A UNIQUE SITUATION IN THE WORLD OF ROAD TRAFFIC, THE BURMESE DRIVE ON THE RIGHT, IN RIGHT-HAND DRIVE CARS—THAT'S TWICE TO THE RIGHT. FOR TWO REASONS.

TO BREAK WITH THE BRITISH COLONIAL PAST, NE WIN IMPOSED RIGHT-HAND DRIVING FROM ONE DAY TO THE NEXT.

IN 1961, THERE WASN'T MUCH TRAFFIC, AND I'VE BEEN TOLD THE SWITCH WAS NO PROBLEM.

BUT FOR EMBARGO REASONS, THE ONLY CARS YOU COULD FIND IN THE COUNTRY WERE JAPANESE MODELS WITH THE STEERING ON THE RIGHT SIDE.

RESULT: PASSING CARS IS A REAL CHALLENGE.

i GET A BETTER SENSE OF WHY THE BUSES ALL HAVE BLOCKED DOORS ON THE LEFT SiDE.

AND WHY THERE'S ALWAYS A COPiLOT TO GUiDE THE DRIVER WHEN HE WANTS TO PASS A CAR.

THEN THERE ARE THE PEDESTRiANS WHO CROSS ANYWHERE. AND iF YOU'RE UNLUCKY ENOUGH TO HiT AND KiLL ONE, YOU'RE LOOKING AT PRiSON WiTHOUT TRiAL.

iT HAPPENED ONCE, AND iT TOOK ALL LEVELS OF DiPLOMACY TO GET THAT EXPATRiATE OUT.

BUT iF iT'S A MONK YOU HiT, YOU'RE HEADED STRAIGHT FOR THE SLAMMER AND THERE'S NOTHING ANYONE CAN DO ABOUT iT.

iT'S A BiT STRESSFUL.

* NATIONAL LEAGUE FOR DEMOCRACY

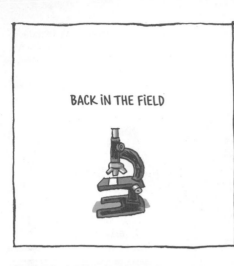

BACK IN THE FIELD

I'M GOING OUT INTO THE FIELD FOR A SECOND AND LAST TIME BEFORE THE MISSION SHUTS DOWN.

THIS TIME, I'VE BROUGHT A HAT.

ASIS

BUT I STILL DON'T HAVE A PERMIT TO TRAVEL IN THE ZONES WHERE THE MSF CLINICS ARE LOCATED, SO WE ARRANGE WITH ASIS THAT I'LL SLEEP IN MOULMEIN, THE TOURIST TOWN, AND THEN JOIN THEM ON THEIR VISITS DURING THE DAY.

THE NIGHT IS PRETTY GOOD, I'M LESS COLD THAN LAST TIME.

KUNG FU FILM →

TOWEL

BUT EARLY THE NEXT DAY...

OUR BUS STALLS A FEW MILES FROM OUR DESTINATION. WE START BY WAITING FOR REPAIRS, BUT END UP, LIKE ALL THE OTHER PASSENGERS, STOPPING LOCAL BUSES TO FINISH OUR JOURNEY.

ASIS AND NADÈGE, WITH THEIR DARKER COMPLEXIONS, BLEND INTO THE CROWD. PEOPLE TALK TO THEM IN BURMESE. THEY PRETEND TO UNDERSTAND AND COLLECT THEIR CHANGE.

OF COURSE, I LOOK LIKE A STRANDED TOURIST AND A KIND TRANSLATOR OFFERS HIS HELP.

HE EXPLAINS... YOU WANT TAKE WITH VILLAGE?

UH... YES, OKAY. THANKS.

OH!

LET'S SEE: NO...OPIUM, SHOOTING UP OR SMOKING ...IS THAT A CIGARETTE?

WE GET TO OUR DESTINATION A FEW HOURS LATE. AN MSF CAR COMES TO TAKE US TO MUDON. I'LL NEED TO MAKE THE TRIP BACK TONIGHT TO SLEEP AT THE HOTEL.

THINGS ARE MUCH QUIETER NOW IN THE BIG HOUSE IN MUDON. THE EXPATS HAVE LEFT AND ACTIVITIES HAVE WOUND DOWN. FOR ALL THE STAFF HERE, IT'S THE END OF AN ERA.

ASIS STAYS TO DO INVENTORY WHILE I LEAVE WITH NADÈGE TO VISIT THE FAMOUS CLINICS.

WE DRIVE PAST MILES OF RICE PADDIES.

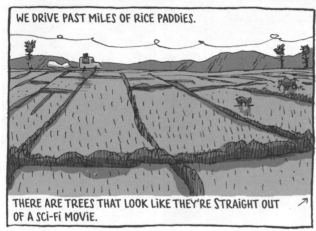

THERE ARE TREES THAT LOOK LIKE THEY'RE STRAIGHT OUT OF A SCI-FI MOVIE. ↗

NEXT, WE PASS BY A SERIES OF RUBBER PLANTATIONS.

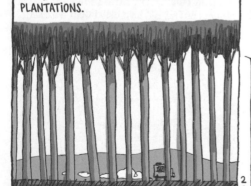

SEE, THE PLANTATION WORKERS OFTEN GET SICK BECAUSE THEY HARVEST THE SAP AT NIGHTFALL, AND THAT'S WHEN MALARIA-CARRYING MOSQUITOES ARE ACTIVE.

IS THIS IT?

THIS IS WHAT A CLINIC LOOKS LIKE. WE'VE BEEN GIVEN A ROOM IN THIS TREATMENT CENTER.

MSF HAS TRAINED A MICROSCOPIST FOR EACH CLINIC.

MINGALABA

MINGALABA

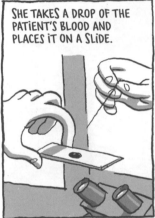

SHE TAKES A DROP OF THE PATIENT'S BLOOD AND PLACES IT ON A SLIDE.

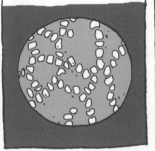

THROUGH HER MICROSCOPE, SHE CAN DETERMINE THE PRESENCE OF MALARIA AND ITS TYPE.

SHE THEN PRESCRIBES A TREATMENT ACCORDING TO ESTABLISHED PROTOCOLS AND DISPENSES MEDICATION TO THE PATIENT.

SOME STRAINS OF MALARIA RESULT IN RAPID DEATH, OTHERS CAUSE FEVER THAT RECURS IN CYCLES. BUT ALL FORMS OF THE ILLNESS ARE TREATABLE.

AND THE MEDICATION IS FREE?

YES, EVERYTHING'S FREE. PATIENTS SOMETIMES COME FROM VERY FAR AWAY, AND SO THEY LEAVE WITH THEIR ENTIRE TREATMENT.

THE SECOND CLINIC IS LOCATED IN A ZONE THAT'S OFF-LIMITS TO TOURISTS.

IT'S IN THESE ZONES THAT THE JUNTA COMMITS THE WORST ATROCITIES, WITH NO WITNESSES TO INTERVENE.

AND IT'S WHAT GOES ON IN THESE ZONES THAT HAS GIVEN MYANMAR THE REPUTATION OF BEING ONE OF THE WORST DICTATORSHIPS ON THE PLANET.

WE'RE GOING TO TRY TO GET IN TODAY. THE GUARDS GENERALLY DON'T MAKE A FUSS WHEN THEY SEE THE MSF CAR.

BESIDES, THERE'S NOT MUCH TO LOSE, WITH THE MISSION SHUTTING DOWN IN A MONTH.

HEH HEH! I MADE IT. I'M IN A FORBIDDEN ZONE.

ADVENTURE, HERE I COME.

IT'S TIME FOR THE REAL DEAL!

I'M WITH YOU NOW, JOSEPH KESSEL!

WE STOP TO VISIT A SECOND CLINIC.

HEY, THERE'S RICKETY GRANDMOTHERS IN THE FORBIDDEN ZONES. DAMN, I WAS EXPECTING MORE OF A WILD WEST FEEL.

THE LAB TECHNICIAN'S ROOM HAS AN EXAMINING CHAIR THAT MUST DATE BACK TO THE JAPANESE OCCUPATION.

WE'VE GOT OTHER CLINICS TO VISIT, BUT THAT'S IT FOR TODAY. WE TURN AROUND AND HEAD BACK TO THE AUTHORIZED ZONE.

HMPF. WHAT A LET DOWN.

BUT FIRST WE MAKE A STOP IN A VILLAGE. THE FATHER OF A TECHNICIAN DIED LAST NIGHT AND WE'RE GOING TO OFFER OUR CONDOLENCES TO THE FAMILY.

WE'RE INVITED INSIDE AND OFFERED A MEAL. NO WORDS ARE SPOKEN.

OH, I GET IT...SO THAT'S HOW THEY FOLD THE DRIED LEAVES TO MAKE THEIR ROOFS WATERTIGHT.

PEOPLE DON'T LIVE LONG IN BURMA. THE LIFE EXPECTANCY IS AROUND 60 YEARS.

WE GO, LEAVING A FINANCIAL CONTRIBUTION IN A SMALL ENVELOPE FOR THE FAMILY OF THE DECEASED.

I GET A LIFT BACK TO MY HOTEL. I'M GLAD THAT I FINALLY GOT TO SEE THE REASONS FOR MSF-FRANCE'S PRESENCE HERE. AND INDIRECTLY, FOR MINE AS WELL.

I SPEND THE NEXT DAY IN MOULMEIN, BEFORE TAKING THE BUS BACK HOME.

THE NIGHT IS HELL. THE GUY BEHIND ME KEEPS COUGHING AND SPITTING INTO A PLASTIC BAG. I PRAY HE DOESN'T HAVE TB.

AS IF THAT'S NOT ENOUGH, SOMEBODY HAD THE GREAT IDEA OF PACKING A DURIAN FOR THE TRIP. THE HUGE FRUIT IS SO FOUL-SMELLING THAT IT'S NOT ALLOWED ON AIRPLANES. IT SHOULD BE BANNED ON BUSES AS WELL.

WHERE'D I PUT THAT HAT?

CONVERSATION

i DON'T UNDERSTAND WHY MSF HAS DECIDED TO LEAVE THE COUNTRY.

YOU TREAT 1,000 PEOPLE A MONTH AT YOUR CLINICS, WHICH IS SOMETHING. YOU'RE FAR FROM USELESS. SO WHY GO?

iT'S NOT JUST A QUESTION OF BEING USEFUL. WE COULD OPEN CLINICS ANYWHERE IN THE COUNTRY AND THEY'D WORK JUST AS WELL.

BUT THAT'S NOT WHAT OUR MISSION'S ABOUT.

FOR 2 YEARS NOW, THE GOVERNMENT HAS BEEN FORCING US TO WORK OUT BY MUDON.

BUT MUDON ISN'T IN A CONFLICT ZONE, AND IT HAS NO MINORITIES THAT ARE THE VICTIMS OF ANY SPECIFIC DISCRIMINATION.

BASICALLY, iT'S A ZONE THAT SHOULD BE TAKEN OVER BY THE STATE HEALTH CARE SYSTEM. NOT BY MSF. AND WE'RE NOT NECESSARILY HELPING THEM DEVELOP BY PROVIDING FREE CARE AND MEDICATION.

MSF'S MANDATE IS TO HELP THE MOST DISADVANTAGED. IN OUR CASE, WE'VE TARGETED A POPULATION, THE KARENS, WHO LIVE IN THE MOUNTAINS NEAR THE THAI BORDER.

THE GOVERNMENT HAS HAD US TURNING IN CIRCLES FOR 2 YEARS. IT'S KEEPING US FROM GETTING WHERE WE WANT TO BE.

SO, IN THE END, THERE'S NO HUMANITARIAN SPACE FOR OUR MISSION.

AT SOME POINT, IF WE AGREE TO STAY, WE END UP ABETTING THE GOVERNMENT'S ACTIONS, AND IN THE PROCESS, WE BECOME AN INSTRUMENT OF DISCRIMINATION.

THE OPPOSITE OF WHAT WE WANT TO BE.

GIVEN THE OPTIONS, WE'D RATHER GO.

233

SO WHY DO THE OTHER NGOS STAY?

SOME NGOS DON'T HAVE THE PROBLEMS WE'VE RUN INTO. THERE'S ROOM FOR THEM HERE.

AND THERE'S ALL KINDS OF NGOS. SOME ARE SO SMALL, THEY ONLY WORK IN BURMA. SO HOW CAN THEY LEAVE?

OTHERS RUN HUMANITARIAN AID LIKE A CORPORATION, WITH OBJECTIVES TO BE MET AS EFFECTIVELY AS POSSIBLE.

AND OTHERS ARE SIMPLY COMPLACENT, BECAUSE LIVING HERE IS EASY.

OR BECAUSE BURMA LOOKS GOOD ON A WEBSITE WHEN YOU'RE OUT FUNDRAISING.

SOME ARE FUNDED BY GOVERNMENTS AND HAVE LIMITED ROOM TO MANEUVER.

AND THEN THERE ARE THOSE THAT DON'T ASK QUESTIONS, EVEN THOUGH OUR ACTIONS, LIKE IT OR NOT, HAVE SIGNIFICANT IMPACTS ON THE POPULATIONS WE'RE TRYING TO HELP.

234

AND WHICH ARE THE COMPLACENT ONES?

MYITKIYINA
(PRONOUNCED MEE-TCHEE-NA)

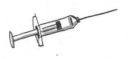

FOR OUR LAST OUTING, WE'VE DECIDED AGAINST THE TOURIST CIRCUIT IN FAVOR OF AN INVITATION FROM TWO BELGIAN FRIENDS WORKING IN THE NORTH OF THE COUNTRY FOR MSF-HOLLAND.

THE ONLY WAY TO GET THERE IS VIA THE NOTORIOUS STATE-RUN "MYANMAR AIRWAYS."

AW, NO WORRIES, GUYS. THEY HAVEN'T HAD A CRASH IN AT LEAST A YEAR.

ONE YEAR!

GREAT, WELL, IF IT'S BEEN A YEAR, THAT'S REALLY REASSURING.

AND JUST TO CHEER US UP, EVERYONE WHO'S BEEN HAS A STORY TO TELL.

...SUDDENLY, AN ALARM SOUNDED AND THE STEWARDESS RUSHED TO THE COCKPIT...

THE DAY OF OUR DEPARTURE, MY HANDS ARE A BIT SWEATY.

THERE'S SO MUCH CONDENSATION IN THE CABIN THAT WATER'S DRIPPING DOWN ON ME.

BEFORE TAKEOFF, I NOTICE COCKROACHES ROAMING THE WALLS.

DURING THE FLIGHT, WE'RE OFFERED DRINKS IN DIRTY GLASSES.

NO...

PINCH ME.

THERE'S JUST A LITTLE CURTAIN BETWEEN US AND THE PILOTS. ONE IS SMOKING, AND AT SOME POINT, WE HEAR A RADIO PLAYING MUSIC.

♪♫♪

A PHOTO OF BUDDHA IS TAPED ON THE FRONT WINDOW OF THE PLANE.

ONE HOUR LATER.

DING!

BLOODY HELL, WHY DIDN'T WE GO TO THE BEACH LIKE EVERYBODY ELSE?

WE DON'T KNOW MUCH ABOUT KACHIN STATE, BESIDES THE THREE OR FOUR WORDS OUR NANNY HAS TAUGHT LOUIS...

...AND THAT THEY'RE CHRISTIAN.

2/3/6

CATHERINE AND THIBAULT HAVE WORKED HERE FOR A YEAR. THEIR MISSIONS ARE ENDING SOON, SO ONE OF THEIR REPLACEMENTS IS WITH THEM.

WE HAVE A LOOK AROUND THE MYIKYINA CLINIC, WHICH TREATS HIV AND AIDS PATIENTS.

I'M RATHER SURPRISED TO SEE ALL THESE CROSSES IN AN MSF CLINIC.

THIBAULT TELLS ME THAT HE PUT A SIGN IN FRONT OF A CROSS UNTIL THE OWNER THREATENED TO CANCEL HIS LEASE IF HE DIDN'T TAKE IT DOWN.

AZG

ON THE GROUND FLOOR, A SMALL MEETING HAS BEEN ORGANIZED TO INTRODUCE THE NEW STAFFER TO THE LOCAL TEAM.

KACHIN GIRLS ARE LESS TIMID THAN THEIR SOUTHERN COLLEAGUES. THEY ASK THE NEW GUY LOTS OF QUESTIONS.

ARE YOU MARRIED?

237

HOW TALL ARE YOU?

WHAT SIZE SHOES DO YOU WEAR?

DO YOU HAVE A GIRLFRIEND?

NEXT UP ARE NADÈGE ("MANAGER") AND ME ("ILLUSTRATOR").

THIS IS GUY WHO ILLUSTRATED THE CHILDREN'S BOOK ON HIV.

OOOOH!

AAAAAH!

IT'S VERY NICE.

THANK YOU.

WE USE IT EVERY DAY.

LITTLE MOMENT OF PRIDE

THERE'S A LOT OF PREVENTION WORK TO DO HERE. WE'RE NOT FAR FROM THE GOLDEN TRIANGLE AND THERE ARE MANY ADDICTS IN THE REGION.
CONDOMS AND SYRINGES ARE DISTRIBUTED FREE OF CHARGE.

70,000 EVERY MONTH!

SEVERAL OTHER CLINICS HAVE OPENED IN NEARBY VILLAGES. INCLUDING ONE IN HPAKANT, WHERE FOREIGN (MOSTLY CHINESE) COMPANIES OPERATE THE JADE MINES.

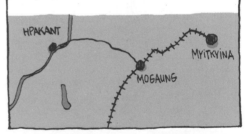

HPAKANT

MOGAUNG

MYITKYINA

APPARENTLY, WHEN A MINE SHAFT CAVES IN, EMPLOYERS DON'T EVEN TRY TO RESCUE THE VICTIMS. THEY JUST DIG ELSEWHERE.

MANY SORDID TALES ARE TOLD ABOUT THIS 21ST CENTURY FRONTIER TOWN. I'D LOVE TO VISIT, BUT THERE'S NO WAY I CAN. IN RECENT MONTHS, EVEN THE MSF PHYSICIAN HASN'T BEEN AUTHORIZED TO GO.

IN HPAKANT, THE MINERS ARE PAID IN SHOTS OF HEROIN.

I'M JUST HERE TEMPORARILY. I'M WORKING IN ANOTHER REGION UNTIL I CAN COME BACK FULL-TIME.

THERE ARE ALSO SO-CALLED SHOOTING GALLERIES, WHERE $1 WILL GET YOU A FIX.

I'VE MET GIRLS WHO COME FROM RANGOON TO WORK AS PROSTITUTES IN HPAKANT. THEY SEE UP TO 40 CLIENTS A DAY.

SAY HELLO TO HIV PROPAGATION.

AT THE END OF THE DAY, WORKERS ARE SEARCHED TO CHECK THAT THEY'RE NOT HIDING PRECIOUS STONES.

IN RUBY MINES, I'VE SEEN MEN CUT SLITS INTO THEIR CHEEKS TO STASH GEMS.

AND THE WOMEN ARE SUBJECTED TO VAGINAL SEARCHES UNDER SUCH UNSANITARY CONDITIONS THAT THEY WIND UP WITH INFECTIONS.

THAT'S CHINA OVER THERE.

OH, HEY, WE REALLY ARE NEXT DOOR.

SINCE WE CAN'T VISIT HPAKANT, WE GO FOR A RIDE IN THE COUNTRYSIDE.

I THINK THIS IS A CEMETERY FOR THE VICTIMS OF BURMA'S STRUGGLE FOR INDEPENDENCE.

AND WHAT'S THIS?

I DON'T KNOW.

WE COME ACROSS A MYSTERIOUS STRUCTURE.

IT'S A LITTLE ROOM, WITH A CHAIR IN THE MIDDLE.

THERE'S OTHERS.

LET'S SEE.

IT'S GOT TWO FLOORS.

WITH AN INNER COURTYARD.

WITH SMALL ROOMS EVERYWHERE.

AND A CHAIR IN EACH ROOM.

THERE'S A CROSS HERE!

HEY, I'VE GOT IT! IT'S A PLACE OF PRAYER.

ASTONISHING LAYOUT, HUH?

IT'S LIKE YOU'RE IN A JODOROWSKY* COMIC.

240

...AND WITH FERVENT WORSHIPPERS IN EVERY ROOM, A MYSTICAL ENERGY TAKES HOLD OF THE BUILDING, WHICH STARTS TO SPIN AND LIFTS OFF LIKE A UFO.

DON'T YOU THINK?

*FAMOUS SCIENCE FICTION COMICS WRITER

OVER SUPPER, WE MEET A FRENCHWOMAN WORKING FOR ANOTHER NGO. SHE INVITES US TO COME VISIT HER PROGRAM, A FEW MILES FROM HERE.

SLEPT WELL?

GREAT, THANKS. THE COOL AIR WAS A TREAT. I ALMOST FELT COLD.

THE ROAD THERE IS VERY DUSTY.

A SHOPKEEPER IN FRONT OF HIS SHOP.

IN THE VILLAGE WE'RE GOING TO, IT'S ESTIMATED THAT AT LEAST 86% OF THE PEOPLE SHOOT UP AT LEAST ONCE A DAY.

IN SOME FAMILIES, JUST ABOUT EVERYBODY SHOOTS UP!

WHAT DOES YOUR CLINIC DO?

FOR NOW, IT'S A DROP-IN CENTER FOR ADDICTS, BUT WE'RE PLANNING TO START UP A METHADONE DETOX PROGRAM.

AN ASSISTANT SHOWS US AROUND. HE HAS US WATCH AN INFORMATIONAL VIDEO ON THE DANGERS OF DRUG USE.

ACCORDING TO THE UN, THE ADDICTION RATE IN KACHIN RANKS AMONG THE HIGHEST IN THE WORLD.

AND WHERE DO USERS GET THE MONEY FOR THEIR DRUGS?

THEY PAN THE RIVER FOR GOLD AND SELL IT FOR A HIT.

THEY GO INTO THE WOODS, WHERE DEALERS GIVE THEM AN INJECTION. THEN SOME OF THEM COME HERE FOR THE DAY.

WE TRY TO DISCOURAGE THEM FROM USING DRUGS.

GOOD LUCK! UNDER CONDITIONS LIKE THOSE, THE RISK OF RELAPSE IS HUGE, EVEN WITH METHADONE.

WE'RE GOING TO TRY METHADONE WITH 7 PATIENTS SOON.

AND WHAT'S THAT? BOXES OF TAMIFLU?

YES, TAMIFLU, IT JUST CAME IN.

YOU HAVE TAMIFLU BUT NO METHADONE?

YOU COULD TRAIN A LAB TECHNICIAN TO DO BLOOD TESTS FOR MALARIA. IT'S AN EASY PROGRAM TO SET UP.

YOU'D NEED TO TALK TO OUR NEXT CHIEF OF MISSION. THE LAST ONE QUIT A MONTH AGO.

WE GO BACK TO THE GROUND FLOOR, WHERE THE REGULARS HAVE ARRIVED. THERE ARE 3 SPRAWLED OUT ON MATS, 2 PLAYING PING PONG IN THE COURTYARD AND ONE LEANING AGAINST A COLUMN, TRYING TO TAKE AN OLD GUITAR DOWN FROM ITS HOOK.

THE VILLAGE IS DEAD SILENT, NOT A SOUL IN SIGHT.

BEHIND THE CLOSED SHUTTERS, THINGS ARE PROBABLY NO DIFFERENT THAN AT THE DROP-IN.

IT MAKES YOU WONDER HOW THE GOVERNMENT CAN PUT UP WITH SUCH A SITUATION.

IN MY HUMBLE OPINION, IT SUITS THE GOVERNMENT FINE. THEY'D PROBABLY PREFER TO SEE YOUNG KACHINS STONED TO THE GILLS THAN TAKING UP ARMS AND JOINING THE RANKS OF THE RESISTANCE.

AROUND THE CORNER

AFTER ALL MY TRAVELS HERE, iT'S GOiNG AROUND THE CORNER THAT FiNALLY TAKES ME MOST OUT OF MY ELEMENT.

A WEEK EARLiER, A MOM AT THE BABY GROUP TOLD ME ABOUT HER MEDiTATiON RETREAT iN A BUDDHiST TEMPLE.

HEY, i WOULDN'T MiND GIVING THAT A TRY.

JUST DON'T GO TO ONE OF THOSE TOURiST CENTERS. THERE'S A WONDERFUL ViPASSANA TEMPLE RiGHT iN THE GOLDEN VALLEY

WHERE?

HERE, ViPASSANA, THiS MUST BE iT.

i BET NO ONE SPEAKS ENGLiSH iN THERE.

244

MAYBE I CAN ASK HERE?

HELLO, I'D LIKE SOME INFORMATION ABOUT COMING TO MEDITATE HERE.

IF IT'S POSSIBLE.

ONE MOMENT.

SHE STEPS OUT AND COMES BACK WITH AN AMERICAN NUN WHO HAS LIVED HERE FOR 12 YEARS.

YOU CAN COME ANYTIME AND STAY AS LONG AS YOU LIKE.

IT'S VERY SIMPLE.

SHE TELLS ME EVERYTHING I NEED TO KNOW.

FOR FOREIGNERS, THERE'S NO CHARGE.

REALLY? I'D LIKE TO MAKE A DONATION ANYWAY. IS THERE A BOX SOMEWHERE?

NO, NO. NO DONATIONS. THE MONKS HERE HAVE EVERYTHING THEY NEED.

SHE IS VERY THIN AND HAS A PERFECTLY SHAVED SKULL. BUT I NOTICE THAT SHE HAS HAIR ON HER CHIN. I FIGURE IF SHE SHAVES HER HEAD, SHE MIGHT AS WELL DO THE REST... BUT I GUESS IT'S THE LEAST OF HER WORRIES, BEING AN AMERICAN NUN WHO HAS LIVED IN BURMA 12 YEARS TO LEARN PALI.*

I'D LOVE TO KNOW A BIT MORE ABOUT HER STORY AND ASK A FEW QUESTIONS, BUT I HOLD BACK.

THANKS.

*ANCIENT INDIAN LANGUAGE.

AS PLANNED, i RETURN THE FOLLOW-
iNG FRIDAY MORNING FOR A BRiEF
3-DAY STAY.

i CHECK iN AT THE RECEPTION. A YOUNG NUN
GiVES ME A SHORT DOCUMENT TO READ AND
SETS ME UP WiTH A ViDEO TO WATCH.

...THE OLDEST FORM OF
MEDiTATiON, TAUGHT BY THE
BUDDHA 2,500 YEARS AGO...

iN HALF AN HOUR, iT GiVES A BRiEF OVER-
ViEW OF THE HiSTORY AND TECHNiQUE OF
THE MEDiTATiON PRACTiCED AT THE CENTER.
i FOLLOW UP WiTH THE BROCHURE.

OK, THAT
DOESN'T
SOUND TOO
COMPLiCATED.

THE YOUNG NUN COMES BACK TO SHOW ME
WHERE i'LL BE STAYiNG.

AND HERE'S
YOUR KEY.

THANKS.

SHE LEAVES AND i'M ON MY OWN TiLL THE
END OF THE RETREAT.

246

IN MY LITTLE ROOM, THERE'S A BED AND WHAT MIGHT SEEM LIKE A LUXURY IN THIS KIND OF PLACE: A FAN.

I MUST BE IN A BUILDING RESERVED FOR FOREIGNERS. THERE ARE TWO TIBETANS AT THE END OF THE HALL, AND AN INDONESIAN FURTHER DOWN.

BUT WE WON'T SPEAK A WORD TO EACH OTHER BECAUSE "WE ARE NOT HERE TO SOCIALIZE", AS IT SAYS IN MY BROCHURE.

I CHECK MY SCHEDULE. WAKE UP AT 3 AM, SHOWER AT 9 AM, LAST MEAL AT 11 AM AND BEDTIME AT 9 PM. THE DAY ALTERNATES BETWEEN SEATED MEDITATION AND WALKING MEDITATION.

THE KEY THING IS NOT TO MISS THE 11 O'CLOCK MEAL.

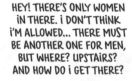

ACCORDING TO THE SCHEDULE, I SHOULD BE MEDITATING. I LOOK FOR THE MEDITATION HALL. ON THE WAY, I PRACTICE THE STANDARD TECHNIQUE HERE OF BEING ATTENTIVE TO EVERY GESTURE. WALKING, FOR EXAMPLE, BREAKS DOWN INTO A SERIES OF MOVEMENTS THAT YOU FOCUS YOUR AWARENESS ON. SO EVERYTHING HAPPENS IN SLOW MOTION.

HEY! THERE'S ONLY WOMEN IN THERE. I DON'T THINK I'M ALLOWED... THERE MUST BE ANOTHER ONE FOR MEN, BUT WHERE? UPSTAIRS? AND HOW DO I GET THERE?

AFTER A FEW MORE TRIES, I FIND THE MEN'S MEDITATION ROOM. GIVEN THE SPEED I'M PROGRESSING AT, THE SESSION IS WELL UNDER-WAY. ALL THE MONKS ARE ALREADY SEATED.

I SETTLE IN. I TRY TO FOCUS ON MY BREATHING AND CALMLY DRIVE AWAY OTHER THOUGHTS, BUT I'M A BIT TOO NERVOUS AND DISORIENTED TO GET ANYTHING OUT OF IT.

I WAIT FOR MEALTIME IN MY ROOM.

I GO DOWN TO THE COURT-YARD, BUT IT'S EMPTY. I GO TO WHAT I THINK ARE THE KITCHENS: NOBODY. WHERE DO WE EAT? HOW DO I GET THERE?

A BIT LOST, I GO BACK TO WHERE I STARTED. LUCKILY MY TIBETAN COMRADE COMES FOR ME.

HEY, DINNER TIME.

OK, THANK YOU.

AH, THIS MUST BE IT.

I GUESS I NEED TO LINE UP WITH THE REST.

THE TEMPLE MONKS ARE AT THE FRONT OF THE LINE, THEN IT'S THE FOREIGN MONKS AND ANY BURMESE THAT ARE PASSING THROUGH, AND AT THE VERY END, THERE'S ME, A STRANDED FOREIGNER.

IT BASICALLY COMES DOWN TO TWO CATEGORIES: SHAVEN AND UNSHAVEN.

OK...

...WHAT'RE WE WAITING FOR?

BONG!

AH, HERE GOES!

THE DINING ROOM IS HUGE. THE WOMEN ARE ALREADY SEATED. I GUESS THAT'S WHY WE WERE WAITING PATIENTLY OUTSIDE.

BEFORE HELPING THEMSELVES, THE MONKS CHANT A PRAYER.

I'M NOT VERY HUNGRY, BUT KNOWING THAT THIS IS OUR LAST MEAL, I LOAD UP MY PLATE.

UP ON A STAGE, TEMPLE MONKS ARE EATING THE FOOD THEY COLLECTED ON THEIR NEIGHBORHOOD ROUNDS.

I TAKE A SEAT WITH THE VISITING BURMESE AND FOREIGN MONKS.

THE MEALS ARE PLENTIFUL. i THOUGHT BUDDHIST MONKS WERE VEGETARIAN. NOT AT ALL. TODAY, WE HAD CHICKEN, AND iCE CREAM WITH BITS OF CHOCOLATE FOR DESERT.

AFTER A MORNING SPENT GETTING ORIENTED, i FEEL MORE RELAXED.

i CONTINUE WITH MY WALKING MEDITATION, BUT i DON'T QUITE HAVE THE HANG OF iT YET.

i SET DOWN MY HEEL...

i SLOW DOWN...

i TRANSFER MY WEIGHT...

i FEEL THE SOLE OF MY FOOT MAKE CONTACT WITH THE GROUND...

i MOVE SLOWLY...

WE ALL MOVE SLOWLY...

WHERE YOU'VE GOT ALL THOSE OLD GUYS WALKING LIKE ZOMBIES...

iT REMINDS ME OF THAT SCENE IN THE MOVIE ZARDOZ...

WASN'T ZARDOZ BASED ON A KIDS BOOK?

OH, RIGHT, THE WIZARD OF OZ.

i SET DOWN MY OTHER HEEL...

iT ACTUALLY LOOKS A BIT LIKE AN iNSANE ASYLUM...

iT'S AMAZING HOW MANY REFERENCES THERE ARE TO THAT STORY IN THE MOVIES.

UH...

IN THE AFTERNOON, i'M IN A STATE OF PANIC.

WHAT THE HELL AM i DOING HERE?

i'LL TRY AGAIN FOR THE SAKE OF FORM AND THEN GO HOME TONIGHT.

i'LL TAKE THE KIDS TO THE POOL TOMORROW INSTEAD OF WASTING MY TIME HERE.

DAMN, WHY DID i TELL EVERYBODY i WAS COMING HERE FOR 3 DAYS?

THE TRUTH IS, i'D LIKE TO GO HOME RIGHT NOW.

HAVING MADE UP MY MIND TO LEAVE, i MANAGE TO RELAX ENOUGH TO STAY.

MEDITATION iS HARDER ON THE BODY THAN YOU'D THINK.

IN THE MANUAL, iT SAYS THAT YOU CAN GET OVER THE PAIN BY CONCENTRATING. FOR MY PART, i CAN JUST MANAGE TO iGNORE THE TINGLING, BUT AFTER AN HOUR, i'M HURTING ALL OVER.

POSTURAL EVOLUTION DURING THE RETREAT.

THERE'S A FOREIGN MONK RIGHT iN FRONT OF ME, ALL DRESSED iN GRAY, WHO iS TRULY ADMIRABLE. HE CAN GET THROUGH 2 HOURS iN A ROW WITHOUT EVEN BUDGING.

THAT GUY REALLY SEEMS TO BE FLOATING iN ANOTHER WORLD. i WONDER WHERE HE'S FROM. JAPAN, OR KOREA MAYBE?

MY FIRST DAY COMES TO AN END. IT'S 9 PM, I'M TIRED ENOUGH TO GO SLEEP.

THE ALARM RINGS AT 3 AM. THE SECOND DAY BEGINS.

BEFORE THE 5:30 AM BREAKFAST, I DECIDE TO PUT ON MY LONGYI. I'VE WORN ONE BEFORE, BUT I'VE NEVER FELT ENTIRELY COMFORTABLE IN THESE LONG SKIRTS.

AFTER A DAY AND NIGHT AT THE TEMPLE, THE AMBIANCE SEEMS RIGHT.

I SEE THE MONKS GOING OUT TO GET FOOD IN THE NEIGHBORHOOD. THEY'LL PASS BY MY HOUSE.

MY STAY AT THE TEMPLE WILL HAVE GIVEN ME AN INSIDE LOOK AT THIS GIGANTIC RELIGIOUS STRUCTURE.

I GET THE STRANGE IMPRESSION OF HAVING STEPPED THROUGH THE LOOKING GLASS.

SEEN FROM HERE, IT FEELS LIKE YOU'RE EXACTLY WHERE YOU'RE MEANT TO BE, WITH EVERYONE ON THE OTHER SIDE SUPPORTING YOU AND ENCOURAGING YOU TO STAY.

ON DAY 3, i GET A NOTE INVITING ME TO MEET A SENIOR MONK TO TALK ABOUT MY EXPERIENCE.

i GO TO HIM IN THE AFTERNOON. THE YOUNG TRANSLATOR IS WAITING FOR ME. i TELL THE MONK WHAT i FELT DURING MEDITATION.

HE GIVES FEEDBACK AND SAYS THAT DESPITE THE SHORT STAY, i'VE MADE PROGRESS.

i'D WANTED TO LEAVE EARLIER, BUT i END UP STAYING TILL THE END OF THE DAY, 9 PM.

AS i PACK MY BAG, i'M SORRY THAT i'LL BE MISSING THE NEXT MEDITATION, UNDER THE MOONLIGHT AND THE MOSQUITO NET.

ALL IS QUIET, i GO DOWN TO THE COURTYARD TO GET MY BIKE. i FEEL LIKE i'VE BEEN HERE A MONTH.

BEFORE LEAVING, I STOP BY THE DONATION BOX AND DROP IN ALL THE MONEY I'VE GOT ON ME.

IF I'D KNOWN, I WOULD HAVE COME HERE FROM THE START OF MY STAY AND NOT WAITED TILL THE END.

AND HERE GOES YOGI GUY, RETURNING TO THE ACTIVE WORLD, TO THE EXISTENCE OF IGNORANCE, TO THE SAMSARA.

AFTER 42 HOURS OF MEDITATION IN 3 DAYS, I FEEL MORE PEACEFUL THAN EVER BEFORE, BUT ALSO VERY ALERT. HOW LONG CAN THIS STATE OF GRACE LAST? IT COULD BE A HARD LANDING.

IT'S NADÈGE'S BIRTHDAY, AND THE PARTY SEEMS TO BE IN FULL SWING.

READY OR NOT, HERE GOES.

FIRST FAREWELLS

I LOVE WORKING AT NIGHT, WHEN THE HOUSE IS EMPTY AND EVERYTHING IS CALM.

HOLY CHRIST! WHAT'S GOING ON? ...WHAT'S ALL THAT WAILING?

WHAT THE HECK ARE THEY DOING HERE?

DURING THE CHRISTMAS SEASON, GROUPS OF CHRISTIANS GO CAROLING FROM DOOR TO DOOR.

ON A HOT TROPICAL NIGHT, LISTENING TO CAROLS ISN'T UNPLEASANT.

LATER, MAUNG COMES AND CHIDES ME FOR HAVING GIVEN THEM MONEY. HE EXPLAINS THAT THEY'RE BUDDHISTS PRETENDING TO BE CATHOLICS.

SO WHAT? IT WAS VERY NICE.

THIS IS THE EVENING MY STUDENT ANIMATORS HAVE COME TO GET ME FOR A FAREWELL SUPPER. ALL 4 SHOW UP.

WE START WITH ONE LAST CLASS BEFORE GOING OUT.

WITH THE BASIC PRINCIPLES WE'VE LOOKED AT, YOU'VE GOT EVERYTHING YOU NEED TO DO GOOD ANIMATION.

FOR OUR SUPPER, THEY'VE CHOSEN A HOMEY BURMESE RESTAURANT. IT'S UNPRETEN-TIOUS—THE KIND OF PLACE I LIKE. AFTER ALL THE HOURS WE'VE SPENT TOGETHER, THEY HAVE ME FIGURED OUT.

WE EAT A LOT, WE DRINK A LOT.

AT THE END OF THE MEAL, THEY EACH TAKE TURNS RECALLING A MEMORABLE MOMENT FROM OUR ANIMATION CLASSES.

...i FORGOT TO DO MY EXERCISES AND...

AND INVARIABLY THEY WRAP IT UP BY HEAPING ON THE PRAISE.

HOW LUCKY WE'VE BEEN TO HAVE BENEFITED FROM YOUR EXPERIENCE!

PFF!

IT'S ALL VERY TOUCHING. AND IF WE WEREN'T SO SOUSED, WE MIGHT EVEN SHED A TEAR, BECAUSE DEEP INSIDE, WE ALL KNOW THAT WE'LL NEVER SEE EACH OTHER AGAIN.

SEE YOU..

UNTIL NEXT TIME.

THE FERRIS WHEEL

86.7° F, THAT'S THE TEMPERATURE i HELD OUT TO BEFORE TURNING ON THE AC.

LOOKING AT MY NOTES, i SEE THAT i COULDN'T GET PAST 79.7° F WHEN i ARRIVED. WHICH GOES TO SHOW THAT YOU CAN GET USED TO ANYTHING, EVEN SWELTERING HEAT.

THE HOUSE EMPTIES OUT BIT BY BIT AS MOVING DAY APPROACHES.

YOU CAN FEEL THE PAGE TURNING.

AND SINCE THE MSF MISSION IS CLOSING SHOP, EVERYTHING NEEDS TO GO. IT'S A BIG SPRING CLEANING, AT THE OFFICE AND AT HOME.

WE HAVE SO MUCH STUFF TO BRING HOME THAT FOR WEEKS, WE'VE BEEN SENDING ALONG SUITCASES WITH ANYONE HEADED THAT WAY.

TO GET OUR THINGS BACK ONCE WE'RE THERE, WE'LL NEED TO DRIVE THROUGH ALL OF FRANCE.

PFF!

AND WE'RE STILL RETURNING WITH MORE STUFF THAN WE BROUGHT.

OH HELL.

JUST A FEW DAYS LEFT BEFORE WE GO. LUCKILY, NADÈGE HAS MANAGED TO FIND WORK FOR ALL THE STAFF. WHICH MEANS WE CAN LEAVE WITH LIGHTER HEARTS.

AFTER MORE THAN A YEAR HERE, I FEEL LIKE I'VE SEEN WHAT I NEEDED TO SEE.

260

IT'S TIME TO PICK UP LOUIS, WHO'S AT HIS LAST DAY OF KINDERGARTEN.

MAUNG AYE COMES ALONG. WE TAKE A SHORTCUT HE KNOWS.

WOW, YOU COULD HAVE SHOWED US THIS ROUTE EARLIER...

SO, WHAT'S WITH THE WEDDING?

THANKS TO HIS HUGE BETEL CONSUMPTION, MAUNG AYE HAS HIS OLD SMILE BACK.

COME TO THINK OF IT, I WONDER IF I DON'T LIKE HIM BETTER THIS WAY.

YES, SHE IS VERY PRETTY.

HE REALLY DID GET MARRIED, BUT HIS WIFE LIVES IN ANOTHER CITY. I CAN'T MAKE OUT IF HE'S PLANNING TO JOIN HER.

THERE'S A LITTLE GOING-AWAY TREAT FOR LOUIS. I SAY MY GOODBYES TO THE PARENTS I'VE MET.

I'LL SEE THEM AGAIN IN A FEW DAYS AT A BIG PARTY WE'LL THROW AT THE HOUSE JUST BEFORE LEAVING FOR THE PLANE.

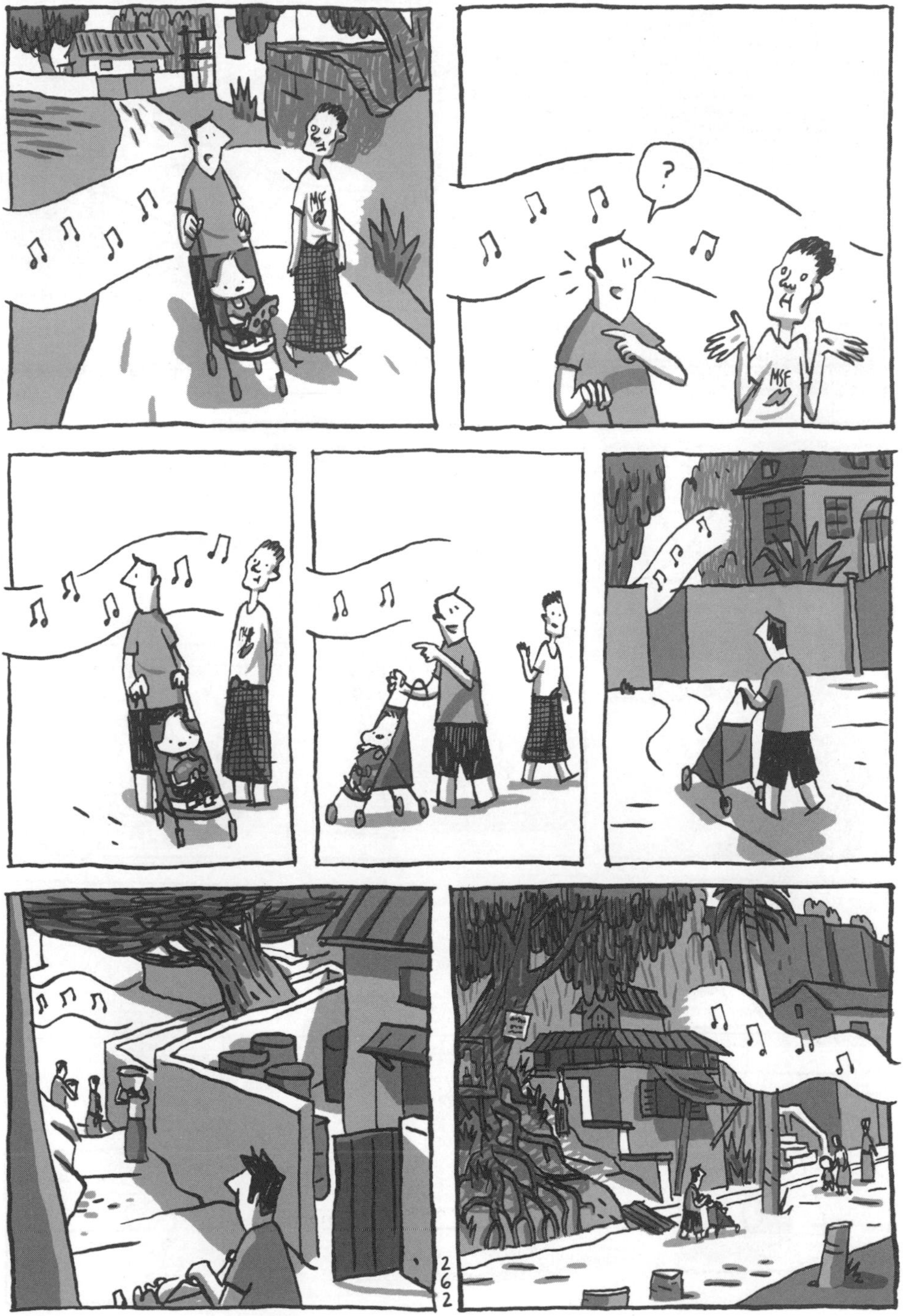
MSF
?
MSF

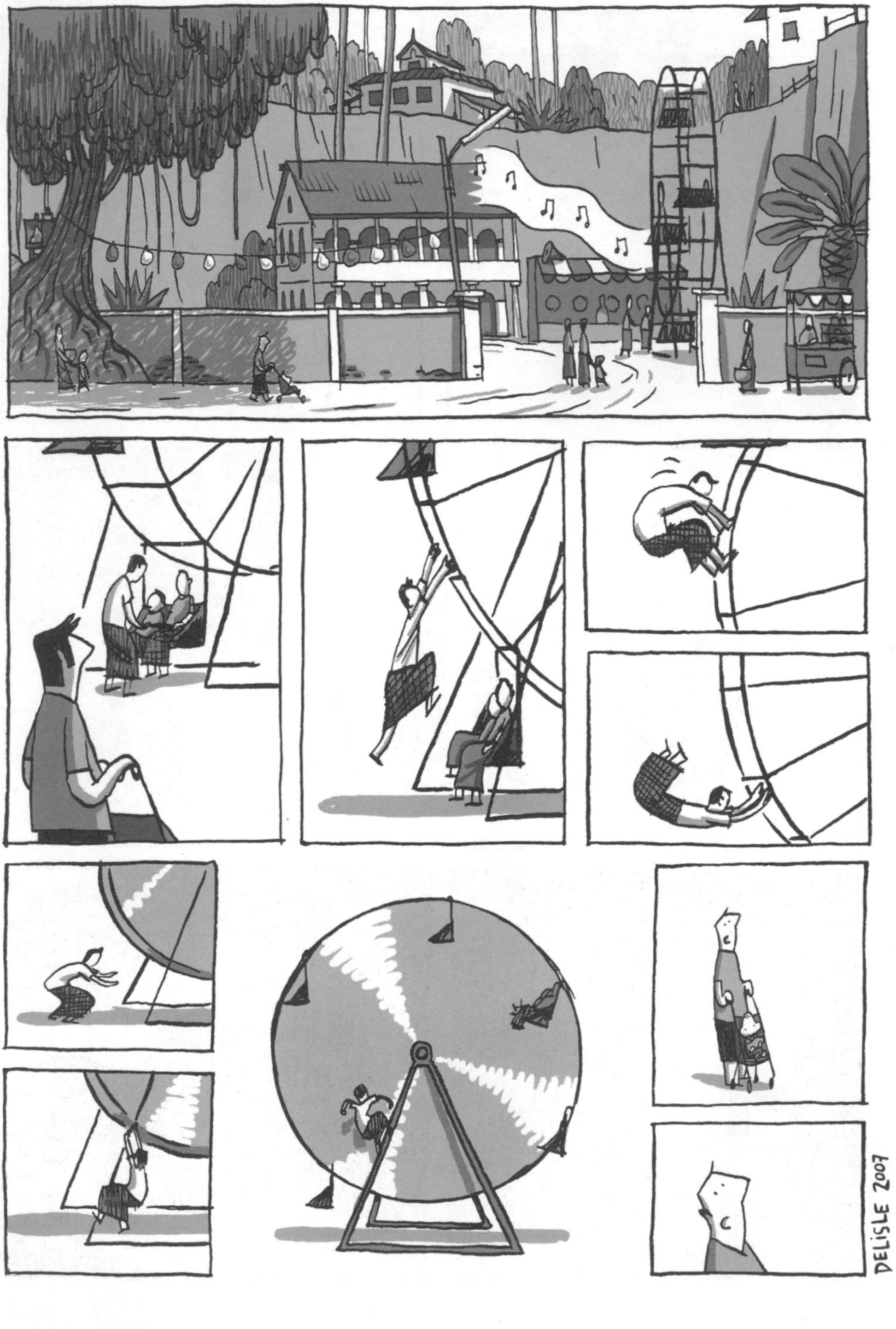
DELISLE 2007